with the
compliments
of the author

A Highland Story
-written on glass.

David Sutherland

**Printed by EPW Print & Design Ltd.,
Simcox Court,
Riverside Park Road,
Middlesbrough TS2 1UX**

**P. V. P. Imprint/UK
276 Marton Road
Middlesbrough
TS4 2NS**

Tel: 01-642-242357

Fax: 01-642-706113

Price: £8-50

All rights reserved. No part of this publication may be reproduced, stored in or introduced into a retrieval system, or transmitted, in any form, or by any means (electronic, mechanical, photocopying, recording or otherwise) without the prior permission of the author.

Copyright David Sutherland: 2008

This impression 2008

Illustrations: Front Cover -A section of Thomas Faed's *The Last of the Clan* in the Glasgow Art Gallery and Museum; the Ancient Old Sutherland Tartan; Rear Cover - MacIan's *Sutherland*; Title page - Croick Church;

ISBN-0-9543698-7-3

This book is dedicated to the wonderful people of the Highlands of Scotland, both past and present.

Introduction

My grandfather was born in the tiny village of Latheron, Scotland, in 1856. This village is in Britain's most northeasterly corner, once called the county of Caithness. It is level with the upper confines of Hudson Bay in Canada and parts of Alaska. The fact that he was born in Caithness and not the adjoining county of Sutherland (his surname and the ancestral home for generations) was due to the Highland Clearances. This was also the reason why his family were involved in a successful Atlantic and North Sea fishing business instead of farming the mountainous lands they had done for centuries. For his parents had been driven out of Sutherland both by force and want, like so many of their northern kinsfolk, in one of the most shameful British episodes of the nineteenth century. My mother waited until she was in her nineties to relate some of these tales, perhaps imperfectly told in part because of her age. Much of the story is based on true incidents although some of the characters' names and locations have been altered, while some events have been compressed in time to hasten and dramatise the narrative.

For those who are not familiar with the Highlands of Scotland the great reach of Sutherland that spreads northwards towards Cape Wrath has, at first sight, a forbidding and daunting aspect. Starting on the east coast at Dornoch Firth it is possible to trace a westerly route along wide rivers and broad lochs (Loch Shin being one of the most majestic) until one reaches the sea inlet on the west coast, at Loch Laxford. Thus it is easy to see how the inhabitants of this remote land felt secure and secluded from the rest of the world, almost as an island. But in these wild acres is some of Britain's most spectacular scenery - the tallest cliffs, the highest waterfalls, magnificent mountains formed with rock that defy their six hundred million years, innumerable lochs, streams and rivers, coastlines with jutting fingers of land bathed by blue or turbulent seas and graced by the most beautiful golden beaches. Mountains like *Foinaven* thrust thousands of feet heavenwards and wreaths of mist play incessantly around their peaks; while hills sparkle like jewels as their white quartzite slabs reflect and refract the noonday sun. Here are wild moors where the capercaillie, eagle, wildcat and deer dwell, in acres dotted with ancient forests. Rivers and lochs teem with salmon and trout, and millions of seabirds scout the tumbling waves and seals bask on the smoothing shores. All this lies beneath an ever-changing sky, so that the landscape varies in shade, colour and apparent texture by the minute.

Here too is the home of the Clan.

Under the old Celtic tenures – the *Klaan*, or the children of the soil, were the proprietors of the soil; the whole of the Highlands belonged to the people of the Highlands.

For there, the Chiefs were the absolute monarchs. They had the right to give *tacks* of land to their men or take them away, according to their help in times of war. Thus, only in the military sense could they reward or punish; but in no way could they alter or diminish the property of that Clan. They were the Chief, not the owner or proprietor, and could not expel the inhabitants from their homes. These people, however humble, could **not** forfeit their dwellings; they had the rights to what their families had possessed for generations- a guarantee in perpetuity.

So let us go back in time, almost two hundred years, and travel to this remote part of the British Isles, the county of Sutherland in the far north of Scotland. There we will hear the gentle, lilting voice of an old Highlander; his face sculptured by the weather, his love moulded by the beautiful land of his forefathers.

Here we will listen and understand.

Aon (one)

'Sometimes you're a vain body, Robbie Sutherland!'
'You think so, Domhnall!'(Donald)
The old man smiled.

The twenty-five year old lay face down, his head inches above a serene stretch of the burn, it was mirror-perfect.

The light was good. Framed in this pale-blue backdrop were Robbie's smiling face, brown hair, and the remnant of six day's stubble. The eyes, deep-set and brown, focused on the shimmering image in the water. He was not in a hurry.   Once his eyes had adjusted to the brightness, the old hill-shepherd came into view.

'Aye, I do!' replied Domhnall.

'You do? Perhaps you do!' Having satisfied his own query Robbie smoothed his chin and contemplated the stubble. 'This is no so good for the wedding Domhnall, I'll be thinkin'.' He twirled his fingers in the cold water and contemplated.

The old man laughed.

Domhnall's wife, who had walked some thirty yards behind, had been lost in her own private world, but as she caught up she laughed also, a purely instinctive response to her husband's happiness.

The heather was purple. The sky's azure sheen had not a cloud to disturb the uniformity. No other sound broke the tranquillity of this Highland summer's day.

The young man brushed the falling hair from his face, nut brown in the August sun, and splashed water over his features. It ran refreshingly down his cheeks and he caught the familiar peaty taste as it trickled over his lips - that peculiarly distinctive whisky-taste of Scotland.

With a shake of his head Robbie threw fine droplets into the air, which held the spectrum's colours for a moment. The delicate ripples that eddied on the mirror-surface broke the stillness of the water. In a second they were lost and all was serene once more. He shook his hair again and a thin spray drifted towards the watching couple.

'I dinna think anybody will notice ye, Robbie, beard or no! It's yer brother Alasdair (Alexander) who might be noticed. But, more than likely, his bride Mairead (Margaret)! Even if y' had one leg a foot shorter than the other and breeks to match, y'd no cause an eyelid to flicker in interest.' The sixty-six year old women pushed back her grey curls and laughed.

Robbie turned on his side and gazed reflectively for a short while. 'My brother's a fine figure of a man; there's no doubting that, and your Mairead's as pretty as a highland loch in spring. But for me in breeks...that's a sight not worth waiting for,' he glanced down, 'but this kilt will look fair bonny today, despite what the Sassenachs say!'

The old man put his hand on his wife's shoulder for a second. He replied dubiously, 'They have no liked the plaid we're wearing since the rebellion in '45, over sixty years gone. I suppose if we're found out, the wedding will not be as cheerful as we wud like it!'

Robbie continued lying on his side supported by a tuft of wiry heather in full purple bloom. His only reaction was to purse his lips. Then he gave a broad grin. 'Ealasaid (Elizabeth), you look as pretty as a lochan on a summer's day in the tartan with that shawl and bonnet. Fair good for the eyes, is she not Domhnall?'

It was the old man's turn to laugh with pleasure.

'I'll not be for the changing of my girl, even after forty-eight years, if that is the number! Sometimes her nagging's like the waves on Dornoch shores, ebbing and flowing, roaring and rattling. But, most times, there's a soothin sound in a woman's voice like the sea that quietens a man's soul, Robbie. That y'll ken one day, laddie and ye'll be better for it! '

Noticing Robbie's wry face, Ealasaid gave her husband a good-humoured push that caused him to stagger slightly on his thin, wiry legs, clearly visible beneath the kilt.

'Look at you now, Domhnall! Unsteady as a newborn calf...and not a drop of whisky has passed y' lips in nigh on twelve hours.'

'I willna be able to say the same by tomorrow morn, with the wedding nigh!' replied her husband ruefully, 'and if man's unsteady by then…it's the Lord's will, for usquebaugh be heaven sent.

Robbie laughed and nodded in agreement.

But the old man's attention was directed first towards the sun and then towards the distant horizon where a narrow cleft broke the sharp contour of the hills. 'It's time we were away,' he said firmly, 'there's a guid one hour's walking to the wedding. Are y'coming now, Robbie?'

The younger man smiled and turned to study the placid water. 'I've still a fair while to lie here and the inclination to do so, Domhnall!'

'Ah well! Ye're in a blithesome way, Robbie Sutherland, lying there an'doukin yerself,' Ealasaid laughed as she waved goodbye.

The old man laughed too. They slowly ambled down the sloping, twisting mountain path; his wife a few paces behind. Theirs was a purposeful walk only hurrying once they reached the maze of paths near the stream. Here the narrow confines of the rushing water left the lonely passage and the land opened into a broad vista at the confluence of the Glens. The way was smooth and clear.

But Robbie was content to let them go, content to lie with the fresh smell of the crystal water in his face and the warming sun on his back.

His mind turned to that morning's wedding. He knew of no finer man than his brother Alasdair. He thought of their childhood escapades together…the tickling of trout on the riverbanks. How they stretched their skinny arms so slowly – barely afraid to breathe - until the wet, sleek scales were firmly grasped. Not that he liked to kill them, for his brother always bent their necks with a faint crack. Then there was the odd salmon, poached from the Laird. And there was their mother in the kitchen, welcoming them back…stirring, beating and scouring; with fresh scones perfuming the air, appertisingly. He liked the fish in oatmeal but he hated those opalescent, fat-scalded eyes - so firmly fixed and reproachful. His mother would chide him for his silliness and, with a deft slice of the broad kitchen dirk, sliced off the head.

Sometimes he would creep through the coarse bracken with Alasdair, stalking the red deer under the very gaze of old McPherson, the gamekeeper. Not that they killed or caught any, but it was fun seeing how close they could get before the old stag came snorting up in its defence. How beautiful were the doe's eyes, how long the lashes. And the fawn, curled and still in the long grass, was a masterpiece in nature's store of beauty.

His mind came back to the present. Then he considered the future. As the eldest brother, Alasdair would inherit the family farm. That was more than likely, it was a fact! But what would he, Robbie Sutherland, do? What could he do? 'While you're fancy-free, Robbie, let the winds and weather be your guide,' his grandfather used to say with a smile. 'As a boy they took me hither and thither. It did me no harm. Then one day it was time to settle down. So drift like the clouds, son, while you can and be as lazy too! For the future can store up a whole heap of troubles, Robbie, as well as joys. And who knows what the Almighty has in store for such as we!'

And it was in his make-up to wander; to be like his grandfather, to seek whatever fortune might come his way. He was philosophical about the loss of the farm, it didn't upset him one bit. As the youngest son –that was the way it had always been in the highlands.

Thus, after further agreeable thoughts and self-justification, Robbie smiled and shook his hand in the water to erase his reflection.

'I'm no married and still free to roam,' he mused, 'in my lovely, wild land of Sutherland!'

He had just come from Scourie, past the majestic dome of Suilven's heights, where the massive curved ridge with its circle of cliffs hurried on with a long slender crest. And he loved this life -to feel the winding stone paths beneath his aching feet; to amble through the bracken with its characteristic smell; to walk down the straths, across the pulsating rivers, swollen by the sudden rain, and to pause in the hanging, spiral waterfalls. And at a whim, it was time for one of nature's showers, however cold the weather. Sometimes, when in its ferocity the downpour enveloped the land in shrouds of mist, it would cling affectionately to his hair, forging tiny rivulets across his face, but never diminish the feeling of freedom.

His nature enjoyed that freedom – rain or shine - never dampened by the harsh winter's blasts and the blizzards that drove him to seek shelter from the kinsfolk in the county of Sutherland, he adored.

Once again he trailed his hand in the cool water. There were no girls in his life, well – no one special; but some quite comely in a coquettish way, some inviting him back to their homestead, where their parents were, by enlarge, welcoming enough. 'But at twenty-five? Alasdair could settle down...he was three years older and wiser. Sometimes staid and sometimes dour, was his brother – but always a friend in need. Alasdair would work Mairead's family's holding near Rogart, now that her father had become infirm with joints crippled by the highland damp. The old man had moved further north, until the time when his grandson would come of age, maybe in twenty years. Then Alasdair and Mairead would move from this temporary abode to his family farm and take over. The timing would probably work out well.'

Robbie heard a curlew wing its way across the heather, and the plaintiff sound echoing from the crags beckoned him on.

He splashed a final handful of moisture on his face, suddenly wished that the beard had gone, but in a resigned and cheerful way, set off for the wedding – some three miles away.

Dha (two)

Tha I breagha an-diugh. (It is a lovely day.)

One could not deny the eagle's cry that day, as it soared mountain high into the mist and was lost in its whispered crispness. A vexed cry that was soon spent in the rock-strewn glens as the dark chaos of hills basked in the first bright rays of morning.

For at dawn the mist had spread along the unfenced moors in total freedom, crouching grey and ghost-like by the tumbling rills, and veil-like draped itself across the highest summit faces. Now an awakening summer breeze dispelled the gloom and in the increasing brightness the eagle's talon-trailing flight was soon lost, if ever observed, by the Chief and Clans folk assembled on the level summit of the hill.

Yet there was nothing grey and forlorn about this glen, for the mood was one of happiness. From the group of almost two hundred men, women and children came their lilting voices and laughter, each clear and cheerful in the warming air. They stood in a half-circle in their brightest clothes, with the Chief and his wife prominent by their finery and displaying the green, blues and reds of the Sutherland plaid. The scene was one of Highland merriment, the anticipation of another union before God and the elders of the Clan. Young men and women - eager in this anticipation and hurrying around in small knots, laughing, gesticulating - shared a moment of true warmth with their neighbours. Robbie laughed as much as the rest, his eyes bleary from the early morning's exertions and the drinking of the night before. How he wished for a good swill of goat's milk to clear his head, it never failed. But his eyes were not so defective in vision that he failed to notice an eighteen-year old girl call Eilidh (Helen) who seemed to gravitate towards him whenever she could. Robbie shrugged his shoulders in a curiously resigned way and stood beside her. Yet in an instant the chattering and laughing ceased. The interest of the men, the growing trepidation of the young girls, and the tears of the elderly began to dominate the scene. Nervousness, sudden palpitations, a ripple of admiration towards the bride and the service commenced.

Amongst the group of near two hundred assembled for the wedding, three people were clearly seen.

Minister McBain, a wiry man in his late forties, with a broad welcoming face and a weary, nervous smile, which waned into sadness on occasions.

The groom, twenty-eight year old Alasdair Sutherland -tall, dark eyed with shock of brown hair, his handsomely strong features part-hidden by a coarse beard. At first glance he looked like his brother but in a less rugged and a more sensitive way. He was not quite so tall, although just over six feet.

And the bride Mairead Sinclair, not yet twenty-two, with an emerald green-eyed beauty framed by the curl of her auburn hair and enhanced by the folds of a blue dress.

But Mairead had eyes for no one but Alasdair.

And when another long beam of light broke through the cleft in the hills, its brightness became reflected in her smiling face.

Her husband caught the mood of happiness. She felt the soft stroke of his hand on hers, and flushed with love. She wanted to reach out and kiss him, if only for a moment's reassurance, but stopped herself. Tonight they would be together for the first time and, in her heart, she knew it was for eternity.

She thought, 'I love you!' a hundred times over, such was her joy. She had never felt more alive, every memory of their time together came flooding back in vivid colour, each event replayed in an instant. Suddenly the Minister spoke her name and it was reality once more.

Marriage was her one desire. Since childhood she had dreamed, fantasised and worried about being married. Now it was becoming a reality. Alasdair was by her side and she was marrying the man she adored. It was natural to hope, and to believe that all would be well - an optimism born of youth and adoration. Half aware of the ceremony, half aware of her inner thoughts and aspirations, Mairead held her husband's hand, gripping it tightly as the Minister's voice rose and fell with each incantation.

As the breeze became a whisper, the light movement of air gently ruffled the women's long hair without disturbing their bonnets and shawls. It was a quiet, reflective group caught up in the emotional solemnity of the occasion.

Then a warm summer wind quickly followed, rushing hither and thither from the mountain pass, picking up the sweet scents of August heather and carrying them on ethereal wings; in its enthusiasm it set a choir of larks winging into song, and the delicate calls seemed to emanate from the vault of heaven.

Now the sky began to fill with a liquid blue even deeper than before.

In such a blissful setting were Mairead and Alasdair being made man and wife.

But their marriage was on a day that was to be remembered for another reason. And that event was destined to become part of the chill folk law of the Highlands in the years to come, although only one man foresaw the dangers at that time.

For when the mist of morning had broken on the highest mountain pass, another cloud tumbled through the glen.

Its noise disturbed the Gaelic, and its sounds were soon to haunt the moorlands forever.

It was the sound of a tumbling, swirling flock that poured down the broad Drover's path, a mass of white by the thousands.

Sheep after sheep after sheep...some pausing to crop for a few seconds, ...some running bleatingly...some ambling inquisitively, all were being swept along in a seemingly unending mass that amazed the gathering by its sheer numbers and intensity.

And as the eagle swept higher and higher above the sprawling flock it watched with orange-eyed curiosity but did not call again - but left the words to Old Domhnall who muttered softly to his wife Ealasaid. 'What manner o'events be this, what hath the Lord provided?'

While she hung her grey head and whispered as the Minister spoke, 'I'm thinking that soon the black of the valley (*An Gleann Dubh*) will be white (*ban*) with grazing sheep.'

'*Tha* (Yes)!' The old man paused and wrung his hands, his eye fixed on the approaching mass. 'I dinna believe guid will come o' this. Aye, I have heard it spoken amongst our kinfolk down the valley,' he whispered 'that this year will be our year of the sheep!' (*Bliadhna nan Caorach!*)

Ealasaid looked for a moment at the earnestness in his face and shook her head.

Then he mumbled once more, 'Nae guid will come o' this!'

*****

The Minister did not look up at first.

His head bent and eyes steadfastly forward, he traced the Gaelic words in the prayer book with a long, crooked forefinger.

It was to be his last wedding.

But this fact he did not know as he rambled through the text, sometimes pausing to smile at the couple, at other times turning to address the Chief and Clan elders, in an almost deferential if not reverential manner.

And so the service continued. His quiet voice was almost imperceptible as the breeze swung round the side of the hill and brought the animals' calls towards them in an increasing crescendo. So that the assembled group craned forward and the periodic faint murmuring amongst them became hushed as they strained to hear the Minister through the noise.

Even Mairead and Alasdair held their breath, as if afraid that he might not continue. Her smile faded with anxiety and disappointment, and Alasdair touched her trembling hand in a gesture of reassurance.

Without warning the Minister paused.

It was not the bleating that caused the interruption, nor was it the apprehension written in the couple's eyes.

It was because Minister McBain suddenly, and without any particular reason, hesitated as he thought of the past.

And his brother's past.

And his future that never became the past!

For in those fleeting seconds, his mind raced back in time and a curious veil of suppressed emotions was erased. And a newfound clarity revealed a precious time gone by. Events of almost twenty years before - when he was to have been the groom in a wedding such as this; and yet that chance had slipped away, and the bride had married another.

The fact hit him with all the force of a pain subconsciously submerged...his twin brother had stolen his wife.

The memory was an anathema to him. He pondered the question, 'What had brought these emotions and events rushing back from so long ago?' In this short reverie he was deeply unaware of the crowd and noise around him, lost in his own solitary world. 'Perhaps it was the girl standing before him, perhaps she resembled the woman he once loved - not so much in her looks, but in her wistful, warm smile!' And still he paused and reflected. 'Something had jarred his memory! '

He gazed towards the approaching flock and the bleating came echoing and re-echoing, tossed like an avalanche of sound from the crags and peaks. As quickly as the memory was born it faded like the mist and vanished into current reality.

Yet those recollections had disturbed him, if only for a moment.

Now it was difficult for him to concentrate on the service and he could only mouth the words in one long, emotionless Gaelic intonation and hurry the service along.

The congregation was aware that the ceremony was hastening towards its conclusion. They looked in consternation towards each other and then towards the sheep, angry that such a noise should desecrate a Holy Union before the God.

But the huge flock continued to spill and tumble down the Drover's road and the earthy, slightly pungent smell drifted ever stronger on the breeze as the animals moved closer and closer.

Four men were now clearly seen pushing the animals remorselessly onward with whistles and calls; while appearing on one side and then on the other, a dozen collie dogs spun in wild arcs pressing the sheep forever forward in close formation.

The dust clouds whisked up by the clattering feet began to swirl nearer and nearer like a miniature whirlwind. Anxiously the assembled Clan's folk looked at their finery and even more anxiously towards the bride and groom.

But the couple stood composed, head bent in a final silent prayer. The minister closed his book.

With a smile, Alasdair suddenly reached forward and taking Mairead in his arms lifted her off the ground, kissing her lovingly while gently turning her round and round in a slow circle as the Clan cheered.

But still the flock came on and on, undisturbed by this commotion.

Now the dust swirled more ferociously about them and covered the purple heather and browning greens of the bracken in a broad expanse of grey.

The Minister had just warmly shaken the hands of the bride and groom, when he stopped short, staring unbelievingly towards the flock some two hundred yards away.

At this point the Drover's path turned right because of a small gully and quite suddenly, to everyone's relief, the animals began to move away from the congregation clustered on the hillside.

Yet the air was still heavy with clouds of grey dust.

And as Minister McBain stared in amazement, so did Alasdair and Mairead; so did the congregation.

None more so than the Chief, who took three paces forwards. He shielded his eyes with his coarse right hand. Muttering to himself, he surveyed the figure on horseback who brought up the rear. A figure who suddenly emerged from the clouds of dust.

It could have been the Minister McBain!

But it wasn't, it was his twin brother.

With trepidations and a heavy heart, the Minister stepped forward as the onlookers listened, and waited; and wondered what would happen next

*****

'How are you?'(C*iamar a tha thu?)* Almost twenty years had elapsed since they had last spoken, and the Minister's words were cold, and yet polite.

The brother reined the broad-backed fell pony in a half circle to better survey the speaker. His expression showed little emotion; no joy of recognition, 'Reasonably well, thank you!' *(Meadhanach math, tapadh leat!)*.

A few laughed but then a hush swept over the onlookers, guilty in their surprise and enjoyment of the Minister's discomfiture.

There was a pause only broken by the slow turning of the horse and the flock retreating down the road.

'What makes your journey here, Murdo?' the Minister asked. He looked up at his brother who returned the stare majestically, the extra height giving him an air of importance. The Minister perspired in his nervousness and dilemma. He gripped the prayer book and tried to remain calm, speaking slowly but firmly, enunciating each Gaelic vowel.

''Tis surely evident to one of the cloth!' His brother replied, 'You're no so astonished to see me that you have not a kind word'. Then he waved towards the sheep. 'They are my flock, and is that not apt brother?' He laughed.

The Minister paused and looked earnestly into the speaker's face. Still the sun sparkled on the droplets of sweat that coalesced upon his forehead 'Your flock, you say, and what good it may bring you and your Master!' There was bitterness in the Minister's voice and a rising confidence born of past hurt. 'You're one to humiliate your own kin in front of this gathering!'

Murdo gave another short laugh. 'Aye, humble indeed...you're humble right enough and poor no doubt. And unfortunate in the eyes of the Lord! What good will these beasts bring you, brother...is that what you ask? In this land of barrenness and waste, what prospects are there? But here,' he raised his voice, 'is something to bring wealth, more than your failures and those about you. Here's a new prosperity, a sheep-prosperity. Something even you can preach about...meat...wool...and a better way of life for these impoverished Highlanders. Men and women who know only life in a one-roomed hovel and sleep with the harsh winds and freezing rain as companions! Those are your flock, Minister, and ill-fed and ill-tended they are too, if I may say, - compared to my sheep!'

'Who is speaking?' (*Co tha a' bruidhinn?*) Old Domhnall whispered to his wife, 'and do my eyes deceive me?'

'Your eyes are true, my husband (*mo cheile*), as true as they ever were!' She replied in a hushed voice. 'It is without doubt the brother that has been spoken about in the Glens but never been seen before. Both created in God's likeness but with different manners and ways, so it has been oft-times said.'

The old man shook his head and stared at the two men with a puzzled look. His eyes settled first on the hardened features of the brother and then on the Minister who seemed incapable of any further bitterness, his head almost cupped in his hands. Domhnall found himself muttering, 'Speak up for ye'sel man, speak up and shut his gab!'

The Minster raised his head and with a more determined step walked to the horse's side. He grasped its bridle to halt the slowly spinning animal. He looked steadfastly into Murdo's eyes. 'You have no right to speak in such a cruel and venomous way! But I'll not be expecting an apology. What really brings you here, brother, tell us once and for all, in the name of the Lord.'

The figure, aloof in uniformly light brown clothes, with grey stockings and silver buckled shoes, replied. 'I bring help and succour, as the Good Shepherd did eighteen hundred years ago.' His hair shone as silver in the sunlight like the fastenings on his shoes.

Without warning a voice in the hushed crowd cried, 'No!'

There was a moment of exhilaration that grasped the onlookers, made the old women pull their shawls tightly around their shoulders almost as a snail draws into its shell – the same primitive, uncalculated reflex. The young women took a deep breath and held firmly onto an obliging man's arm. It was the Chief of the Clan who spoke. He stepped forward in the moment's confusion and hesitation, scowled and half-pushed the Minister to one side and addressed the man on the horse. 'Hold y' tongue brother or it will be the worse for ye! I'm saying man that there is no place for such talk and blasphemy...and likewise no place for such beasts. Sheep and their shepherds 're no welcome in such numbers...they canna stay. They're no welcome now, and ne'r will be! Ye have my word on that! Take this plague off the lands and in the name o' God leave the Glens, let them be!'

The horse began to turn in slow circles once more, but the rider remained calm. For a moment he ignored the remark and, shielding his eyes against the brightness of the sun, he finally deigned to address Chief. 'By my word and my blood if you wish to spill it, they have come to stay. That much has been decided.' It was delivered with such an evil sternness and unmitigated unswerving conviction that all eyes turned first to the speaker and then to their Chief and finally to the Minister.

Alasdair overcome with apprehension held his new bride in his arms, not knowing what he could do, or say, to alleviate the unexpected hostility. Mairead bit her lip. It formed a small red globule in one corner. She felt no pain, only loathing for the man on the horse who was now swollen with confidence and ruining her day. With a supercilious smile he stared down, it seemed, from an even greater height. People glanced at each other, nervous, fearful glances. But Robbie, in his unconcerned way, simply waited and, while waiting, smiled at the pretty dark-haired girl, Eilidh, who pressed next to him and whose long black locks brushed his shoulder. He paused to push her hair aside and when it hung free the girl acknowledged the gesture with a smile; and the perfume of her hair distracted him even more. He thought of kissing her on the cheek, but noticing her parents nearby, desisted. With nothing better to do, he closed one eye and thus, for a second, lost the Minister from his gaze, retaining the harder image of the brother for future reference.

The Minister had lost his voice, his mouth firm in a face suffused in anger. But the Chief was not to be outdone. He waved his arms, a rapid, horizontal, threatening gesture as if he was wielding a sword, 'It is the voice of the Devil himself rushing forth from y' lips, dinna deny it man!' He gazed fixedly into Murdo's face.

But there was no emotion in Murdo's cold eyes. He stayed silent. The pause had the effect of disarming the Chief who, on expecting a retort and used to physical rather than intellectual combat, looked round at the assembled throng for support. Then, collecting himself, continued in more subdued and rational tones, 'By what authority do ye speak...by what command?'

'By the authority of His Grace, the Marquess of Stafford, the Great Laird of Sutherland!' Murdo's reply was crisp and factual.

The statement had the desired effect. The old Chief hesitated. 'The Great Laird, y' say?'

'Aye, that is what I said! The orders are that the sheep are to graze in the Highlands.' He laughed, 'Well-rounded beasts that can only enrich our lives! But let me warn you,' his voice became deep and cold, striking fear into many of those who listened, 'that no man is to interfere with the flocks! They are to remain in peace! You understand...in peace! Otherwise his Lordship will deal with those that transgress so severely that no one will ever disobey this command again. Transportation, the gibbet, if need be, and I will have pleasure in seeing to either or both!'

The Chief looked steadfastly ahead for one moment like one vanquished. At length he replied 'Is what ye say of honesty and truth?'

'Aye,'tis true.'

'And honest?'

'Aye, and honest! The Great Laird talks kindly when not displeased.' Murdo paused for a moment as the horse spun slowly. 'Frequently have I heard him express his benevolence towards his Highland people and what he and his wife, a true Sutherland, can do for them. They're kind and generous a couple as any can be, but do not like to be thwarted. Neither do you, Chief, I suspect.' He said it in a condescending way and smiled, but his tone and gesture were lost on the congregation apart from his brother.

There was a pause and the Clans folk watched the Chief, waiting for the response; but he only gave a nod of the head and stepped back - uneasy in mind and spirit - next to his wife.

Old Domhnall had listened with a fixed expression and another customary slow shaking of his head. He turned to the young man by his side, 'I nae like what I hear, Robbie, not one word did please me!'

The dark-haired young man moved closer to his friend, 'Why, Domhnall?'

'It's no the words that a' spoken, I dinna like, but the words that are no spoken!'

'Which words?' The twenty five year old man asked in a whisper.

'Our Chieftain...he speaks tae little and reasons nought! Most o'the Chiefs speak tae much as a rule but as t' his argument...well!' The old man shook his head again in disbelief. 'But a Chief that says nought gives me precious little hope. And why he does it puzzles me, Robbie, it puzzles me! For I ken that such monstrous flocks will strip the lands o' its goodness. Why, I had but a few Highland sheep on part o' that moor, and scrawny they were at times, I trow, and there was little enuf to feed them in the harsh months o' winter and just a wee bit mair in the best o' times.'

As Robbie turned to face the speaker the resemblance to the groom became obvious. His strong physique belied the kindness written into his face. 'Perhaps things will work out Domhnall, for they seem a fair sturdier breed of ewes (*Cheviots) than I have ever seen in these Glens. They might be our salvation!'

But the old man placed a thin hand on the speaker's shoulders. 'Laddie! What the stranger hath said may be o' little consequence to me and my wife. What is etched in the future is God's will, but this land is a land of rock and stone, and its future is ordained in the fine grass that shields it - trampled, eaten and destroyed our land will vanish as surely as the grass ...mark my words, Robbie! Yet my wife and I are auld and thus, in some ways, we care little about what is to come; but take heed...for the Great Laird's ways are foreign to ours, he being a Sassenach by birth. That is quite clear!' (*Tha sin gu math soilleir!*)

While the whispering would have continued for some time, the young man being curious as to what further words of wisdom Domhnall was about to say, their muted conversation was broken by the sound of the horse galloping off down the Drover's track after the sheep.

The Minister turned and, tucking his prayer book under his arm, quietly started to leave the assembled throng, giving a final prayer and a deep bow.

Even Mairead's entreaties could not make him stay for the festivities.

She held his arm for a moment and then in an impulse kissed him quickly on the right cheek. Alasdair shook him warmly by the hand.

Thus with other tokens of friendship the Minister slowly made his way along the Drover's track in the direction of his twin brother.

Yet he did not smile, but walked with his tall, angular frame stooped forward as if in silent contemplation.

The guests watched him depart.

Then the sun really broke free, and the Glen sparkled in the light, while the eagle's cry sounded plaintively in the distance.

Tri (three)

To understand some basic facts.

Barely able to walk, the baby girl toddled into a fortune.

For in1766 she succeeded to the estates of her father, William, 21st earl of Sutherland and became the Countess, at the age of one.

She was the premier aristocrat of Scotland.

In 1785 she married an English man, the Marquess of Stafford and took his title in addition.

In the years to come their wealth grew and grew and in1833 The Marquess was created Duke and his wife Duchess-Countess of Sutherland, one of the largest acreages in Britain was at their disposal.

The family mansion in that county was Dunrobin Castle situated on the eastern seaboard in the southern section of the County of Sutherland, close to the county town of Dornoch in the Highlands of Scotland – that ancient landmass that first emerged at the beginning of time.

Their home was England, their language English, and their loyalties to the English crown. To them, Scotland was almost a foreign land; and when they came - which was an auspicious and rare occasion in the lives of the poor tenants - they came only to the Castle. Those stonewalls were their horizon. The tenants were denied access and in their humility generally sought none. Petitions were ignored if not signed by a man of the cloth; yet the ministers paid deference and courted no disapproval of the Marquess' wishes while the factors, who managed the land, were equally unapproachable in their blind servility, eager for any favours that might come their way.

Such was the schism between the nobility and the peasants.

*****

Three hundred thousand a year!

That was some income indeed! (* it was when the average wage was about £10-20 per annum.)

Although he recognized that wealth had to be protected in 1809, even when bloated to this degree.

The Marquess of Stafford pondered the facts in his self-indulgent way.

Nearly two thousand square miles of land in the Highlands– and only bringing in fifteen thousand per annum!

The Marquess paused. That piffling sum of fifteen thousand could not support his staff - this thought was melancholy enough.

Never mind the luxurious mansion in London, and his family seat at Lilleshall. (* Shropshire, England).

He recognized that he owned a huge chunk of Britain, including a northern landmass in Scotland that stretched from coast to coast, the district of Sutherland.

What a strange, sinister area it was to be true. A place where no one travelled or ventured to travel, unless unduly curious or foolhardy.

He acknowledged that in polite society, the far north of Britain was too horrible to contemplate or even mention– a barbaric land as wild as any place on earth. For beyond the mountains the Highlanders were feared, ridiculed, despised and hated by those who did not understand them. It was not a place to venture!

The Highlanders live in the midst of smoke and filth, Lord Stafford had been told, which has been their choice for generations; poor, ill-educated and illiterate as any desert nomad or village African.

But the feudal system was slowly changing and the wily lord knew it.

For in the place of the old chiefs who had died, the newer more ambitious leaders were starting to develop lowland aspirations. Stafford knew that many dreamed of an Edinburgh house and their wives pondered over having exquisite silks and satins gowns, monogrammed cutlery and children secure in the armed forces and making a mark in society.

And as the new chiefs considered the current reality, they realized they had to increase their income.

*****

The Chiefs knew they could prosper in two ways; first by increasing the rents and second by reducing the number of people working on their land. The tacks men were the vital link. They shared out the land. They had to be brought to heel. If they resisted or dissented in any way, they had to be removed.

Some died, infirmity removed some; but many tacks men left of their own freewill once they realized the impossible situation they were being driven into. They were the honest managers, unable to pass on the extortionate increase in rent. How could they double or treble the dues, they asked themselves. They felt nothing but sympathy for the sub-tenants and cottars – those most humble of Highlanders- whose lives they oversaw. Not wishing to be part of the new order they decided to leave and, in doing so, break the old feudal ties that bound them to the chiefs and lairds. Liberty beckoned, but liberty was often many thousands of miles away. Thus tacks men of free spirit and enterprise took the gamble and left their native land. They spread the gospel and were often eagerly followed by the people they had employed- simple families who trusted them implicitly. These poor people realized that the rising rent prices were designed to benefit the chiefs in their extravagance, or to drive them off the land. Such was the rapid exodus that by the year 1809 almost seven thousand people had sailed from Highland shores. While Lord Stafford's plans meant that sheep were taking over and a way of life which had been loved for generations was being slowly deserted. Houses crumbled, small acres rapidly became festooned with thistles and weeds, while fences rotted as the slow trickle of emigrants began to strike the first death knell for the Highlands and Islands

Nova Scotia and the Carolinas, places so far away that they were beyond the simple comprehension of the

Highlanders, were the first and popular choices. There, it was felt, would be the better life. At first they left, as cheerfully as such an upheaval would permit. But as the years went by this optimism was replaced by the necessity of having to leave - as starvation, poverty and neglect drove them from the Highlands. They left to seek new lands; bitter were the tears, and even more bitter were the recriminations later.

As always there were many tacks men who obeyed their masters and did not have a conscience or feel any resentment about the hardship they were inflicting, arrogantly thrusting the rising rent onto the subtenants; while the chief or lairds' right-hand man (the factor) made sure that the rules of payment were rigorously enforced.

Throughout this execution of the plan to harness the wealth of the Highlands, the Marquess and Countess stayed as remote as the mountain peaks the cottars gazed upon in their humble lives; as far removed again were the jewels that festooned the Countess compared to the primitive iron crucifixes that hung in the cottar's tiny homes. The Lord and Lady Stafford were in essence remote – both in manner and location. The South of England was good enough for them, where the affection in dress and language gave them a sense of superiority. Wasn't the Gaelic tongue uncouth, the language of the uneducated?

What was this land they ignored? What were the people they neglected and hoped to suppress? The Gaelic language told of a land scoured into mountains and lochs by the coarse grinding hands of ice. Where winds flew in from the sea and Sutherland clung to a restless edge of the world laid siege by water on three sides. But this land and weather could temper the spirit, hardened the sinews and strengthened the resolve. Arctic cold, freezing gales, deluging rain, storm and tempest, hurried summer days - no race on Earth like the Sutherland clan had such an iconoclastic molding by the elements. People tall and hardy, tallest by far in Britain and in most of Europe, with resolute yet phlegmatic characters, were able to fend what life threw at them. This race, a mixture of Gaels and Norse, cut off from the outside world, with not one road of note but the drovers' tracts to the lowlands, dealt with the elements in simple huts of stones with grass, sod or peat roofs. Through this moss covered thatch the smoke curled from an opening that could let the elements in and disturb the animals' slumbers as they sought sheltered before the peat fire they shared as members of an extended family. Within the small fenced area – a fence of crude branches – the scrub land was used to contain the black cattle, goats and scrawny sheep. The meager crops of oats, turnips and small potatoes, the rough beer and sharp whisky gave a basic sustenance and constant cheer, which just kept famine at bay - year in year out.

Theirs was a contrast of contrasts! For the Marquess and Countess held court amidst the finest furniture, finest pictures of the day (now priceless in countless museums and art galleries), gold and silver ware, butlers, coachmen, maids and all the paraphernalia that filled the Dunrobin Castle and their other stately houses.

At first the Highlanders hoped that things would improve. But as times passed even their faint hopes that some of the clergy might help them in their hour of need began to fade; and to the grief, anger and bewilderment of the people, the Great Laird and Lady (as the Marquess and Countess were called) began the uprooting of families for sheep. And as the other landowners and chiefs prospered, so did the clergy. For the ministers were an important cog in the wheel of suppression, for they propounded that God's authority backed the Marquess and his henchmen's plans, and many of the Highlanders who detested the sheep at first, relented in piety and soon fell in with the rich and powerful to become rich and powerful themselves. Others, in true scriptural style, fearing the Holy Word were struck with religious hesitancy about future damnation. Believing there was nothing that could be done, they accepted their fate with a resigned patience.

The Marquess recognized servility and hard work; those who were industrious were praised although they gained little in material terms. But, at least, they did not have to forfeit all that was theirs by birthright. 'Children come into the world without any covering or defence against the weather,' he wrote, 'is it too much to say that for every person born a certain number of sheep must be lambed? On this principle, with a good conscience, I grow wool on mountains that are covered with peat bog, believing that I thereby benefit my fellow men.'

If only all the land was peat bog and alpine scrub, these plans would have not caused any hardship. But the animal that survived best, and had done for generation upon generation, was the Highlander. Such plans may have changed the economy, may have enriched a few pockets including the Marquess (later a Duke and by far the richest man in Britain) but they did not enrich the cottar and his wife one iota.

It was the first seeds of a proud clan's destruction.

Ceithir (four)

The young girl pulled her skirt high above her knees as she sat in the heather.

Her hair was long and dark, her smooth skin equally dark, her body curved but plump and well rounded at hips and thighs. She had black and mischievous eyes, long eyelashes and a full and sensual mouth. Robbie had a sly kiss on that mouth after the wedding. At first inclination she had been taken aback and, in feigned annoyance, refused a second, yet longing to kiss him again. Whether she would or would not succumb in future depended on her caution. Eilidh (Helen) had been caught unawares before and nearly paid the price. She never knew if it was an early miscarriage or not. Perhaps not, but she was unsure of her instincts now.

Looking at her in this preoccupied moment, one would note the suffused blue of her lips and tongue, the discoloured mouth, her face appearing as if the Devil had tried to hold her in one long and suffocating grasp.

Her fingers were equally indigo and purple, up to the palmar creases.

The basket by her side gave the clue to her unusual appearance. For it was full of bilberries –rich and plump like her body and equally tempting, she liked to think, to the men of that Glen.

She had enjoyed their lingering looks, their furtive glances as she wandered past, their high spirits. The smiles and agitations as they fumbled for words when trying to impress! The lost composure of youth, the firm composure of middle age, the accomplished loose-tongued platitudes of old age, which impressed no one!

She paused in her picking but not because most of the green wiry shoots had been stripped about her. No, she thought of the wedding the day before and it was the noise of the revelry, the sound of the drunken masses, that still rang in her subconscious – and she smiled for she had been as drunk as the rest; weaving round and round the throng, jubilant in its witnessed happiness. A debauched reel, which spun in her head now as it did then; face after face whirling before her. Some were kissable, some not – but that's always the way with men. And so much to drink - they had run out of goat's milk, that perennial cure. Her head had ached when she got up that morning at six, but not now. She had washed her hair and let it dry with a neat curl about her face, waved by the August sun.

Her dress was black…so what did the stains matter? She laughed.

She held to one aim above all others, and she was no different from the rest of her friends. She longed to be married…away from the uncertainty of it all, secure in her own croft.

Probably to one of her neighbours – someone she had known for most, if not all of her life. That was the rule! One hadn't to wander far to find a husband, not in this remote corner of the world where people, especially eligible, handsome men were few and far between. She smiled as she contemplated her future. Perhaps married to Robbie Sutherland? He was so fly at present and a wanderer born. But still he was a fine kisser and looked a romantic, braw man.

She liked to consult the future through the portents of her clan. How often had she used eggs; the first laid of a young pullet were the best and had to be dropped into fresh spring water. The white would slide through the crystal water. It was easy to take a mouthful without swallowing. Hold the wobbling jelly mass on the tongue and walk about the countryside. The first single man's name she heard called would be the intended.

Eilidh laughed.

Someone had called for Ciaran, perhaps his mother. She laughed again. He was ten and in short pants and of no future worth to anyone. Hadn't they made him drink from the skull of a man who hanged himself, the way to cure his fits, or did they bury a black cockerel alive at the spot where he first writhed and foamed, she could not remember. But it was to no avail anyway – that was the point. Poor Ciaran! Poor Ciaran!

And herring fat? It slid down the wall in a series of whorls so that her friends said she threw it deliberately to marry a crooked husband, and others told her to learn how to throw!

She would go to a Holy Fair, she decided with a pursing of the lips, and meet someone of good repute in the week of Sacramental Days. He would be a good man! Someone away from her makeshift, drunken father; a truly good man could be found that way.

Eilidh gazed over the valley and saw the red grouse winging their stiff-winged flight onto the heather opposite.

She liked such communion with the wildnerness of the Highlands, such undisturbed reverie! As she gazed her mind reverted to the preparations for marriage. She smiled at the thought of bundling together, when a lad and lass shared a bed before the wedding. It would be too late in her case! She shook her head.

But the sheer enthusiasm of the sunshine and the bird song made her feel alive. Eilidh laughed and started picking the blue berries. She thought of the strange enactment of sharing a bed fully clothed but with her legs firmly tied to a long double pillow; so that the time spent was talk and more talk, and so she had been told, the couple got to know each other for better or worse. She could think of nothing worse than being tethered to a highland man in a lumpy bed.

She considered her options. There were but a few strangers to meet in the Highlands. 'Go and ask the lowland boys over,' she had said at one gathering and Criosaidh (Chrissie) had obliged. Laughed and talked and tickled and chattered like wrens! Bright virgins, so those strangers thought; with a strange tongue to puzzle the lowland cattlemen who brought their beast up to the hills for some extra grazing!

A few clouds drifted lazily across the blue sky and fretted the crags and hills, just above the shallow tree line where the junipers twisted convulsively towards the earth again. A fleeting set of shadows, with another hint of a bird song in the distance and the sound of bees hunting the shimmering honeyed-heather fragrance.

She felt a slight change in temperature as the shadow crossed her reclining body and then the sunshine whipped free of the transient gloom.

But the chill remained.

She puzzled for a moment and turned round.

A red-coated soldier stood behind her and smiled; then bowed politely, 'Sometimes it is not fair to spoil such beauty outlined by the rich colours of the fell.'

The girl sat silently contemplating the stranger, unafraid but not unmoved. His fine, fair features, pale-blue eyes tempered by the smile hidden within and the even teeth looked even more romantic against the scarlet tunic of the infantry.

'I startled you, my apologies, please!' He spoke without condescension.

The second, more truncated bow, made her laugh. 'Aye, ye did and ye didn't!'

She was unused to such manners and slightly abashed and unsure of the response. But her laugh was so unaffected, so totally naturally, that the soldier unceremoniously went to sit by her side.

'Take care!' she said firmly.

He straightened up suddenly and the gold of the buttons caught the sunlight.

'There's mickle juice from the bilberries to ruin a fine pair of trousers like that!'

It was his turn to laugh. He surveyed the girl. 'She's only a few years younger than me and spirited in that unabashed Highland way,' he thought.

Yet, from that first moment he felt a bond between them as if he had known her for all of his twenty-six years. It was so strange, he was to think later.

To Eilidh the brightness on his buttons formed a series of distinct halos, so that like the Nordic chiefs of old from Valhalla he seemed to exude an aura that aroused all her latent feminine instincts. She felt for him as an innocent child, an ethereal and delicate being suddenly thrust upon her. It was both a beautiful and disturbing experience.

While lost in contemplation the soldier had removed his jacket, and taking care to place it over a rock above the heather-line, he lay back shading his face with his hand against the sun; not speaking but simply contemplating the shadows, crags and hills.

Eilidh had stopped picking the bilberries for a few minutes. In the silence she returned, working as dutifully as any wife. But she was conscious of his gaze from time to time, but did not turn round. She would occasionally, and slyly, glance over her shoulder. 'The jaiket is sae bonny,' she repeated to herself, 'and he's a braw figure of a man, indeed. More's the pity,' she thought 'that I dinna have any of my Celtic incantations and omens with me, to test the truths o' matrimony. But he has a Sassenach way and speech despite the Scotia manner and looks, which might no be so guid, after all'

He broke the silence. 'You're as fair a maid as I have seen above the north side of Perth, are you not! In my kirk you would cut a fine figure amongst the auld dames!'

She smiled and half-looked at him. 'In these auld black clothes, and I've little else, I can tell ye! And y' in all that finery.' She pointed to the jacket.

He stood up and reached for the coat. In an instant he had slipped it around her shoulders and stood back to admire the picture. Not content he reached forward and smoothed the black hair neatly on each side of the gold epaulets. She liked him touching her hair, why she couldn't reason, but instinctively she liked it.

He only said, 'There!' and nothing more.

There was a silence until she bashfully took off the scarlet coat and handed it back. 'If the folks round here see me in a Sassenach jacket, they'll have me whipped or some such, I can tell ye!'

He laughed. 'I mean no offence…and the picture was of true beauty, believe me!'

She wanted to believe him and she did. Was she being naïve and impressionable, she could not decide? Suddenly the strange intoxication of the moment made her laugh and laugh, in a curious nervous release of tension.

The young man looked perplexed.

'Y're a handsome body yersel, soldier and the manners of a born laird. For a wee moment I fancied myself a lady in the congregation, with fine clothes and airs and graces and a' that! But it'll never be me, not until old Scotia sinks in the sea. No! Never! I trow! But it's a dream, if only fur a moment. And I thank ye kindly fur it.'

'Think shame on yourself, miss, for having such a low opinion! Perhaps your beauty and strength of character will carry you through and beyond the expectations you imagine now.'

'I dinna think sae soldier; and I ken myself better than anyone, if anyone can ken oneself!

There was a short pause.

She glanced shyly round and he looked up and smiled, not just with his mouth and eyes but his whole being seemed to radiate warmth. It gave her a sudden instinctive thrill of pleasure and she caught the light in his eyes, and it was another strange primitive experience, one she had not felt before.

The girl resumed her bilberry picking, smiling to herself, and the soldier surveyed her intently. Curious, he asked, 'Do you have a boyfriend?' He paused and said hurriedly, 'Anyone in particular?'

She shrugged her shoulders and put the berries in the basket, now half-full. She sucked the juice off her fingertips and looked towards him.' Aye, *aon!*'

'Only one?'

'Tha!'

'That's a mystery, I would have expected more', he smiled, 'what's his clan?'

She resumed picking, pushing the green shoots aside for the last lingering berries. 'Sutherland, as I am!'

The soldier inclined his resting head to one side so that the blue eyes directly faced her. 'And…'

'…Robbie'. Content with the knowledge the soldier turned and stared at the valley in silence.

*****

The soldier lay back and thought about his relatives, and considered his plight.

He thought of cheese, bitter and slightly pungent with the smell characteristic of ewes' milk.

The soldier knew that there had always been sheep in the Highlands, scrawny, poor boned creatures that lived in the higher reaches of the mountains and provided grizzly meat when killed; not the rich red-blooded venison or hare or kyloe beef. And these sheep were few and mixed amiably with the cattle in the grazing lands.

The sheep from the Borders and rich fertile areas of the lowlands were a hardier breed but considered unfit for the harsh winters of the north. He recalled that his uncle, John Lockhart, had thought differently a year or so ago – a plain, sea-faring man, but with a plan to graze the highlands. At first there were doubts. Cautiously, and watched with interest, Lockhart had explored the possibilities. For he had become, in his early forties, the great laird of the area, buying up land that stretched from Dornoch Firth to the County of Ross where the winds were warmer, and the grazing better under the milder, more conducive climate of the western coast. His holdings were known as Balnagowan – a land of mountains, marsh and intermittent green pastures, bathed by the warm mists of spring and summer that drifted in from the Atlantic Sea. As his importance and prestige grew his name had recently stretched like his property to an imposing Sir Lockhart-Ross.

He liked the black-faced Lintons and then the Cheviots.

'Enclose those hills!' He had ordered. 'Drain the marshes! 'But my Laird…' The soldier had heard from the Highlanders of the objections, the commands and more objections. It was the talk of his homeland.

However, there were only a few 'buts', for the labourers were southern men who had no truck with the highlands. A shilling a day, and the grip on the reclaimed fenced land that had survived for generations in Ross was tightened as if a noose had been placed around its neck. The local families cried out in despair as the noose was pulled even tighter, and more and more pastures were given over to the bleating flocks. Lockhart-Ross had said that he meant no offence. But within a liberal breast he harboured wealth and ambition. There were no intricacies of guilt in this man. He thought no thoughts but those of himself and family. There were no alternate ascendancies to power but through the wealth of wool.

But were the sheep hardy enough to survive? The local crofters laughed, thought not, and tossed back the wee drams of usquebaugh.

The soldier smiled at their naivety, for they were wrong.

And the sheep had the last laugh, warm without any spirit or spiritual help, comfortable in thick wool, and dreaded by the Highlanders as they wrenched the tough grass and laid waste the higher grounds.

So, as he lay and contemplated the girl, the facts rolled over and over in the soldier's mind.

*****

The soldier who watched the girl picking bilberries could be described as above average height and muscularity with a shaven face and pale complexion. The apt description of his manner and bearing could be summed up as felicitous. By maintaining a pleasant companionship and an ingenious aura of silence Eilidh seemed drawn to him by instinct.

Like a cat, he waited and thought.

The redcoats of the 42nd Black Watch were his men, companions in good times and bad. They had paraded; tired and perspiring, face coated with dust, through the streets of Dingwall. The only enemy, they were told, was some of their own simple folk, people generally obedient in the Glens. Poor men and women, who barely survived with a cow or two and a small strip of grazing land. He had felt the pain, the humiliation of these people as he paraded past, many who called after him, 'Awa with ye Andrew. Y' call yersel a Lockhart as well, after that greedy aud laird who has taken the land. A lowland nephew but as bad! Y're a traitor to thine own folk!'

And these old women waved their fists and the younger ones threw water, mud and stones. He had the bruises yet!

He could recall that the Colonel had made one thing absolutely clear! There was to be no insurrection in the Highlands. Especially not on his lands, or his cousins!

But he knew the men of Ross had hardened in their opinion and felt slighted at being told what to do. At the time he sensed they were determined to act and they did. Like a smouldering ember they required only one catalyst of energy to burst into flame.

They needed a spokesman, someone to drive them forward; and they found him in a burly blacksmith who beat the sparks out of the iron day after day, brawn upon brawn. Niall MacIomhair led them on.

Niall saw the hills were overstocked with the scraggy cattle and were confined into smaller and smaller acreage. Niall had watched the relentless march of the sheep as the grazing suffered. And the crofters knew that for the last few years the crops had been bad and many of the starving cattle slaughtered. Now these crofters were barely able to eek out a living, and had to face renewed hardship and empty bellies day after day. They had had enough.

The soldier's thoughts left the dismal past and he looked up to study the girl. But she was content to fill her basket, the plump fruits had almost reached the top. The only sound was the occasional sucking of her fingers.

This vision did not end his ruminations. He was annoyed to contemplate the recent past in this way, but the beauty and contentment of the girl and the surroundings, brought the events of the last few days into an even sharper focus.

For in early summer the cattle had been driven up the strath towards Glen Morie for summer grazing; only to find that this fertile land was taken, unavailable, invaded by Cheviot sheep. The local Cameron brothers had seized the initiative. The soldier could appreciate that

MacIomhair's anger on hearing this news would have known no bounds.

Within the hour of MacIomhair's call to action, thousands of bleating animals were being pushed away from the glen. Not only by the cattlemen, but workers cutting peat downed tools and joined in the foray just as the soldiers arrived, rifles at the ready with Captain Cameron in command. It was his battalion and he had been one of them!

He recalled his hand trembling as the gun was raised and pointed at one of his own folk, an old crofter from near Adross. And the look of hatred, defiance and despair in the old man's eyes as he saw his meagre living in the process of being destroyed – perhaps forever!

One of the Camerons had armed themselves with a dirk as long as his forearm. Another, Captain Cameron levelled his musket. He had suddenly felt afraid for the Highlanders.

There were taunts, gibes and parleying between the sheepmen and the Highlanders. But Niall MacIomhair, tiring of such blathering, just waded forward through the throng. He stood foursquare in front of the Captain, looked him in the eye, and in a second had grasped the gun. The Captain was too astonished to act. With a grunt Niall bent it over his knee as if it were a reed. With another blow he sent the dirk spinning into the air.

For a second he remembered levelling his gun on the blacksmith. But the man's look conveyed no fear, as he gave a contemptuous shrug of the shoulders and ambled off down the valley by the twisting beck.

The scuffling mob had been subdued.

He later heard that within a few days five honest Highlanders were sentenced to transportation to Botany Bay, for seven years. It did not seem fair!

The soldier looked up again.

She had finished picking now, stood up and smoothed her dress.

'You'll be going then?' he asked with a symbolic gesture of the hand.

'I'll be of a mind to, the berries are all done!' Nothing was spoken for a few minutes.

'The deepest feelings are oft said by silence!' the soldier was surprised at his poetic eloquence.

The remark spoken in such a tender, yet off-hand, way made her pause before replying, 'It's no true!'

'You'll not be agreeing then with the sentiment?' He looked apprehensive as he said it.

She laughed; a short laugh and rolled a few berries round and round in the basket as if collecting her thoughts. 'No! It's aboot Robbie Sutherland...he's no my boyfriend. It was said to tease. I ken nae why!'

He laughed. 'I don't know the man anyway!' He paused. 'Now, Niall MacIomhair, he's a man I would like to know!'

But she didn't reply.

The crofters had their code of silence.

Feeling uneasy with the last remark, Eilidh hurried down the hillside, while the plovers dashed back and forth in their confusion and alarm.

Coig (five)

Standing in isolation, and whipped by the harsh Highland winds, was a small, stone cottage. The walls were a dirty white and stained peat-brown by the thatch, which was of tinder dry heather, held down by stone-weighted ropes.

This cottage had once been part of a small township of six houses and two barns, but the swampy land had encroached on the hollow of the fields and sphagnum moss and bell heather now invaded what was once meagre pasture land, at the best.

So the inhabitants had moved on, taking with them their scrawny sheep and a dozen or so kyloes. Over the ensuing twenty years the other houses had fallen into disrepute, so that their main wooden beams had rotted and snapped, and the thatch lay crushed within their tiny rooms, now open to the sky.

However, a peat fire still smoked in the remaining dwelling, the slow blue-black cloud drifting up from the centre of the room and out through a small opening in the ceiling.

The fire made the living area even more cramped. Measuring only twelve feet by eight, the floor was of compressed earth, rising slightly at the far stonewall to give some drainage towards the only exterior door. The windows were only a few inches wide and about two foot high, slits which kept out the cold but barely let in the light - hence the need for the door to be open at most times.

In one corner stood a roughly made pine table harbouring a few utensils and two bowls. In another corner was a spinning wheel with a few fleeces draped over it, while in another corner was a wooden bed set three feet from the floor, the whole surrounded by a rough spun brown curtain to keep out the draughts. Into the supporting beams and the furniture were driven iron nails, in the shape of a cross, to ward off evil spirits. In pride of place was a rusty horseshoe retrieved from a shipwreck in years gone by.

However, the room was not empty.

For behind the drawn curtain, half-propped on the wooden bed by a large pillow stuffed with wool, was an old woman - toothless, palsied, and dishevelled. A tattered bonnet covered her sparse grey hair; a dark plaid shawl was wrapped around her shoulders, while a long stained dress stretched to her feet. Into the hem of her garment were other small nails to ward off the pain that wracked her body. Morag, Domhnall's elder sister, had been unable to attend the wedding of Alasdair and Mairead.

Her eyes slowly focussed on the cross of nails, and in a sudden compulsion she snatched at the air to try and grasp the crucifix before her. But the rapid movement of sitting up and reaching out fatigued her and, with an imperceptible sigh, she slowly sank back onto the pillow.

In such a bemused state she contemplated life, seeing only fragments of the distant past - sometimes as a young girl running through the heather and plashing along the shore frightening the gulls, at other times as a woman strong in middle age, yet sad and alone after the death of three of her children. She could still hear the harsh, rapid breathings of each child, one by one afflicted with a tuberculous chest; one by one passing away in her arms. And the cholera outbreak, the violent pains that had mysteriously settled with the extract of wort before it took any more of them off, although five had died in the township. Then her mind took another diversion in the past and she was wandering free with her mother, fetching in the black cow from the long pasture, feeling the warm milk rush down her throat, hearing her mother's laughter, comforting even today.

There was a faint clattering of hooves in the distance.

'*Hello!* There's that Shetland pony, and Auld Jock the carter calling,' she mused to herself smiling at the man's cheek. 'He would take anything for nothing and turn it into something. 'With a wee nip o'whisky forever by his side.'

She called faintly, 'It is me, Morag, Jock…it is me!' *('S mise, Morag...Jock....'s mise Morag!)* But there was no reply.

Only a confused babble of voices, and more clattering of hooves.

For a few moments the noise was suspended, and the old lady began to dose, her pale face resting gently against the side of the bed's wooden frame.

Once again Auld Jock.

She heard him clearly, a friend from her youth.

''S mise, Morag...Jock...Jock!'

And she heard a faint reply, but in her confused mind it seemed the strong voices of men calling and calling, their voices echoing around her head.

Then suddenly there were hushed whispers, then shouting.

And as she craned forward to see what was going on, she saw a golden glow light up the crucifix of nails.

With the brightness of Calvary a thousand suns seemed to shine as halos around her face.

The brown curtain twisted and gnarled in the intense heat, the bedclothes leapt in reds and whites and yellows.

While the men outside went on calling, 'Burn the thatch, burn the thatch...and let us be rid o' this hovel.' Someone called, 'Is there anyone inside, factor?'

'Damn her, the old witch, she has lived too long, let her burn!'

So factor and his men paused to survey their handiwork of orange flames and black smoke leap wantonly to the sky.

Thus the final derelict homestead, in a township of no worth, was destroyed to make way for more grazing land.

And in such manner did one old woman meet her Maker.

*****

'No matter how hard the work was (*Air cho cruaidh's a bha an obai*), no matter how poor they were (*a dh'aindheoin cho bochd 's a bha iad*), Domhnall and Ealasaid had always maintained a simple faith that one must accept what the Good Lord provideth.

It had been their parents' creed and that of the generations before them. They had lived in a society dominated by the Chief and his family.

Just below the Chief, were the tacks men –sometimes family, sometimes friend - who held enough power and wealth to lease meagre strips of land to the tenants. These leases, based on service in kind and good will, formed the small townships in which so many lived. These were tiny, often isolated, communities where a half a dozen families or more worked a farm in common. But it was no great area to speak of, only a humble plot on one side of the glen sufficient to graze thirty cattle and a small flock of bony sheep. While arable land was often so scarce that the strips (or runrigs) were generally proportioned at intervals by the drawing of lots.

But as poor as these people were, there was another layer in this primitive society. For below the tenants were the cottars. Landless people who were from birth destined to labour as servants. With enough land for a cow and a small potato patch, they were the workers - herdsmen and weavers, blacksmiths, woodsmen and hill shepherds.

Domhnall knew how to work and how to suffer hardship and hunger in a life of servitude - and be thankful. His indomitable spirit was as unshakeable as the relentless surroundings, moulded for generations by the elements, pleased to be part of a small, hardy fraternity, seemingly separated from all others by a water divide.

It was a windless and warm day, and the sun shone - highlighting the mountains and casting a green and purple glow almost to the rocky summits - as the old man and his wife picked their way among the stones of a dried out riverbed towards a delve in the horizon. Here they would begin their descent into another valley. They made their way purposively in the heat, measuring each step up the winding incline which less than a month before had been filled with the rushing tumult of a summer's flood fed by a dozen storms. Pausing every hundred yards or so they surveyed the surrounding valley, which must have been a witness to their slow deliberations so many countless times before. Yet theirs was an uncritical gaze, and they still found time to admire the majesty, solitude and beauty. Familiarity bred no contempt! Quietly they would point out a familiar landmark commenting on how it had, or had not, changed. The old man would observe the folds of the hills, the freshness of the grass upon them, the encroachment of bracken and he would quickly calculate its grazing worth. As they climbed higher and higher each stop gave a further few moments of peaceful contemplation. The love of this land was in their blood. It was the only land they had ever known. To them no other place existed.

Few Highlanders ventured far from their place of birth and the relatively small number of people who lived in the immediate vicinity shared their knowledge, beliefs and ideas to a great degree. They rarely travelled far. Superstitious and naive, they knew that their future was always unpredictable. To them the hand of fate was ever present. Only through signs and omens could incipient evils be quickly recognised. Thus Domhnall felt uneasy that August day. For he had heard a cock crowing near midnight, and knew it foretold an imminent death. He waited for other signs with apprehension but none had come that morning. Although Ealasaid had noticed his initial silence and quietly walked by his side throughout the journey, as his spirits rose and the conversation developed, her replies had become almost mechanical.

For she was thinking of the previous day's wedding. There the omens had been good! The ceremony had taken place on Venusday (*Friday) and there had been a good show of presents on the Thursday. How plentiful were the oatcakes, honey, meats and fruits...what prosperity they heralded for the future. Also the bride had made up her own bridal bed...and what amount of salt had been scattered on the floor for luck. How she smiled as she remembered her own wedding in the Kirk those many years ago, with the nervous Domhnall standing by her side. But they were poor people and it was a penny wedding (* when each guest defrayed the cost of the food, drink and fiddler with a contribution). 'And what's ta'en and what's gane, life had been a bit o' a struggle, but mostly all guid,' she mused to herself stopping to breathe in the pure mountain air and survey the surroundings.

Suddenly she noticed Domhnall hurry on. Within moments he was a hundred paces ahead.

Ealasaid was puzzled by this new haste. She called out, asked him to slow down; but he did not pause. He only turned for a moment and impatiently motioned her on.

As they strode forward the summit of the hill came into view, and by a curious slight of perspective it seemingly appeared from nowhere, having been hidden for most of the way by a narrow ridge. Just before the summit the ground sloped steeply towards them and the wind, not present on the lower reaches, gusted suddenly and lifted the plaid shawl from the woman's shoulders.

As she paused to smooth it down, her husband gained the summit. He stood motionless, his fading sight scanning the ruined township below.

At first he thought it was mist, but as its blueness was woven into the tendrils of grey it became unmistakable, even to his failing vision.

Slowly the smoke curled in fine, wispy columns, a pointer to the charred shell of a house. He turned to his wife; she also gazed in disbelief. They did not say one word, but hurried in their alarm along the downward path. In his haste Domhnall strode across a boggy area, squelching through the mud between the bulrushes and in the effort of dragging his feet from the morass he taxed his frail frame. Anxiety drove him on - taking the most direct route to the homestead whatever the terrain, breathing rapidly in a mixture of anxiety and fear. His momentum quickened as he approached the smouldering house. With his wife following the longer, dry route Domhnall arrived about a minute before her. He stared in disbelief and anger at the slowly burning timbers, the thick, blackened beams and peat roof now degenerated into grey ash.

But the wood was still hot and it was only with difficulty that he dislodged some of the charred timbers, which having snapped, had fallen to block the entrance and criss-cross the rough mud floors. He tried to pick his way through the debris, despite the smell of wood and flesh and confusion around him. He could see that the bed and the coverings were gone; all that remained on the ground where it had stood were a small metal ring and a mass of nails. With a start he saw the body, or what remained of charred tissues, and he turned back to the entrance, tears rolling down his face.

Meanwhile his wife called hysterically, 'Morag! Morag!' - until her voice was hoarse. Only then did she slowly sink to the grass outside the ruin, weeping softly and rocking gently to and fro.

'Oh! For the Minister,' the old man said softly when he had composed himself, 'for he wud give us a decent answer to a' this!'

But the Minister could not reply, although he was only a hundred feet away.

Sia (six)

Robbie Sutherland sat on a small crag with his back against the rock and enjoyed the August heat in a sublime solitude. He closed his eyes, his head still pounding from the wedding festivities of the day before and from the whisky and ale that had freely flowed. There was tranquillity - a sweet calmness- in the gentle current of air that played round him on the small promontory, some two hundred feet up the cliff face. He sat there like a mountain goat in all its solemn and acrobatic majesty. Directly below his dangling feet the ground shimmered with haze, and only the occasional faint warbling of some moorland birds broke the stillness. It was a low whispering sound he had heard so many times before. The coolness of the rocks soothed his aching body. Idly he searched the tough green shoots that clung to the ledge for bilberries and their sweet juice soon purpled his lips and tongue. For once the Highland silence had tamed the mountains and he lay back against the rock face in a blissful dream only concerned with the moment and nothing more. Even the glen seemed to sleep in the sun. Robbie stirred lazily. He was the youngest in a family of two children. His father was a half-brother to the Chief, and this relationship conferred certain rights and privileges that included a large, fertile strath of land some twenty-five miles away, close to the southern boundary of Loch Shin where the River Tirry flowed swift and pure.

It was not in the Highland spirit to feel restless about events, the pace of life was slow amongst the hills and Robbie was not anxious to hurry on. There was an eloquence in the silence about him that he enjoyed, in the pure air and gentle rushing of the streams as they poured down the steep inclines into tinkling waterfalls within the distant hills. It was a beautiful noise to his senses, as reassuring as his mother's lullabies. He was feeling very grateful for the life he had been given, and the feeling strengthened the strange bond with nature and with the deity.

The sun has moved stealthily forwards in the heavens, and a shaft of brightness aroused him from his dream-like state and he felt hot. Thus on opening his eyes, yawning to clear his head and stretching to give life to aching limbs, he slowly sat up. Robbie was surprised to see two figures picking their way amongst the rocks of a dried out burn. Although some distance away and far below, he could easily distinguish Domhnall and his wife. He recalled the old man's words of warning, 'Flocks will strip the land o' its goodness!' Robbie puzzled over this remark.

He had heard of the Marquess wishing to hire good, strong men for work on the land and he felt tempted to apply. Once more he ruminated over his future, the wedding having, in a curious way, made him conscious of his own current restlessness. There was little prospect of him inheriting land on his father's death. He knew that their farm was, in many ways, too small to be divided into two useful holdings. Even if that should happen, which he doubted, the poorest part, the dampest area, would come his way for Alasdair would have his pick. Despite the long held reservations there was a glimmer of optimism, a ray of hope. 'Perhaps his brother might stay on the land he was farming now, which had been tenanted from Mairead's father?' This thought made him reflect for a moment as he surveyed the valley.

The flattened bracken showed the route the recent flocks of sheep had taken. The fact that the animals had spilled off the broad drover's track and onto the moorland was an indication of the enormous numbers involved.

Then he considered the work that was needed to tend such flocks. The more he thought about it, the more hopeful he grew. He would apply for a shepherding post to the Laird's factor. As he dwelled on his vision of future -prosperity, new friends and hopefully a holding of his own or promotion to a factor's job - he smiled broadly with an inner confidence. After all, he was well versed in the best grazing, often taking their meagre flock into the hills for summer grass. He could read, taught by his mother and the Minister. And he was the strongest of the three men in the house, and his cousins and friends too. It was no mean feat to hurl the caber in last summer's games farther than anyone had for years.

In such optimism did Robbie arise, having rested for half an hour, and after stretching once more he set off in an eager step towards the pass. As he looked up he saw the old man and his wife standing on the brow of the hill, but when he looked again, after crossing behind a small crest, the old couple had disappeared. The clouds came in broken wisps and the gold of the sun was not affected. He stopped and bathed his brow with the water from a small stream that ambled falteringly along a broad stony course. The water was warm and unfit for drinking.

But a spring shone in earnest, glinting in the morning light, as it spurted from a crack in rocks. The side was so steep that even a feral goat would have faced it with trepidation, but Robbie got a finger hold and with one heave hung suspended, his parched lips just inches away from the slit. The iciness felt so good in the heat, and he swallowed slowly letting the cool moisture trickle down his beard and onto his chest.

After a few minutes, Robbie dropped stealthily to the ground. Still somewhat unsure of his future, he lay on the bank for a further rest and the time to reconsider his options on life. The first and most obvious fact was that he was single, not even remotely attached to anyone. There was nothing to stop him moving on and he was gripped by an urge to move on. But such was his limited knowledge of the world that the only sure solution for his future was to work in the area he knew best; and that meant working for the Laird who, he had heard from several of the Clan, was a fair-minded and generous man. 'Hadn't the Minister's brother, Murdo McBain, said as much?'

As he lay on the coarse grass, facing the placid water, he studied his face from one direction and then another as if seeking some reassurance about himself and his destiny. A small reddish-brown butterfly seemed to hover around his dark curling hair for a few seconds before fluttering off in a sideways loop towards a clump of heather. Robbie watched the deflected flight with an idle curiosity and then, after standing up and stretching himself once more, he set off up the hillside at a brisk pace. It took him only ten minutes to reach the pass. There he stopped and gazed down at the glen below. In an instant his eyes focussed on the smouldering ruin and the couple standing close by, the old man's arm around his wife's shoulders. Robbie wondered what was happening, paused for a moment and ran down the fell side as fast as he could.

Ealasaid was the first to hear his footsteps and turned with a frightened expression. 'Thank the Lord it is only ye!' she said softly through her tears. 'Dinna alarm yerself Domhnall, it be young Robbie from the Glen.'

But the old man was still mumbling to himself and slowly began walking round the smouldering ruins. He seemed oblivious to his wife's voice.

'It be Robbie, *mo cheile* (my husband).'

But the old man did not look up. (*'Tha e coltach gun robh...*) 'It seems that my sister is dead. Perishing in the flames of her own making, like Satan himself', was all he could say over and over again. Robbie looked towards Domhnall and held out his hand in friendship. Putting one arm around the old man and the other around the wife, he held them closely for a few moments and said to comfort them. 'I would like (*Bu mhath leam...*) to say more, to help you in some way, but I'm lost for words. Only God can help her now in His Mercy.'

His voice trailed away as the woman sobbed. 'We will inform the Minister and have the ceremony here. Morag would have liked that!'

'Aye, she wud,' said Domhnall turning towards the young man for the first time, 'she wud have liked that a lot!'

'And the finest piper to play a lament,' continued Robbie, warming to the fact that he was lightening the man's mood.

'Ay, that wud be guid,' the old man replied, nodding his head in agreement. He paused. 'See how the heather hath burnt as if it were St John's Eve*, there's no such luck in these embers!' (*June 24th was a ritual burning of a festive, good luck heather torch in each village)

After this sombre remark Domhnall kicked up a small cloud of dust with his leather boot and some red embers swirled in the light breeze. 'No luck!' he kept muttering, largely to himself.

Robbie watched the fine sparks glow as they touched a clump of dried coarse grass some ten yards away. Suddenly a small flame appeared and ran a narrow track through the dry grass.

Then it petered out thirty yards on.

The young man strode over to the faintly glowing embers and stamped them out. He was about to say, 'One such fire is all we need!' when his attention was caught by a dark object in the bracken. At first he supposed it to be a dead and decaying sheep or a stag, but as he got nearer he saw a coarse black shoe sticking out of the tangled vegetation. 'Come here, Domhnall,' he cried. 'See for yourself!'

The old man hurried over, alarmed by the agitation in Robbie's voice.

'What's bothering you, Robbie?' *(De tha a'cur ort, Robbie?)*

The young man had reached into the bracken and, grasping the shoe, pulled out the lifeless, recumbent form of the Minister McBain.

The old lady began to hurry over but was stopped by the cry from her husband, 'Stay!' (*Fuirichibh!*) But she continued in a half run until she reached their side. 'Perhaps there's mair evil in this than meets the eye!' she said with emphasis looking at the two men.

She paused and whispered a short prayer.

'The Devil has struck o'er once in such a wee place. I think that these last two days are bringing mair harm than guid! (*barrachd call na feum!*). This be a word o' advice fur ye, Robbie! Stay clear a' the Laird in the big house!'

'Perhaps so, Ealasaid,' replied the young man with feeling, 'perhaps so!'

Seachd (seven)

They buried the Minister and Morag in shallow graves amongst the heather, and covered the area with a few rough stones in the shape of a cross.

The old man recited a short prayer, intoning the Gaelic in a deep whisper. His wife and the young man stood head bowed. Domhnall would inform the authotities

In his sadness Robbie was lost for words and only muttered the briefest of goodbyes as he set off along the green valley floor. Even the sky had become overcast, so that by the time he had climbed out of the glen by a narrow path and was able to look into the distance towards his family's home - some eighteen miles on - the rain had just begun to fall and a dense mist began to impede his progress. The elements took up the symphony and a roll of thunder stopped the moor birds' songs in their tracks; while the mountain paths became soaked and the hills sullen in the downpour, as the lightning flashed. The shale and scree soaked up the water so that these very routes became an exit to infinity as he criss-crossed the mountain summits, where far below the abyss harboured the hissing torrents.

Knowing the futility of walking through the mountains in such dangerous conditions, Robbie settled down in the lea of a large rock overhang, which shielded him from the sudden downpour. The vertical rain splashed off the rocks above and trickled vigorously into the small gullies, so that within minutes there was a miniature cascade on both sides of his shelter. He pulled himself close to the cold rock face and tightened his jacket to the top button, thrusting his hands deeply into the pockets. Like a sphinx he sat there, defiant to the weather, his face cold and expressionless.

Robbie's thoughts did not return to the prospects of employment in the Laird's estate, for his mind ruminated uneasily on the deaths of the Minister and Domhnall's sister.

Minister McBain certainly had not injured himself by falling masonry. The clothes were free of burn marks and there were no signs of charring on his face or arms. Also, if he had been badly injured when attempting to save the old woman he would not have been able to drag himself so far from the cottage. Those facts were plain to see!

But there were no signs of any struggle in the bracken. 'On the other hand,' he reasoned. 'The ground was hard and footprints would not linger.'

He waited for half an hour in the makeshift shelter until the heavy rain had stopped. Then he set off in the grey drizzle of the mist that rose from the still warm land like the breath of the glens; mist that clung in fine glistening droplets on his dark hair, kilt and black jacket. His stout leather shoes, well versed in the ways of moorland walking, crushed through the cropped grass and tough heather stems.

At times he would stop and brush the moisture from his face with the back of his hand, pausing to contemplate the peaks around him part hidden by the low cloud. He could hear the lonely croak of a scavenging raven in the gloom and the occasional piping buzzard's call, but little else.

Over another break in the ruggedness of the mountains Robbie strode, scrambling along a narrow gully in a short cut he knew so well, kicking up a fine stream of pebbles that cascaded down the steep mountain face behind him.

Then down another narrow path he went, towards the valley floor. Although he would have normally been able to see the hills near his family's township, they were invisible in the mist which seemed to have settled and compacted in the narrow confines of this glen.

Still the raven's call broke the silence.

But Robbie's mind was still preoccupied with the event of the last two days. So it was with a start that he felt two rough hands grasp his shoulders as a voice cried out, 'How are you Robbie?' (*Ciamar a tha thu, Robbie?*)

'Fine thanks!' *(Tha gu math, tapadh leat)*. He paused and laughed once his surprise had settled. 'It is very cold!' *(Tha i gle fhuar!)*

He surveyed the speaker - a tall, broad man -Niall MacIomhair (McIver) with a shock of long curling black hair and brown eyes that surveyed him from a thatch of greying whiskers. He was about forty and his muscular arms had swung many a hammer against his blacksmith's anvil over the years. 'How's yourself, Niall? But you fair frightened a body in the mist, that I know.' Robbie gave another laugh and put out his hand.

The man took it, held it for a moment in a tight grip, then shook his head. 'If ye are frightened by this, what about the others who have been tormented by sae much more in the weeks ye have been away! They'll not forget the Cameron fiasco in Ross, I'll bet, fur a lang time and other matters as weel!'

Robbie looked the speaker in the face. 'What other events, Niall?'

'The happenings in my village by Loch Ailsh is a bad business, Robbie! We have had to move on!' Niall's voice was a mixture of anger and disgust.

'When?'

The blacksmith shrugged his broad shoulders. 'T'wards the end o'May.'

'And how many have had to move on?' Robbie asked cautiously looking the huge man in the face, whose very strength seemed to emanate from his resolute expression.

'Thirty- six *(Sia deug air fhichead)* men, women and children! Th' young and th'old, th' fit and th'infirm! It burns me to my very soul, Robbie, and I'll have vengeance one day!' His words rang out in the grey gloom like sparks from the anvil.

There was a pause as the younger man contemplated the situation. 'But why is it happening, Niall? Why?'

The blacksmith stroked his beard, 'I ken'd yer father's father, and nae better Sutherland took breath! Many a bairn was fed from the herring he sent, and many a buck or capercaillie he took frae the hills for those people. And y' father and yersel, Maister Robbie, ye're an honest lad. But there's a fair trouble brewin' in the hills now. For the drover's have tain our land for the sheep and frae the very outset Bailie Galbraith has set his mind agin us.'

'Bailie Galbraith?' said Robbie in astonishment, 'Our family knew him right well, and a fair and decent man he seemed.'

'Aye, the very man! But to us he came all mealy-mouthed and offered us a price for the land, by the Laird's command. Well, the devil take him, Bailie Galbraith and his kin! For ye may think him an honest man, and the great Laird a Highland gentleman! But I tell ye, the bailie, he comes with drovers and a score o'soldiers. So sae far we have been driven fra'our homes and our land and nothing is left but charred wood and blackened stone.'

'You mean that nobody can save the timbers and take them away...which is a given right?' asked the young man.

'No! (*Chan eil!*) Fire took every thing that canna be removed, and in an instant! But there was a worse deed that came to my knowledge!' Niall replied.

'What was that!'

'Old man MacBeath, bed-ridden with infirmity and the ague, had a' the roof knocked out fra' over him, and what with the unusual wind and rain for that time of year it was no many a day until the cold and damp put pay to him!'

Robbie listened in increasing anguish as the man slowly emphasised the horrific tale.

'Aye, they came the heathens...they wrecked the barns, kilns, sheep-cots and all! And some o'them were driven oot towards the coast but then were told they could return within a few days to grow their crops. But when they went back to their auld homes the sheep had been driven onto the lands, so that the green shoots were being eaten as soon as they came, and some puir beggars sat in the storms, fair frozen, watching their corn being destroyed bit by bit! Some wandered in the woods, to God knows where! They were as skinny and as raw-boned as the cows that wandered aboot with them!' Niall paused and shook his fist. 'Aye, the factor and the men - they're the devil incarnate, there's no doubting that!'

'I don't want to hear any more just now, Niall. I've had enough!' Robbie replied quietly.

The two men walked on in silence.

The rain came down in earnest once again but lacked the venom of before. Robbie's mind was in turmoil. His imminent plans had been suddenly thrown into confusion. They walked side by side.

They had descended about five hundred feet and quite suddenly as they cut through the line of the mist, the valley became clear and bright ahead. The heavy downpour had ceased as suddenly as it began.

'The truth is that we hav' mair misfortunes than the Lord Almighty usually sends o' us. But I wud love to see every Lowland sheep in the Highlands hang by its own shank! That I wud!' Robbie waited for the blacksmith to continue but he remained silent.

A patch of pale blue suddenly appeared as the dark clouds were being swept along the far mountain peaks. Alongside the blue a hazy shaft of sunlight began to make progress through the gloom.

'Aye, the land is fur sheep now Robbie, fur sheep! Those men are a disgrace to their kin. May they hang by their buckle belts too!'

As they approached a low thatched building that Robbie knew was generally deserted, other than by travellers or herdsmen who used it as a shelter on their way to the mountains around Creag Mhor, he saw the dark curl of a fire from the squat chimney and caught the sharp smell of peat smoke.

Niall hurried towards the building, much to Robbie's surprise, and on reaching the door he pushed his way in. The young man followed, wondering who would be inside. What Robbie saw took his breath away.

A squalid, ragged bunch of humanity.

He glanced from face to face. Before him was a huddled group of about thirty Highland men, women and children - cold, soaking and miserable. Almost from the first glance Robbie had recognised a dozen or so of them.

The blacksmith placed his hand on the boy's shoulder. 'So ye see, Maister Robbie, the plight o'them. They've trudged many a weary mile to seek shelter and food. For they're sae afraid o' the future! But I ken the good deeds of yer father in the past and I hope he can help them fur a wee while until we get to see the factor or the bailie, in one of the houses by the Castle of the Great Laird.'

'Aye, but what will you get out of either of them?'

'At least to speak to someone and ask fur help! But for myself, I canna go for I'm a marked man in recent months and mair marked in recent days. And if it's help we need - then it's help we'll seek!' He paused. 'You know, I was cutting across the Glen to find ye all coming from the wedding and the very man I most wanted to see was you, Robbie, and I did by the Lord's will! Ye can speak in their tongue Robbie! And I ken it's a guid omen! I mean finding y' sae quickly! For y're the very man who can get help if anyone can. I feel it in ma bones…and brae bones they are two!' Niall laughed.

But Robbie found it hard to laugh as he looked around, for his spirits were sinking by the minute. It was not just the gaunt faces and sunken eyes that unnerved him, but the curious apathy that seem to rise with their dampness and hang as a cold mist around them; and when he tried to talk to them, only those who knew him well would reply, and then in a subdued and hesitant voice. The majority sat on the rough earth floor in a cold and hungry silence. Even the children remained quiet and suppressed. The silence was intermittently broken by one old woman in a black tattered shawl and dirty dress who rocked incessantly backwards and forwards on bent knees as if in prayer. Apart from her wail, the whole room had a sepulchral stillness about it.

In a moment of complete silence as the moaning ceased, a young woman with long dirty hair about her face and white lips, reached out towards Robbie and began to speak in a whisper, 'I would like to ask a question!' *(Bu mhath leam ceist fhaighneachd!)*

Before she could say any more the old woman burst forth in another loud wail. The shrillness and despair in the quavering voice made Robbie jump; but there was little effect on those around her. 'The factor...' she almost hissed the words and a few dull eyes turned towards her; the name had added a momentary look of fear to their faces. 'The factor,' she repeated, 'and those tacks men...if they ever return, by the Lord, I'll take the old flint stock t' them, that a' will!' She looked round, her haggard expression for a moment defiant; then she lapsed back into the rapid mutterings, which unnerved the young man by their very persistence.

Confused and uneasy, Robbie sat in a small group. He closed his eyes and, despite the cold, began to abstractly think about the moorland, his home and his childhood, trying to put the surrounding harsh realities aside. But, try as he might he could not escape the horror around him. Then the strange silence became oppressive as the wailing and moaning ceased! And the dank and fetid smell in the room repulsed him! 'You ken me man!' a youth with thick black locks and dark eyes tugged at Robbie's elbow.

He paused for a second, 'Aye, I do now! What troubles ye, Chalum. I saw you but four months back!'

'You did that! But my parents ha' stayed on in the township tho' I couldna stomach it no longer.' He rubbed his hands for warmth and continued slowly. 'One o'the factors men came and he was all huff and pride until my father tackled him aboot the rent and if our dues were guid why had we to move on. He was full of froth so father threatened the whip o'him if he returned and sent him on his way!'

'Did he come back?'

'Aye, in a manner o'speaking! Fur some beasts were shot in the hill pasture, two guid cows and a horse, to show that the factor meant business. So Father didna resist after that, but agreed to all they asked! As I said, I canna stomach such ways!' The youth leaned, placed his back against an old man, who had wrapped himself in a coarse blanket and seemed oblivious to everything around him.

'I'm sorry to hear that...' Robbie responded but the youth interjected.

'Spare me y' pity, Robbie Sutherland. I'll make out, I'm young and strong...but fur the rest...' he stopped short and gazed into the distance, 'they expect to be leaving Sutherlandshire (*tha duil aca a bhith a'falbh*)...but where to is another matter!'

Robbie had heard enough! Now his seemingly simple and serene world was one of pain, hunger and despair. He glanced around at the shivering figures, some huddled with arms around each other to keep out the cold, others coughing, some silent, some occasionally sobbing - and he felt his heart racing in anger. He knew that penalties for engaging in resistance could be serious or even catastrophic, his conscience told him that he had to take some action. What manner of resistance or revenge as yet he could not determine. But he faced the fact that something had to be done!

Suddenly a voice broke his meditation.

'Rouse y'selves, kinfolk,' said Niall brusquely and with a brisk clapping of his hands, ''twould be a darned sight mair cheerful in a wake than this, by the Lord!'

At the sound of the voice the old woman suddenly reached forward and mistakenly grabbed hold of Robbie's hand. He noticed the thin fingers like icy tendrils wrapped round his skin and felt the faint trembling of the palm. There was a curious stale odour as she bent towards him. Instinctively he drew back and released her grasp. Realising what he had done, Robbie gave a faint, apologetic smile, and attempted to take hold of her fingers once more. But the woman did not notice and turned her bony arms towards Niall.

He brushed them aside.

'Aye, there'll be many a wake to come, fair weather or foul,' replied a sallow faced man between coughing bouts, 'or ma names not Lachlan.'

'Wist man, I am tired (*tha mi sgith*) o' that...and such talk is of no use to man nor beast,' answered the blacksmith.

'Aye, Niall MacIomhair ye speak like a man o'strength. But there's no future in this land fur ourselves, no future! That I tell ye! How can we live on fresh air alone, I ask ye that? Where do we go?'

'To the shores and the fishing villages,' said a youth firmly, 'for the herring will see us through - people are saying!' (*-thathar ag radh!*)

But the sallow man shook his head and sighed, 'There's no hope fur the poor such as we, I tell ye!' He spluttered for his breath for a few seconds and turning to the youth inquired, 'Are you good at fishing?' *(A bheil thu math air iasgach?)*

'Och awa with thee, man! Coughin' has befuddled whatever mind ye had!' said Niall impatiently.

Annoyed by the rebuke the sallow man attempted to rise, still watched by the others in an apathetic silence. But his frail legs did not support him for more than a few seconds and, exhausted, he collapsed back coughing. Large beads of perspiration clung to his clammy brow. The rattle in his lungs sounded like a feeble crack of thunder.

Robbie reached over to comfort him but he was pushed away as the sallow man bent forward, retching for breath. 'May the Lord deliver me soon!' was the eventual reply to the gesture as he gasped and groaned.

Throughout it all, the blacksmith remained unconcerned, shaking his wet hair then wringing out the long locks so that small trickles of water streamed down his face like sweat on a summer's day. His clothes were black with the rain and within minutes steam rose imperceptibly from his chest like faint wisps of mist. He neither acknowledged nor addressed the sick man again.

Robbie got up and sat down in a corner by the wall, away from the rest of the group. It was colder there but he felt more detached. His body was soaked so much that his teeth chattered. He watched the old woman swaying to and fro muttering a Gaelic hymn she had learnt as a child, wringing her hands as she came to the end of the only verse she knew. Round and round came the monotonous incantation. It had now become the incessant background sound to the man's unceasing cough. A small child whimpered with hunger until his mother pulled him close and wrapping her arms about him hushed him to sleep.

'Lachlan is fair sick, Robbie, and not sae long o'this world, I'll be thinking,' whispered Niall at length.

'I'll be thinking that too,' he replied. 'And many more if we can find no food or good shelter'.

'By the morrow we will eat,' continued Niall in a whisper, 'for I ha' tain a ewe from the old Laird and hidden it by the waterfall of Creag an Daraich (rock of the oak tree).

Robbie paused and looked the man earnestly in the face. 'It is a risk, Niall, that I know! Would you like me to help?'

The blacksmith laughed. 'If you wish!' (*Ma thogras tu!*) But he put his arm round the younger man's shoulders. *'Ma thogras tu!'*

Ochd (eight)

As the weather is wont to do, as they say in the Highlands, it will not do it for long.

Thus by midnight the squalls that beat the down pouring against the stone walls and turf roof, suddenly fell silent. Only the steady dripping of the pooled moisture from the eaves remained and, within the hour, even that had ceased. So by first light, the summer sky was more blue than grey, broken only by a faint yellow glow in the east as morning shook off its mantle of night. On the previous evening Robbie had been well over half way home. But now he decided to stay and accompany the blacksmith on the expedition.

He had hardly slept. Not from lack of comfort for he had been brought up to sleep on whatever surface he found, but by the depressing scenes around him. Worries and fears, and fears and more worries, had tumbled through his mind in an endless reel. He could not fully comprehend all that was happening, but felt -as in the evening before- the need to venture on, and by his travels acquire a more stable and more prosperous way of life. Despite misgivings he was still inclined to go to the Laird's great castle for work. The fact that he was to be a partner in robbing this estate of a sheep, did not affect him at all. These animals were increasing at an alarming rate on all the best grazing moors, driving the finest stags and hinds into the high mountains. He had no conscience about taking a sheep or two to feed the hungry.

Niall had slept soundly with his back to the wall - oblivious to the sounds and moisture around him, for a small puddle had darkened part of his jacket and soaked one side of his brawny arm. Yet in an instant he was awake and with a sudden stretching of his back and legs he had taken three strides to the door before Robbie realised what was happening.

'We will have to go!'(*Feumaidh sinn falbh!*) said the blacksmith abruptly.

The morning air felt cool against their cheeks as they hurried out of the crude hut and up the mountainside. But the sweetness and freshness of the air pleased the younger man so that he walked with a half swagger. They hurried along in silence, for Niall was either deep in thought or simply subdued by tiredness. Before them the horizon gradually assumed its outline of jagged peaks and steep indentations of the glens, increasingly lit by the brightening sun. The narrow rivers cascaded down the rock faces, freshened and forceful from the night's rain. Their sounds seemed a harsh echo in the stillness of the dawn.

Once the two men stopped for a moment and both drank from a glistening, spilling stream. Robbie worked the liquid round and round his face, and the cold felt soothing. He bathed his brown eyes, the eyelids puffy from lack of sleep, and the very sparkle of the water seemed to give strength to his gaze and transfer its lustre to his smile. He looked cheerfully round and said confidently, 'We will sit for a minute, Niall!' (*Suidhidh sinn airson minaid, Niall*)

But the blacksmith was impatient, and with a quick gesture of the head that flicked moisture from his dark wet hair, signalled his desire to hurry on. Within half an hour of leaving their crude dwelling, they reached the destination. Robbie recognised the gnarled branches of a solitary oak tree, some of the boughs having become rotten so that its greenery showed patchily and gaunt against the sky.

In front of the tree were six large boulders, deposited by a glacier in times long past. They gave refuge to the tree against the frequent storms, with the largest boulder almost touching the trunk, which sprang precariously from a vertical rock face.

It was in the direction of the boulders that the two men strode.

The entrance to the cave was almost hidden by the rocks, for the drooping branches of the oak spread, canopy-like, almost to the ground. Niall pulled the leaves aside and cautiously entered the gloom.

Robbie followed two steps behind, his feet slipping on the wet, mossy stone floor. Inside, the dank earth and slime-covered walls gave an unwholesome putrid smell. He could hear the steady dripping of water from the roof and feel the large drops landing on his shoulders and head. From there they slowly trickled down his face and body in fine, rancid tracks. Still his companion did not speak but made straight to a heap of dried bracken in a small recess. On it lay a dead ewe, not yet skinned.

The blacksmith with a deep grunt hauled the animal across his shoulders and grasping the front and back legs steadied it on his back. 'Push hard, Robbie lad, and give strength to my arms! The beast is as strong in death as it wer' in life, that I trow!'

The younger man walked behind the half-crouching figure, supporting the sagging carcasses as best he could. For a few minutes they squelched through the slime, Niall grunting and swearing in his exertions. The fresh air was welcome as they ducked under the overhanging leaves and back into daylight.

They staggered on a few paces and then stopped.

'I've never held such a ewe, 'twill feed a fair few!' Niall smiled. Robbie took a deep breath and laughed. But in a second the dead animal had crashed into him, knocking him to the ground.

For in the same instant there was a cry! A volley of shots! And fire seemed to spurt from behind one of the rocks. He saw the blood jerking from his companion's legs and chest, and heard the dull thud as more shot crunched into the dead beast.

Robbie was down but only for a second. Not even glancing in the direction of the gunfire, he raced head-low past the entrance to the cave. This briefest of moments under cover of the hanging foliage was sufficient to deter the gunmen. Then, as he broke into the open once more, a further volley of shots rang out, whistling harmlessly into the heather. Luckily a tangle of shrubs and high bracken was not thirty yards away. Into this cover Robbie disappeared, throwing himself full-length. In a moment he was on his feet running in a scrambling crouch, the greenery whipping into his face, the blood trickling from small cuts on his brow and cheeks. He felt no pain, no sensation, but the fear to survive drove him forward as he had never run before.

However, he was now aware that he had to cross a small, open swamp. For a moment he hesitated but there was nowhere else to go. Summoning his strength Robbie burst across the squelching moraine. More shots rang out but the distance was too great and to his relief they pattered harmlessly about him. But each step in the quagmire seemed an eternity and it was with a beating heart that he reached more cover, a large rock acting as a shield. As he scrambled through the rocks, small pebbles cascaded down like further shots.

He could hear the soldiers yelling, some in English, some in Gaelic. But he did not listen, content to plunge on through more high bracken and into a small wood beyond. He felt curiously elated, and stopped for a second to wipe the sweat and blood from his brow and to listen for the sound of men behind him.

There was no sign of pursuit.

He paused again hoping to hear any sound of Niall.

Yet there was none! A curious stillness had enveloped him, even the rapid beating of his heart seemed muted. Collecting his thoughts he set off in a steady run and within ten minutes had reached the brow of a hill. There he fell to the ground panting. He lay, straining every muscle for any indication that the men were following. Then as his breathing settled, Robbie cautiously eased himself up onto his elbows to see if he could identify his adversaries.

By slowly crawling to one side and resting under the low branches of a broom bush he could see a group of seven men, some with rifles and others with muskets. Two were preoccupied with moving the dead sheep while the others cautiously searched amongst the rocks and bracken. Try as he might he could not see his friend. Robbie's first emotion was of bitter anger. Then he derived some consolation from the fact that Niall had escaped.

But that escape was only of a few yards. For Niall stood crouched in the mouth of the cave, weak from loss of blood. For the crimson tide flowed fresh and unrelenting down his abdomen from a wound in the chest. Blood also poured from a deep wound in the thigh and his left foot felt numb and weak. His large frame rested helplessly against the stone wall for a moment. Then he staggered on for a few more feet, straining in his agony to hear if the gunmen were following.

But there was no sound of pursuit.

Dropping to his knees the blacksmith paused for breath, his ribs moving erratically with each inspiration, his left leg stumbling behind.

The floor was wet with slime.

After a few seconds he tried to collect himself, despite the unremitting pain, and set off on a slow crawl towards the recess in the cave where he had previously hidden the sheep. He felt he would be safe there and could rest. It seemed an eternity as he dragged himself forwards through the slime, each laboured yard taking him nearer and nearer towards his goal. Reaching out into the darkness with trembling hands Niall felt the sidewall of the recess.

For a moment his spirits rose.

Still bleeding profusely he collapsed onto the dry bracken that had been placed there the night before. As he lay softly breathing and numb with pain, the darkness seemed to shimmer and blur, with flashing lights.

It was a curious sensation, as if an unseen anvil was awash with the furnace glow. He gazed at the brightness before him, and it began to dim. Yet the vegetation felt comfortably warm and soft.

He lay still and silent, the only sound was the steady dripping of roof-water in the main part of the cave.

But the darkness was increasing, and Niall realised to his horror that his sight was failing. For a moment terror gripped him. Then he tried to think straight.

For what faint vision remained was rapidly vanishing with each drop of blood.

Niall knew he must stem the tide of red.

He groped on the recess floor for a rope that he had used to bind the sheep's legs. With it he could bind his own!

His left hand moved slowly round and round in widening circles as he lay on his sound side.

Then, almost unexpectedly, Niall felt a rope against the back of his hand. He reached out, pulling it slowly towards him. His mind clung to the one hope of making a tourniquet to stem part of the bleeding that spurted from his thigh.

But even in his confusion the rope felt thin and cold. And the rope was almost as black as the darkness, with venom in both fangs.

With a whipping movement the viper struck, piercing the blanching hand.

In his confusion, Niall did not seem to notice.

But sat staring vacantly into the gloom - puzzled, afraid and dying.

Naoi (nine)

The thatched barn was old…very old and the thatch bore testimony to that fact. The straw had collapsed in the northern corner, moss had stained the overhang with a wretched dirty green and decaying stones allowed the wind to gape through the cracks and crevices.

Not that it mattered on a bright sunny September day.

The Scots pines had for generations bent their robust, scaly trunks and writhed their gnarled boughs so that shards of needles had showered down on the men who gathered beneath to rest their backs and enjoyed a dram or two of whisky. The old ones sat contented with lugubrious wreaths of pungent smoke drifting out of the tips of the long chalk pipes. Each exhalation was savoured as much as the inspiration. The rich aroma clung to the waistcoats and trousers, stained the front of their shirts to the annoyance of the women folk, and gave a strange laid-back tranquillity to the eight men assembled.

The dusk crept in slowly, day was reluctant to become night, and a crimson sun hovered an hour or so above the fine line of the horizon. The men knew the hour, even the day, by the sun's rolling course. Each mountain was like the marking on a clock face, each peak indicated a day in the year. Behind the towering dome *Meall nan Con* at sunset meant the September solstice, when the direction of the sun towards the south heralded the beginning of the shortening days and long Highland nights. Little else mattered in their terms of time and space.

'I heard that it wouldn't be dry today at all! (*Chuala mi nach biodh turadh ann an-diugh idir*)' was remarked at length without much feeling.

The puffing continued until Tomas replied, 'I wouldn't be too pleased if it rained!' (*Cha bhithinn ro thoilichte nam biodh an t-uisge ann*).

There was silence for a minute.

Then the cattle bellowed in the limpid shades of another spinney near by and the odd goat, tired of the tedium and slow pace of life, suddenly hurried off with a wild jump onto the dyke backs; their momentum scattering the top stones in a small flurry that disturbed the stillness.

Tomas looked up and took the pipe from his mouth. His frame was bent as an oak bough, his round back had been seen working the fells for six generations. 'That dyke will no stand such a bouncing of feet, I'll be thinking! If Sinclair canna hold his goats in check I'll take him for a sovereign or two, or a goat or two fur that matter!'

The others laughed. 'Aye, so y'will!'

'Aye, so I will!'

Content with these truncated observations the group resumed their smoking, perfect contentment etched on the craggy features. Another spoke. 'There's little grass for the lowlanders to graze the cattle, for I was on the fell-top today and took careful note of what it was aboot!'

'Did you now!' Tomas resumed smoking.

'Aye! To be sure I did!'

'And what else were y'busying yersel with?'

His friend took a long draught of smoke, let it linger in his lungs for a moment and then blew a fine blue-grey mist into the cooling air. 'I'm a thinkin' that the sheep are roaming everywhere and naught to watch them stray hither and thither on to any man's land.'

This remark was considered in silence for a short while.

Their contemplations were interrupted by the sound of footsteps on the hard baked earth of the street, a rutted line which wound its way through the small stone and white-washed cottages.

'Good even' to you Eilidh,' said one of the younger ones, 'it's a fair night fur walking out, is it not?'

The girl laughed and tossed her head. 'Aye! That's about right!'

'And where might a bonnie lass be heading to at the gloaming hour?' Tomas was the spokesman for the group.

'Nowhere in particular!'

'Aye! That's an easy place to find then!'

'It is!' The girl threw back her hair once more. 'Well, then! That's about sums it up, does it not!'

There was no reply and the girl was soon lost behind the house as she slowly climbed the hill.

*****

She felt a deep longing, and had done so for weeks.

She scanned the cleft in the hills, where the rough grass gave way to mountain bracken. She looked for the familiar redcoat.

All was so secretive.

At first the furtive encounters had excited her, added another dimension to their romance.

Yet sometimes it filled her with dread.

Dread that they might be caught, found out, reviled; shunned by her own clan.

But no sooner did her fear make her tremble than an overwhelming desire to be with him banished all misgivings. The trip up the hill towards the crags had become a weekly routine. In the last three weeks Andrew Lockhart had not turned up, she had sat staring at the hills, too numb to weep; certain that their love was over – or his love for her was over. But she felt sure of one thing - and that was her love was as abiding and eternal as the mountain before her. She would try and lift her spirits by recalling how tenderly he would put his arms around her waist as she leaned back, how softly he would kiss her neck, running his lips towards hers, but always in a restrained, gentlemanly manner, so unlike the uncouth directness of the men she knew. He respected her, and that made her respect him even more, made her admire and adore, even when feeling low. He was like no other man she had ever met, his slight reticence was the key to his appeal.

There was one eagle soaring above the horizon and no other signs of life. She sat and waited as the dusk began with muted calls. The darkness crept in. Furtive at first like her romance, slowly erasing the braes and the juniper bushes low slung to the ground. Then the invisible hand smudged the undulating hills, then the pointed outlines where the pinnacles of stone thrust skyward.

Still she waited, felt cold and pulled the plaid skirt tightly around her legs. Eilidh looked round slowly, deliberately going over the encroaching blackness bit by bit. She stared in fascination as the intense shadows of the crags were lost in the darkness, only their tips protesting within the blood red of the sun. She slowly looked up to the invisible void above her and imagined eternity spent there in the dying glare of the sun.

The eagle had gone and apart from the odd bleating of the sheep a subdued stillness had taken over her life.

Half an hour, then another that seemed even longer.

Now blackness made the route ahead difficult and she turned, sighed, and walked mechanically down the winding path towards the old thatched barn – two miles away.

*****

Eilidh lapsed into silence, and the old man paused.

'I have nothing to say. Nothing! Can y' no understand!

Tomas asked again, his voice kind but firmly probing. 'I was just wondering in a quiet sort of way where ye hav' been?'

She shook her head and the dark hair moved apologetically around her shoulders and across the corner of her cheek in embarrassment.

'If ye must know...with Robbie Sutherland!' She stared defiantly at the group.

The old man laughed. 'I ken he's many a mile fra here!'

'Ye're wrang!'

Thomas laughed. He noticed the tenseness in her voice.

'Ah! Weel he'll be an easy man to ask when I next see him, will he not?'

'Aye, he will, and a curt reply ye'll get, knowing Robbie! So that's that then!' Eilidh replied with a toss of the head. 'You'll be finding out soon enough in y'r prattling ways'.

But the old man gave a slow smile. 'Perhaps I believe y', Eilidh, perhaps not!' He contemplated the stem of his pipe. 'Someone had told the soldiers aboot the sheep stealing, aye and alerted them aboot Niall. That's no in doubt. But I'll be askin' you, who do ye think it was?'

Eilidh remained silent for what seemed an eternity, thoughtfully replied, 'I dinna ken, how could I ken? And why are ye asking all these questions from a body who's minding her own business?'

She noticed Tomas' eyes were as cold as ice as he surveyed her intently, and his hand shook as he reached out to grasp her arm. She did not like being held and with a sudden movement of annoyance broke free and was about to walk away.

'I see evil things abroad on this braw night.' He said sharply.

She tried not to listen but she knew what was going through his mind. The skin puckered on his wrinkled brow as he contemplated her face in the darkness. 'Ye're hiding the truth lassie, and I know it! My eyes are growing dim, but not sae blind as to ken someone in love...that man wouldna be a military man...would it?' He had reached out to grasp her arm once more but she stepped back. His cold, gnarled fingers just brushed hers. She now stood defiant. 'I walk where I want! There's no law agin that! And who I see is my affair, is it not?'

The frown overshadowed the coldness in his eyes. 'Aye...but if you be lovin' a redcoat... many's a word's whispered in love, lassie. Tek heed o'that! For if they (and he waved towards the cottages) find oot that ye've been blabbing to a soldier man about the clans folk…let's say Niall MacIomhair…and he is teken or worse killed because of it…then I pity ye truly, in the name of the Lord, I do!'

But Eilidh did not reply. She hurried off, in a vain search to find Robbie.

Deich (ten)

'Tek snuff, Mr Sutherland? Snuff, well is meat an' music an' maist as guid as a dram when cauld.' The young crofter looked up from the fire, where he sat warming his hand in the glowing peat. His auburn-haired bride of two months sat on the floor by his side, her black skirt wrapped round her legs for warmth. He gently stroked her hair in an almost abstract way, almost unaware of the old carter sitting on the stool at the opposite end of the hearth.

The rough coated, brown collie stretched lazily across the interval between them.

'*Chan eil!* Not today, Jock!'

'Ah well! In such hard times it is pleasant for soul and body, as y' ken.'

The wind rattled the croft door so that the wooden cross latch seemed to shiver momentarily. Alasdair Sutherland gave a brief sigh. His wife glanced his way for a few seconds and then resumed sewing. 'What is the news from your glen, Jock?' she said in a quiet voice.

'Not so guid, Mairead.'

'Why so?'

'Oh! There's been five families driven off the land by the Laird's men, and their hames burnt to a cinder- a' in the last week, by the Lord.' The old carter wrung his hands almost in an apologetic way. Alasdair rose from the stool and walked over to a small cupboard set high on the wall. He reached up and brought down a bottle and two glasses. Placing them in front of the old man he poured out a crystal-clear measure of whisky. Having done this he reflectively began sipping the raw liquid, all the while gazing into the embers. His wife and the old friend, noting the mood, also lapsed into silence, which was only occasionally broken by the dog twitching its paws in some unfathomable dream.

Jock cleared his throat as if to speak and then stopped.

'What's bothering you, Jock?' (*De tha a cur ort?*) Alasdair said quietly.

For a moment there was no reply, so he went on sipping his whisky, and looking at the flames. 'Yer wonderin' what a body shud dee,' said Jock at length, chiefly addressing Mairead.

'Aye!' she replied.

'I'm no feared for mysel', but for you and Alasdair, Mairead, for you and your husband.'

Alasdair spoke first. 'Tush,' tis nothing Jock. As I ha' said in the past we are capable of looking after ourselves in this small township, and we have a clan chief who will support us whatever the odds. As a relative I can speak weel o'him!'

Mairead became restless. She felt her husband was skirting the issues as he had done in the past few weeks

The old man paused yet again and sipped from the glass. He smoothed his grey hair, which hung loosely about his brow. 'I thought y'might think there's no danger in it for ye.'

'Much ye seem to be making of it, Jock', he replied.

Mairead gave her husband a bold, hard stare that the visitor noticed. 'If there's danger we will know it only too well, when it comes.' Her voice rose in agitation and annoyance. 'But all the lootings and burnings must be stopped. How I dinna ken! But our lands are being destroyed...and the Clan's folks with it! I have thought much aboot it in the last few weeks and the truth is that they will no stop until we make them. Such wickedness has never been known before, not even in the barbaric days when Clan was set against Clan.' Her voice trembled at first, but with each word and gesture she gained confidence, the truth of what she was saying was almost palpable to her. She gave a slight toss of the head that shook the curls. Alasdair thought she had never looked lovelier, her eyes aglow with a strange determination tinged with anger. She glared at her husband whom she thought was not listening.

'Aye,' responded the old man slowly, 'there's much to be said and little to be done, I mind t'think!'

Alasdair pursed his lips and leaned back on his stool, the fire-glow lighting his eyes. 'If the Marquess will no speak himself, then we must take the matter into our own hands! We can yet raise men to stave off the factors and their rogues.'

Mairead smiled. 'Well said, my husband! There's but one way to grasp the sword and that is by the hilt and weald it strong.'

Alasdair agreed. Instinctively he took hold of her hand but she impulsively dropped it.

The carter raised his hand in caution, 'Those that follow the Marquess are like tares in the corn, hack one doon and twa will spring in its place. Mark my words!'

'Hush, Jock,' replied Mairead. 'We will have none of that way o' thinking.' She was on the point of asking him what plan might work when her husband interrupted.

'What other way do you think there'll be?' he asked cautiously, for the first time loosing some of his confidence, and annoyed at Mairead's abruptness. Jock pondered the question and they sat for a few minutes in silence.

The carter took another long sip at the whisky, prepared to speak, then looked reflectively at the glass for a few moments.

The couple waited. Mairead was anxious to say more.

After a short sigh, Jock continued. 'Perhaps it be none of y' liking' but it might be o' some use if we cud have asked a minister to talk to the factor face to face. The one who looked like Minister McBain to a shadow would have had something to say.'

Alasdair and his wife gave a short laugh.

Her husband spoke. 'The brother? He'll do naught! As for the Minister, he's dead! What would he have done, even if he had wanted to do, which as the way things are going with the men of the cloth, is not always a sure matter. Yet there's reason in what y'say, and there may be some minister that cud help us!

The old carter rubbed his chin and nodded. 'I believe it is the only way to stop the blood from flowing o'er this land.'

'Och!' Mairead replied contemptuously, 'before you realise it, blood will flow despite our entreaties. We can protest all we like alone, but unless we stand together,' she continued impatiently, 'not a word'll be acknowledged by the lairds and such like! Who has ever seen the great Laird in the castle? Not one that I've heard of, not one soul has ever been allowed within...unless they be in the pay of this man!'

Jock looked at her, but it was a searching look, full of inquisition and unsure about her intuition. Her husband broke the silence. 'Let us pray for guidance and help, Mairead,' said Alasdair in a nervous voice, 'let's no speak so surly on such a matter, though we all ken that it may come true. But we can do without the bloodshed, I canna see myself party to killing, can ye?'

Mairead stared at the fire and then gave her husband another searching glance. 'Maybe "no", but maybe "yes", who can say now until some calamity befalls us. But shud we a'sit here and wait for it to happen? I dinna ken! Do ye?' She said the final words with such bitterness and contempt that Jock placed his hands on Alasdair's shoulder in a gesture of support.

'It's terrible decision!' the carter said ruefully, 'a terrible decision!'

Alasdair bent towards his wife to emphasise his point. 'I dinna believe it has to come true! It's no an inevitable consequence in our township, there must be ways to solve the impasse. I've told ye that many and many a time in the last month, Mairead. All I say is that we need to be strong. All of us! Every family in this glen and the next! Surely that's not impossible if we all get together and reach some compromise with the factors!'

But his wife became tense and her face went white with emotion. She turned to her husband. 'Surely, you willna fail me in this matter.'

'Fail ye!' retorted her husband, 'in what way?' The anger in his voice was all too evident.

'By seeking a compromise so that the land is destroyed by the very animals we are trying to keep out,' was her rapid reply

'I never said I would fail you and I never will!' Alasdair collected himself and reached out to take her hand. The apologetic gesture was rebuffed. Mairead pulled it away.

He looked at her for a moment then shook his head. 'We can fight the factors and lairds, I ken that as well as anyone else, but if we fail, then it will be the end o' us in this glen. Where would we go? (*Cait' an d'rachamaid?*) Can't you see, Mairead that I'm trying to steer a path down the middle.'

'And I say there is no path down the middle!' she replied abruptly with contempt.

'Perhaps...'

'Perhaps nothing! In these desperate times we need desperate measures...and men to see them through. That's what I think!' She tossed her head defiantly. 'The more I listen to the men of these glens the more I think that the women-folk have the fire in their bellies, there's no point in those men skulking about like wounded hares!' She took a deep breath and stared towards the fire.

Jock stood up. He looked at the couple for a moment and raised his hand. 'Let us keep the peace before the Lord. It is not three full moons since you became man and wife.'

Alasdair collected himself, pulled a wry face and stared at the ground. Mairead kept her gaze towards the glowing peat.

There was another long silence.

Jock swallowed the last of his whisky and put down the glass. 'I think I will be going home! Goodbye!' (C*ha chreid mi nach teid mi dhachaigh! Mar sin leibh*) The carter, with a slow stretching of his legs, set off stiffly towards the door and into the darkness of the chilling night.

Aon deug (eleven)

The uneasy silence was only broken by the dog stirring on the floor and the occasional hiss from the peat fire. How long this depressing situation would have lasted is anyone's guess. Alasdair shuffled nervously on his stool while Mairead stared fixedly into the fire. However, some relief was at hand.

For no sooner had the carter wandered off into the darkness then there was a rap at the door, which slowly opened. The dog looked up for a moment, arching its neck as it lay on its side. But the animal recognised the figure that entered, and the husband rose to greet him. *'Ciamar a tha thu, Robbie?'*

His brother replied, 'Fine, Alasdair, fine! It's been a fair walk to Rogart today, for whatever reason! How are y'good selves?'

'In guid spirits!' replied Alasdair but his voice lacked conviction.

Mairead quickly got up and kissed him on the cheek. 'Ye look weary, Robbie, and what are those deep scratches on your knees and arms, not yet quite healed?'

The man glanced towards the sores and shrugged his shoulders. 'From the wiry heather and a few branches that I tangled with, a wee while back! But before I tell you all, a dram of the *usquebaugh* would no' come amiss!'

'By the Lord, where are our manners,' replied Mairead hastening to the small wooden cupboard, 'heaven help us indeed!'

Robbie had settled on the floor but his brother was insistent that he took the stool. 'No, it's all fine here,' he laughed patting the dog who had acknowledged him with a furious licking on the face and arms.

Mairead placed a glass of whisky in his hands and sat on the floor beside him.

'What's doing? *(De tha dol?)*,' she asked, waiting until he had taken a long draught and put down the glass with a sigh.

'Well! I had a good run for the money in the heather a short while back with some soldiers placing the shot after me...' he saw the look of alarm in the couple's face and hastened to say, ' tho' none of it was of a mark.' There was a pause. 'But Niall...well...I suppose they captured him for he did not make it through the heather.'

'Niall? asked Alasdair.

'Aye, Niall MacIomhair!'

'Niall, the blacksmith?' asked Mairead.

'Aye!'

'What was he doing about here?' continued the brother, 'he's usually about the west coast and works a fair bit around Lochinver.'

'So he does, of a rule! But they have torched the lands and driven two score or more good souls from their glens. I've seen them myself, and a poorer more miserable batch of human beings I've yet to see.' Robbie looked down for a second.

'Was he hit? *(An deach a bhualadh?)*

'That I don't know!'

'Nobody was killed?' *(Cha deach duine a mharbhadh?)*

Robbie paused, 'Not as far as I know!'

Mairead clenched her hands tightly together, 'See, people disappearing without trace, is this what our future is to become...?'

But her husband interjected brusquely, 'Please be quiet Mairead, while there is a tale to be told, then we will hav' our say! There's so much going on about us we must listen hard and think with a clear mind.'

Robbie glanced at their faces, it was a brief glance but discerning. Noting the discontent and anger between them, he started to stroke the dog as a distraction.

'Well, I decided to lie low for awhile, and what better place to rest than Domhnall's and give the old man a hand with his farm for a few weeks!' he said at length. 'But the factor and his men are the devils themselves! Driving sheep to the hills and pastures, while driving out poor souls to no end o' misery and famine... aye and robbing the cottages and burning the thatch. I have seen the terrible consequences of that for myself! Surely God must strike the wicked down soon!'

But Mairead could no longer hide her anger and burst in, 'Aye, we've said as much earlier this night…and many a day before that! There will be no stopping them until we meet force with force. The men o' the glen must rally and drive them back, blood to meet blood if all else fails. And it will!'

Alasdair set his jaw and said nothing for a few seconds. 'Aye, if all else fails, we fight! But would it no be wise to speak with the Laird or his men first.'

'Aye, the first time we talk with them will be the last, the auld Laird will see to that!' continued his wife in a hard voice. 'That's what I've been saying all evening. You've just spoken of action, Alasdair, but it seems that it was only for a moment…for old Jock has set out his own ideas on the matter and as soon as y'think about them you want to retreat to your lair like a frightened cat.'

'I didn't say I would retreat but there is a time for reason…which is something that you cannot see!'

Robbie looked from one to the other, perplexed by the anger that suffused the atmosphere, he had arrived wanting rest and relaxation.

She gave a mock laugh. 'More's the pity! (*Bu mhor am beud!*). I see naught but starvation for the people of the Glens. Oh! A few will be taken to tend the flocks and do odd piffling duties but what of the majority, which will probably include us! What future do we have? Answer me that!'

Robbie held up his hands. 'Such prattle will help no one! I have hardly begun my tale and all fury is released about me.'

His quiet voice defused the situation. Mairead apologised.

'What shall we do, Robbie?' she asked. 'Talk or walk away, or fight?'

'It is difficult, Mairead. We have to think of Niall for the present and get his release. For the word is that he could have been captured, but I'm not so sure. Anyway, if the talking fails, we must fight to a man…although servants, factors and soldiers will be sent again us even though most are our kith and kin. But God has given us another kinship and that is with the mountains and glens...our family and succour for centuries. In the past many a lowlander has perished for his greed of the Highlands and, if all goes ill, then many mair will perish before this matter is through!'

Alasdair simply shrugged his shoulders and remained in a sulky silence. When he realised that his brother had nothing to say, Robbie continued, 'It is true that some men, women and children starve, that the crops are not yet gathered, that the animals are weak from a long dry summer and a poor spring. Some families are without homes or chattels, even the barest necessities are taken from them. And why did Niall risk all? For one scrawny ewe, to feed those sheltering up the valley! One scrawny ewe! That is the desperation that grips many in the glens. And we need a concerted plan that cannot fail!'

Mairead instinctively took hold of his hand and held if for a few moments. Her eyes filled with pleasure.

'If it's fighting one day, then I'm prepared to help the cause,' said Alasdair firmly and with a brief smile noting her pleasure in Robbie's remark. 'I'm no afraid of the Lowlanders or Sassenachs.'

The thought of the deaths from the fighting that might ensue caused Mairead to drop her aggressive role for a moment and ask, 'Who will speak to the factor or his ilk if we try conciliation first?'

Robbie threw a piece of peat onto the glowing embers. 'I will! Someday!' (*Lath'-eigin!*)

'But they know you now as a trouble maker, Robbie.' His brother rubbed his hands in nervous anguish.

'*Chan eil!* (No!) I was like a mountain hare, gone in a whist! They have no idea who was with Niall, I'm certain of that!'

'Are ye sure?' inquired Mairead.

'Aye, fair certain! Anyway they'll have to take me as they find me...and they'll never find me,' Robbie laughed, 'unless someone's around to betray me, and I doubt that!'

His brother smiled, 'There's no one as far as we ken, is there Mairead?'

'Not that I know of,' she replied doubtfully after some consideration.

Robbie tried to lighten the proceedings, 'On such a long night let us enjoy a bit of warmth and company for I've had a belly -full of the Laird's men for the last few weeks, don't you think?'

'We've no seen you for so long Robbie, and had few visitors other than those o'the township, and that being but a dozen or so, that we have forgotten how we should welcome guests!' Mairead continued with a laugh. She had pleasure in his company, for he lifted her spirits with his unconventional manner and speech.

Alasdair also laughed but in a fraternal way. 'You're always welcome, Robbie! Ye ken that! But the troubles are makin' everyone a wee bit irritable with themselves these days, aye...and others too!'

'There's no point in fretting any more tonight, you two,' replied Robbie with a smile. 'I have such news to tell you both and I cannot begin for the bickering! But let me say that mother and father are well, and so are Domhnall and Ealasaid.' Mairead brightened at the news of her grandparents. 'All send their love! But it was a strange happening with Minister McBain and auld Morag. But here are the details as I saw them myself, which may be a bit different from what you've heard!'

Dha dheug (twelve)

Eilidh rested her head against the cow's belly, fat with calf. She sat on a stool, comfortable against the soft-breathing body that chewed diligently from the hay thrust in a compact bundle before it. The byre was comforting, out of the chill November wind, a wind that had sprung from the Shetlands and beyond. The udder was flat and the teats shrivelled with age. The milk was poor and came in irregular spurts. The calf that wandered in the byre and called occasionally in frustration was nigh on eight months and another was due in a few weeks, it would renew the flow for the coming spring and summer.

She heard a movement behind her and paused.

'How are ye Eilidh?' (*Tha gu math, Eilidh?*).

The girl recognised the voice and did not look round. She had never liked the voice or the person that went with it.

'Fine!'

'So y' are!'

'And how are ye Mairead? A married woman in the eyes of the Lord!' Her voice had a hint of sarcasm that was not lost on the listener.

'Fine!' replied Mairead approaching the sitting girl, who had paused in her milking and now began again in earnest and annoyance. 'You'll like being married, that I know for sure, Eilidh.'

The milkmaid paused. 'Will I now? If you ken it's fine, well maybe I will!'

Eilidh began squirting the fine white jets into the pail once more. The milk bubbled down the side in its velocity. She laughed, 'Open your gob Mairead and I will give ye a taste, if ye have a mind!'

The listener stepped back hastily. 'They say you're awful fond of Robbie Sutherland!'

'Do they now!'

'Aye they do!' replied Mairead colouring up a little.

Eilidh noticed the pink suffuse the cheeks and spread as a wave towards the corner of the mouth. 'Perhaps they do! But what has it to do with anyone, that I ask?'

Mairead moved a pace closer. 'I dinna believe it for a minute!'

The girl stopped milking once more. 'And why not?'

'He's tae much of a dreamer and a drifter for ye, Eilidh.' Mairead spoke hurriedly and in broad Gaelic that was not lost on the girl.

'He is that! Anyway, who say's I'm fond of the man?'

Mairead seized on the change of tone in an instinctive feminine way. Suddenly she saw a chink in the armour. 'So there's somebody else now, is there?'

Eilidh rested her head against the cow's soft belly. For a moment she was unsure of her reply.

Mairead waited, her green eyes fixed on the girl's face.

There was a long pause, the only sound was the milk sloshing around in the pail, still hammering against the chipped metal.

'So what they say is true, then!' Mairead spoke slowly and with conviction.

'No, whatever it is!'

'Ye dinna ken what it is, Eilidh.'

'I dinna wish to know! What these folks say is barely true at the best o'times and barely worth knowing at the worst. Hell can freeze over fur all I care!'

Mairead could hardly contain her impetuosity. 'Well, who can tell what the highland weather has in store for us all, and Hell might just do that if the truth be out!

'Might it now,' replied Eilidh unconcerned, 'and charcoal sprout too, nae doubt!' She laughed which annoyed Mairead.

'They say there's a soldier who's mightily fond of strolling this way!'

For a second Eilidh's heart missed a beat. She composed herself against the animal's side and took a deep breath as quietly as she could. 'Do they indeed!'

'You canna be evasive with me, Eilidh, I ken the facts!'

'You have no right in here with a'your prattling woman!' she answered angrily. 'Have y'naught better to do with y'time?'

'Aye I have…than talk to a floozie like yersel!'

Eilidh turned, her face now so suffused with red that it seemed to colour the whites of her eyes. 'So you think you're a cut above us all, now that the bans have been spoken, don't ye! Aye! You do! But I'm no fooled! You would have married either o'them brothers but y' picked the one who will get the big farm one day instead of that poor, rundown patch of your father's. I no so blind as all that!'

'What insolence to speak of me and my family like that!' Without a moment's hesitation Mairead flew forward and struck the girl as hard as she could across the face. A deeper red crossed the right cheek. 'There's enough red there to make a match to the coat that you're so keen to be with. Aye! We ken who tells the soldiers where the brave men are! You're a traitor, Eilidh, a traitor! Mind what I say, there'll be a sorry price to pay!'

With those words Mairead turned and stormed out of the byre.

Tri deug (thirteen)

The evening mist settled in by eight and the heavy black clouds foretold of a downpour once the easterly wind had mustered up enough strength.

The climb from the loch was easy in the cool of the dusk, and the soldier, glancing back occasionally to view the darkening water spread out below him, was blissfully unaware of imminent trouble.

At the junction of two paths - both heavily rutted and impassible in the wet - a series of boulders and crags diverted the unwary towards the cliff edge. There the fall was a good thousand feet onto the scree slopes that slid to the shoreline of the loch. The soldier hurried purposefully on, worried because he had been unable to see the girl for the last two weeks.

He hoped she would be there.

His mind played on the last time they met and how she made him laugh in a curious off-beat way, chiding him and teasing him in turns. He loved Eilidh. She had become the sole purpose for his existence.

The path slowly turned towards the angular, needle-shaped rock and a narrow gully. A cleft half way up the dangling face gave the rock the outline of a raven's beak ready to pounce on the unwary who walked beneath. But they had to do so, in order to slip through the twisting cleft in the cliff face. There was a second path, a detour made during the last two or three years to avoid this projecting overhang. This subsidiary path bent to the right and after an initial steep decline it sloped more gently in a serpiginous curve to rejoin the original way. Then came a short sharp climb of two hundred feet that made, in all, a quicker and easier approach to the summit and the glen beyond.

Andrew Lockhart paused. The easier route would be that bit longer, and no walker on the fells likes to loose height. He turned towards the gully and the more treacherous route. As he approached the two massive boulders he paused, thinking that a fox or mountain goat had sent a fine smattering of pebbles into the void. His highland instincts made him stand still for a moment like a beast of prey.

All was silent.

Reassured he slipped through the gully in the cliff face and turned the corner. Without any warning he felt two strong arms grasp his neck and another pair about his waist. A further hand was clapped over his mouth. Instinctively he tried to bite the palm, but a short bough crashed into his right eye, making the mountain spin for a moment and, when that sensation ceased, it appeared bleary and indistinct as if a mist had suddenly descended on one half of his world.

'So soldier, what brings ye here?'

The speaker was a huge man with a grey beard and broad head. The eyes looked curiously small set in such features. Andrew tried to break free but the forearms tightened around his neck. The third person released the grasp on the mouth and Andrew tasted blood on his lower lip welling between his teeth. He shook his head to clear his senses.

Before he had time to speak another two men in rough Highland dress and coarse beards appeared. Between them struggled Eilidh.

'Aye, y'see her full well now, Mr. Lockhart, don't ye.' The leader who spoke stared at the subdued girl, as tears rolled down her cheek.

Andrew instinctively reached out to hold the girl's trembling hand but was restrained.

'You're fair brave the lot of ye against one man and a girl. But if my dirk or pistol we're at the ready I would soon take you to hell and damnation with me.'

The five clansmen smiled and the leader continued. 'So y' might, as y' took my brother and nearly Robbie Sutherland.'

'In what way?'

'I'm Micheal (Michael) MacIomhair. And the way is...by telling that evil Captain Cameron their whereabouts. Niall's no been seen fur a few weeks and that's no like him. He's no been heard of either! It doesna tek much to determine he's either locked away or, more than likely, dead.'

The others crowded round.

Andrew gazed at the speaker. 'If I was free at this minute, you'd pay a fair price for what you say, MacIomhair. There would not be a normal bone in your face.'

'So y'say,' came the matter of fact reply, ' but first I'll be after a few mair facts ye can tell us lassie.

'I can tell y'naught,' said the girl impulsively. 'So let us be about our business.'

'Perhaps Mr. Lockhart, in a manner of speaking, will tell us!' With a sudden twist of the body Micheal MacIomhair swept up Eilidh and made to throw her into the chasm a thousand feet below. She let out a scream that reverberated into the rock overhangs and repeated itself a dozen times in the mountains.

'So you're no so keen to keep quiet when dangling o'er this wee ledge,' laughed MacIomhair.

Andrew cursed, threatened and begged him to stop by turn. But the huge man continued to swirl the girl round and round in a wild dance that took them both close to the very edge of the precipice. How long this uncouth merriment would have gone on without interruption is difficult to guess. But the clear voice of Robbie Sutherland stopped them in their capers. 'What on earth are you doing dangling and dancing o'er the cliff edge, Eilidh. Don't encourage Micheal in that manner!

The girl was hanging head down a foot from the path, perilously close to the drop. 'Don't talk ridiculously Robbie Sutherland, as is oft your want!'

'There is never a time to insult a man, and certainly not now!' he replied blandly.

'Stop you blatherin' man and do something aboot it,' replied the girl still clinging for dear life to MacIomhair.

'It's a strange way to a man's heart,' surmised Robbie with a long laugh, 'and not as neat a way as this dirk in my belt.' He looked significantly at the others as he spoke. 'Anyway, is this man the soldier laddie I've heard tell of?'

Eilidh, who had surveyed the young highlander from an upside-down perspective while vainly clinging to the hem of her dress, was slowly being turned towards a normal position. 'Who from?' she yelled above the roar of laughter from the others.

'Does it really matter?'

'Aye,' replied the girl, 'it does!'

'You're one for the etiquette, Eilidh.'

'And ye're one for the blatherin, put me down, you goat of a man!'

'I'm not holding you!' Robbie replied with another laugh.

'Stop being stupid Robbie! Micheal MacIomhair, please put me down!'

She was gently lowered to the ground amidst further roars of enjoyment. 'I've only one mair thing to say, Robbie Sutherland.'

'And what's that now?'

'This!' and she kicked him hard on the shin.

Robbie hopped up and down for a few moments and then rubbed his bruised leg. The roars of laughter reached a crescendo. 'What's that for?' he asked surveying the swelling area.

'For makin' a fool o'me, that's what!'

However acrimonious the meeting had been the group's mood had ameliorated with the laughter, no one had enjoyed it more, in a perverse way, that the young highlander. Andrew was released but his mood was soured by the treatment he had received and the tomfoolery with Eilidh. He waited until the laughter had subsided. 'I can say on my life that Eilidh has never told me any facts about anyone or anything…and if she had (his voice trembled a little) …I would never tell another soul!'

Robbie looked at him hard and then nodded. 'I will say one thing. That Murdo McBain and Factor Sellar are the men behind all this…old Domhnall and I found McBain's brother dead. It's my opinion that Murdo had something to do with it. Perhaps he got more from his brother before death than we bargain for, that we'll never know! But it could explain how the military men ken some of our secrets. But I shouldn't speak ill of the dead, for the minister was a good man and had the confidence of all of us. So I'm telling you friends, before God, that Murdo McBain is the evil among us!' Robbie walked over and kissed the girl on the cheek. 'I did not mean to upset you, Eilidh and, anyway...a bit o'fun and laughter makes things seem no so bad after all and keeps us away from mischief...for the most part,' he added with a wink.

With this homespun advice, and another wink towards the others and a smile towards the girl, Robbie departed to where, he knew not at the time!

Ceithir deug (fourteen)

The twenty odd miles were easily taken in the young highlander's stride. Mountains came and went, lochs sparkled in the tranquil sunlight; bracken, dead heather and rough drovers roads were crossed at random. The odd eagle's cry, the wheeling buzzard or the cackle of the moorland grouse hardly disturbed his thoughts. The road for the great part ran up the valley between the sharp outline of the crags and peaks, with a hasty stream that broke into falls and pools where the trout lazily basked. Midges brought out by a brief burst of autumn sun, plagued the water and set store on the man as he wound his way up the valley. Here and there were gaunt oaks, half dead in the ceaseless struggle with the winds, their lower branches stripped bare. Sometimes a small path would branch off to some outpost – a small croft or herdsman's hut. Willows stood intermittently at the odd flat patches of land by the river, finding harbourage from the thrusting rocks. The silence was only broken by the drone of innumerable insects and the odd rock pipit that flew into their midst in twittering flight. All beyond him were hills and crests, seeming thrown up in strange rows by the primordial folding of this ancient land. There were no boundary walls to halt the herds of red deer as they ambled down to the lush riverside grass at dusk. The heather's carpeting and moor birds knew of no restraints. While the plover's cry and the plaintiff strutting-call of the blackcock broke out intermittently as he wandered near their domain. The bogs looked treacherously green, smooth and fresh; and filled the air with strange, sweet stagnant odour.

Sometimes these narrow paths led to a small exposed cottage, beaten and buffeted by tempest so that the roof looked melancholy black and squalid.

Rarely did Robbie pause.

Only on one occasion did he stop to buy food from a thatched cottage, and he was given it free of charge - as is the local hospitality towards one of their clan - some rough oatcakes smothered with honey, and a tumbler full of goat's milk to wash them down. However, he did insist on buying for later three strips of dried smoked herring and a loaf of bread, which he filled with a curd-like cheese.

He enjoyed the freedom of the walk, for such freedom was in his being having little to occupy his time apart from the family farm, which although bigger than many around, barely produced enough work to occupy his parents and him for much of the year.

Thus he was a wanderer at heart; often spending long periods away from home, obtaining work wherever he could -shepherding, shearing, crop picking and sometimes helping with the kelp collecting or fish-curing at the coast. Solitary as his life could be, Robbie often craved company, with bright hearth fires and congenial chatter and the pleasure of the warmth within. Thus he had begun to tire of the journey and of his mission, not certain of success and more certain – he believed- of failure when his destination -the Laird's great house- came into view. All beyond and about was in neat order- fields, hedgerows, buildings and forest; with the sea as a permanent backdrop to a building of magnificent sturdiness. It stood out majestic and defiant against all else, proud of its power and heritage

The Marquess and Countess of Sutherland's castle was clearly visible from five-miles away, the pediments and towers etched against the level blueness of the sea.

When he saw it, Robbie's impression was of its overwhelming grandeur. And he smiled as he thought of the township cottages with their tiny windows and small, crudely thatched roofs. He had seen it before but not paid as much interest. Why should he? There was never the slightest chance he would go inside, not the remotest possibility he would ever see the reclusive couple who dominated the land he loved. Yet, for once, he decided to rest on a broad flat stone and gazed at the building, not at all afraid of the consequences of his visit but determined to find whatever he could about stopping the clearances and to ascertain the whereabouts of the blacksmith, Niall, once and for all. His darkest thoughts soon gave way to musing about the grandeur of the castle and the people that lived within, but he was not filled with anything but an idle curiosity devoid of envy. To live in such a place had never entered his mind, nor was he overawed; and as to the reception he might get - he felt confident, in his usual optimistic mien, of handling the situation.

His musings were interrupted by the sound of horses' hooves on the rough-stone road. Robbie glanced round, stared for a moment and then lay back on the grass.

A party of nine men approached with a woman prominent in their midst. She so stood out from the rest, in appearance and manner that he half-sat up to inspect her more closely. A broad crimson cape caught his attention first. It was loosely fastened over a black dress, but it was her hair that made his gaze linger for an unusual length of time. He noted that it hung in fair ringlets around her shoulders other than at one place where it was pushed back with a comb to stop it winnowing around her face as she rode. She looked so graceful on the horse that the contrast between the girls he knew and this 'lady' was immediately apparent.

Robbie would have continued to watch had it not been for another surprising fact. For his gaze wandered briefly to the group of men riding behind her. Then it was not the girl who arrested his attention but one of them – Murdo McBain himself. Robbie whistled softly in amazement.

He collected his thoughts, decided on his plan and prepared to wait until the group reached the spot where he lay.

He heard the sound of the horses' feet getting nearer and nearer.

Robbie rested quietly on the grass, listening with his eyes closed and enjoying the warmth of the autumn sun on his face. A few clouds scudded by intermittently and broke the brightness.

It was not until the jostling noise became overwhelming that he opened his eyes and caught the gaze of the young woman looking down at him from the elevation of her grey stallion. 'He's not dead then!' She laughed as she turned to the factor, McBain.

The man shrugged his shoulders. 'Seems not, Catriona, although idle no doubt when he should be working for his Laird and Master.'

Robbie ignored the conversation and continued lying with the sun shimmering in his eyes. The light glinted off the coloured cape, giving the fair hair an unnatural reddish lustre. He smiled to himself as he observed her beauty, which had a compelling serenity about it. Her blue eyes were so different from his and other highlanders, he curiously acknowledged.

He waited.

Murdo spoke again. 'If you have no other business about the place, be on your way, young man!'

The rest of the group steadied their horses, and some were impatiently wheeling round and round; for the younger men were irritated at having to stop because of the rough highlander. They muttered amongst themselves but seemed afraid to speak out.

Robbie kept silent to heighten the tension. Finally he said. 'I was almost falling asleep!' (*Bha mi gu tuiteam nam chadal!*) That seems to be my business at present on this hillside.' He spoke in Gaelic with a wry smile, glancing at the girl.

'Can you not speak in the royal tongue,' retorted Murdo also looking towards the young woman, 'and not in this incomprehensible Highland brogue?'

Robbie smiled and replied with composure. 'I can! But are we not in the Highlands or do my eyes deceive me? I have come far on foot that I ken, but no so far as to meet with Lowland manners and ways. Anyway, if it pleases you,' he turned to address the girl in English, 'I have come to speak to the Laird or one of his factors.'

'I am the factor!'

'Aye, I thought you were!' Robbie replied in a composed manner that irritated McBain.

'Well, speak on man if you have much to say!'

Robbie paused once more. 'Not much...now that I see you! Just to enquire as the whereabouts of Niall

MacIomhair, the blacksmith who was fired upon by your men a few weeks back and...' he remarked with a shrug of his shoulders and another smile at the girl, '...and to say that I am fair pleased to hear that the lootings and burnings are stopping in the glens.'

Murdo took a deep breath and his face blackened with rage.

One of the riders picked up the mood. In an impulse he drove his horse forward to threaten Robbie but Murdo waved him back. The factor surveyed Robbie who noticed the same penetrating cold eyes as on the wedding day. 'Such impudence from one so low born! "Pleased" you say!'

'Aye, pleased!'

'And why so?'

'For no good will come of killing and burning!' Robbie spoke slowly, part in Gaelic, part in English.

McBain retorted angrily as the girl watched intently. 'Listen, you ignorant, lazy cottar, tell your people that this land is for the sheep. Animals with more brains and manners and usefulness than the lot of you; animals that will make these barren places prosperous again which is more than all of you have done for generations. And that's a fact! This is the good that will come. And if you all do not willingly leave those parts of the Glens that the Laird has decreed are for grazing, then force will follow as winter follows summer.' He paused to smile, a fixed unwholesome movement of the mouth. 'Finally, as for your friend, I neither know of his whereabouts...nor care!'

'Aye, force will follow, no doubt' Robbie interjected. 'The highland people are sure of that, more and more force but it will not be all one-sided, by the Lord! And fire will meet fire!' He spoke calmly, his voice rising to emphasise each point.

But his attention was not solely directed towards the factor. For out of the corner of his eye he saw a broad-chested man leave the rear of the group and canter forward. 'Excuse the interruption, maister, but I ken this man. He was one o' those said to be sheep-stealing and was fired on some few weeks back with the man he has spoken about, MacIomhair. He seems to hav' escaped like the other he speaks of, for naught has been seen of either of them since, although the older man, it is said, was clearly hit in th' chest.'

Robbie bit his lower lip as he felt a shiver of disappointment but remained calm.

'Does that give you the answer you seek?' Murdo pulled his horse closer and nodded briefly to his companions in mock triumph.

Robbie did not reply. He felt a pistol being pressed into the back of his right shoulder.

Robbie tried to turn but a voice said, 'Walk, cottar, walk slowly before me.' The speaker was a stout man who had slid from his mount unnoticed. 'Walk slowly, as I tell you, towards the castle!'

Still the girl watched the scene unfold without commenting. McBain sat immobile on his horse.

'This man's a liar factor.' Robbie continued calmly ignoring both the insult and the danger, although being pushed along.

'Why say you, so full of confidence?' McBain asked.

'Because I was no there!' Turning towards the girl he remarked with a smile, 'I was at a wedding, though the bride was none so fair...'

'Silence, I want not of your lame Highland excuses and impudence.' The factor replied in disgust.

But the girl, who had gently eased away from the group, wheeled her horse round and reined up beside the factor. 'None so fair?' She gazed into Robbie's face for a moment. 'So that's the truth?'

'Aye, as I stand here!'

'You stand there right enough, but as for the truth, I think you know little of that!' she replied firmly.

Robbie laughed. 'Do you eat gruel?' He corrected himself, 'porridge!' The girl looked puzzled. Robbie liked the curious expression in her blue eyes. They held him in a strange fascination. Then he recovered his composure. 'My grandmother said that eating gruel made a man healthy and truthful, and I have swallowed a fair bit in my time, I'll be thinking!'

He said it with such a strange matter-of-fact innocence that the girl laughed for a few seconds and felt a slight triumph in compelling his gaze to remain on her face. Suddenly she remarked, 'Oh! Let him go, Murdo! There is no point in taking him. My uncle the Laird of Sutherland will be displeased at such an interruption. He has no stomach to be bothered with Highland riff-raff at present...and this man can take a warning back to his people, can he not? Providing he does not lie! Anyway, there is no proof of his involvement with the sheep stealing. And if he is born to hang, then he will hang eventually, by the Grace of God!'

Robbie felt a sharp blow on the back of the shoulder from the butt of the pistol. It made him wince as the pain shot down his arm. His first instinct was to strike back at the stout man. Instead he ground his teeth in pain while maintaining his gaze on the girl's blue eyes.

She noticed his fixed expression despite the momentary wince. 'Think yourself lucky,' she continued, 'that your impudence has not been your downfall!'

But Robbie did not reply.

She remained equally composed. 'Have you anything to say?'

'One thing!'

'And pray what is it?'

'That we will meet again...and I know we will!'

She shook her head and motioned Murdo away.

But the factor could not still his curiosity. 'What's your name?'

'None for the moment! And my advice to you factor, is that every hog has its trough before being cured and smoked.'

'Aye, and every man has his jail before being transported or hung!' With a coarse, derisive laugh the factor turned his horse, and the party rode away.

In a minute Robbie was alone on the hillside, at first watching them go, next idly staring at the sky. He paused only once to rub the bruised area. Strangely he did not feel angry at their taunts. They were from people who meant nothing to him. From the failure of his mission, he felt great disappointment. He had achieved nothing and let his friends down! Had he gone about it all in a naive way? There was little else to do than formulate another plan.

And he gazed into the firmament of deep blue above for inspiration. 'He who speaks softly hears the best (*'Am fear as isle a bhruidhneas,'s e as fhearr a chluinneas!'*). I'll say little mair to these *coin* (dogs) in future, but fur the girl, we'll see if chance will come my way agin.'

Then he laughed confidently.

The idea amused him for an hour or more.

*****

The next morning's chill had cast a frosty shimmer in the shadow of the hillside and, as Robbie sat gazing at the coast not half a mile away, he listened to the breakers' roar and thought of what to do next. He was not shy or discouraged. He had a difference of opinion and was determined to make his point. Even more determined after the events and humiliation of the day before.

So far he had no plan.

He had stayed the night with a cousin and their two children in a small cottage within the boundary of the Castle's Great Park.

His cousin had worked for the Laird for many years and was fearful of any criticism. 'Hold thy thoughts to thyself,' he had demanded angrily, 'fur my days be numbered if I am caught speaking so!'

Robbie had begun to outline a plan and seek moral support. But the cousin's wife had ushered the teenage children to bed, embarrassed by the conversation, and contented herself in making a small pan of gruel for three adults. Realising the futility of any further talk, Robbie had contented himself in listening to their general prattle for a while.

He had noticed the fear in their eyes. But felt disappointed, none-the-less and hurt. However, after some reflection he appreciated their concern and let the matter rest.

Now, as he sat gazing out to sea, he wondered how many clans folk could be relied upon to shed their deference to the noble lord and resist the inequity and hardship imposed on the people of the glens.

But, he knew that there was a stoical spirit bred into a Highlander. With it went the submission to authority and a fear of trespassing against the Holy Scriptures.

It would be a hard task to raise resistance although some would fight.

'But how many?' was the question that plagued his mind. 'How many?'

The last thing he wished for was bloodshed. His earnest hope was for a negotiated settlement on both sides, and that the land should be as it always had been - with the people free to live out their own simple lives as best they chose.

As the waves rolled in and broke with streaming white manes, his thoughts wandered back to the previous day.

Especially the girl and the grey horse slowly turning in a mesmeric wheel then the thrill he experienced as it cantered back towards him!

That was the dominant and clear image that filled his mind. He wondered in a quixotic sort of way what had been her impression of him, away from the critical banter of McBain. Somehow, he had an instinctive feeling of attraction towards her that transcended his previous emotional escapades. Yet it was only a hint of attraction, no more, he reasoned agreeably – which satisfied his conscience. He knew it would not be reciprocated and that fact consoled him in a peculiar way. But her very remoteness, perhaps haughtiness, he could not fathom out, was both fascinating and challenging at the same time.

The breaking waves reinforced the image of the girl on the horse. As the waves poured and leapt on to the shore, the spray in its foaming white projected a vision of the girl wheeling and leaping, aloof to the point of being supercilious, erect with contempt. And still the spray swept though the waves, constant and eternal and the image came back and back. Despite his nonchalance, and her patronizing approach, the first foundations of his new plan began to materialize. Suddenly the possibilities crowded together one by one. Slim, graceful, fair and haughty, she might be, but as the thought struck him, he laughed. And as Robbie sat forward he laughed and laughed again until his side ached at the impudence.

Quickly getting to his feet he hurried to the wall of the Great Park four hundred yards away.

Furtively he clambered over the twelve feet wall. Looking for a place to land safely he glided towards a pile of dead bracken. He quietly made his way through the firs. The fallen pine needles were soft beneath his feet, and his footsteps raised a sweet pine scent from the gentle covering. A jay chattered overhead in its quest for acorn seeds while the light slanted through the thick foliage in irregular patches, striping the trunks and the ground ahead.

A dozen fallow deer, speckling into winter coat, stole off through the trees with hardly a backward glance.

Robbie watched them melt away into the gloom of the forest. He appreciated the strength and grandeur of the Highland red deer, and dismissed these creatures as feeble invaders introduced from the southland (*England).

He had not walked more than two hundred yards into the wood when a voice shouted, 'In what manner o' business bring y' here?'

Robbie waved. 'Oh! Cousin you fair startled me!'

'Do you no ken man, that if one o' the Laird's gamekeepers sees you that you'll be tain for a poacher and risk all manner o' punishment.'

'*Tha*! (Yes!) But I would simply say that I was visiting my cousin who is always pleased to see me and forever polite,' replied Robbie sarcastically.

'A cousin who cud risk his neck and his family's too, if he listens to thy wild schemes!'

'Aye, the very man! But tush, I am only passing through to the meadow yonder. Is that a crime?'

The other man shook his head. 'I must say this...(*Feumaidh mi seo a radh*) ...'tis folly on thy part to take the risk, walkin' about in a kilt and...'

'The same plaid as the auld Sassenach Laird wears, yet I'm of the Sutherland blood for generations and so are you...but I would not think so right now or even yester night!'

But the cousin had tired of the conversation and strode off with a shambling gait, muttering and pointing in the opposite direction, 'You see the big park gate *(Chi sibh geata mor na pairce),* get out while you can!'

'Some goodbye!' laughed Robbie to himself as he watched the man leave. 'Still it's better that he's gone. He's nought but a hindrance to himself and everybody else,' he said indifferently.

Undaunted he strolled on until he reached a broad wall at the edge of the forest and, with a leap, was quickly astride the top stones. Making himself as comfortable as he could on the broad, rough expanse Robbie settled down for what he considered would be "a fair wait".

He looked this way and that, shifted position several times and generally felt bored, which was unlike his normal disposition. He glanced up at the sky and noticed a heightening brightness in the east; followed some fifteen minutes later by a warm breeze filtering through the Scots firs, causing them to swish their branches in the softest murmurs.

Then he gazed fixedly into the meadow as part of his quest.

At first he could not make out the horse amongst some dozen mares. However, from behind a small copse the grey stallion suddenly appeared, its neck at full stretch and its hooves drumming across the ground. Round the field it ran with a flowing mane and snorting breath. Some of the fillies joined in for a short distance and then broke off to crop the grass with a graceful swinging of their tails.

The young man observed the animal closely, fascinated by the sheer power of the white blur before him.

Robbie watched for an hour or more. Once in a while the slow rasping-crop of the horses was punctuated by a flurry of cantering around the field. Then it would stop and all was as peaceful as before.

He had an instinct to remain and watch.

And watch he did, forever conscious of the sounds about him.

Another burst of cantering and after a few minutes the pace slowed. This time the grey was the first to stop. With a brief shaking of its long neck and a twisting motion of the shoulders it looked around.

Robbie waited with bated breath.

Then the animal slowly walked towards a small gate in the far corner of the field.

The man's eyes followed the animal.

There stood the girl!

He had not been aware of her presence until then. 'Had she seen him?' There were no signs that she had! He remained motionless.

Now she had arrived, he was undecided as to what to do next.

That she intended to stay was evident; for she was warmly dressed in a long blue coat and a dark shawl pulled firmly over her head.

Still he waited!

But her attention was firmly fixed on the horse, which plodded towards her.

He saw her reach out and stroke the animal's mane, letting the white strands fall softly through her fingers. Then she let the shawl slide down to her shoulders and he watched her gently embracing the smooth neck as she combed each strand, entwining them with her own blond hair.

Thus preoccupied by her love for the horse, he could only sit and wait for the girl to look round.

A few minutes passed.

Robbie took a deep breath. 'Whatever be her mood, it is best I see for myself,' he suddenly thought.

With a soft, almost cat-like movement, he jumped down from the wall.

Still she did not look round.

Slowly he approached, partly afraid he might frighten them, yet eager to call and attract her attention. Undecided, he kept the animal between himself and the girl.

He was now only a few paces behind the horse.

Robbie was beginning to wonder how long the situation would have continued had it not been for a black mare slowly plodding forward. With a characteristic brusqueness it tried to thrust its head between the girl and the stallion.

The grey wheeled around impatiently and, in an instant, his presence was revealed. He breathed a sigh of relief.

To his amazement she ignored him. Was it anger or surprise? He tried to fathom out. She looked away.

Robbie felt deeply embarrassed.

For a second or two he paused; then said boldly, *'Ciamar a tha sibh?'* (How are you?) And not waiting for a reply continued in a self-conscious way, *"S mise Robbie Sutherland!'* He was not aware in his nervousness that he was speaking in Gaelic.

To his amazement she replied without looking up, 'And this is September.'*('Agus 'S ise an t-Sultain)*

The cool, off-hand manner, in which she had ignored his name and referred to the horse, stung him; but out of politeness he waited for her to continue. However, she said nothing more and went on stroking the animal's neck.

'It is pretty!' *(Tha e snog'!)* he said at length trying to break the silence.

'The horse!'

To which he muttered quietly, *'Chan eil!* (No!) I was thinking a little about...(He hesitated)...your face!'

If she heard the remark or not, she did not respond.

He stood waiting, regretting what he had just instinctively said.

Still she did not look his way. But after an impatient movement of her hands she stopped stroking the horse's mane. 'You are as impudent as you were yesterday and equally rude in your personal opinions. I have come to this field to be alone for a short while...and to be with my horse. Now you are here and, in this case, three is more than a crowd, it is an imposition.'

If the girl thought that Robbie would understand what she said in such voluble English haste, she was wrong! He tried to follow the gist of the conversation but failing he gave an apologetic smile. This angered the girl even more.

The animal shook its head and stood motionless for a moment. Then it slowly wandered off to join the mares on the opposite side of the field.

Now they were alone, with the girl abstractly looking towards the trees, the young man gazing into her face. In her anger she had never looked more beautiful he thought; an instant angelic image of blond hair and blue eyes, an image of grace and serenity that slightly unnerved him.

But his smile did not hold her attention, just the reverse. She fixed her mouth and gazed at the horse. Eager for him to walk away, she turned, sighed and gave him as withering and as cold a look as was humanly possible. She said impatiently, "Well, are you going or what?'

'Where?'

'What do you mean "where"?

'I understand that you asked me, non-too-politely if I was going and I asked you where.'

'There's no need to keep going over the conversation, we're getting absolutely nowhere! Would you like to leave!'

Robbie weighed up her immediate distaste, but at the same time was determined to remain. He did not reply, and thinking a smile was inappropriate, perhaps even rude, he simple gazed blankly towards the horse.

In her mind she was more than curious about his strange manner and pleasant face. She had noticed the colour rising in his cheeks, despite their tan, and that gave her a feeling of superiority. But the more she looked at him the more resolute became his face and she became irritated again.

At last he spoke. 'Not so soon!'

'What do you mean 'not so soon'! I asked if you were leaving and you reply, 'not so soon!''

'Aye, I did that!'

She gave a grunt of dissatisfaction.

'The reason I said 'Not so soon'... is because I have something to ask.'

'Have you now?'

'Aye, I have!'

'Well, you take a long time in saying it,' she said haughtily.

'Perhaps I do! But it's hard to get a word in edgeways without some sort of retort...if you don't mind me saying.' Then he smiled. It was a sudden smile of warmth and familiarity that made her blush. And within a moment she felt angry with herself. But Robbie did not seem to notice, or if he had, gave no further indication that for an instant he had seen her show weakness.

At length she said, 'You speak English then!'

'I do!'

'Very good!' (*Gle mhath*) she replied in Gallic to show her linguistic skill and superiority. Suddenly she felt ashamed at her brusque manners and smiled for the first time. She noticed the dishevelled brown curls clustered about his forehead and the features that displayed in an instant such varying emotions. But his eyes were forever smiling and alert, and that held her interest, if only in a curious way.

Robbie paused for a second and considered the situation, his confidence rising like at lark in the morning. 'So you speak the Gaelic then?'

'Only when I have too!' She replied quickly.

'That's a pity then,' he said earnestly. 'For it's a beautiful language!'

'You have just said you speak English and that is good enough for me.'

'It is true I can speak! But it is only little, and infrequently used, at the best of times!' He paused and collected his thoughts, forming the words slowly in his mind, once again self-conscious of the girl's smile. ' My mother worked in the Lowlands when she was young and always said that if ever I hoped to improve my situation I would have to know some of that foreign tongue.' He smiled. 'Since I find myself addressing a lady, I am trying, as best as I could...is that right?'

'Can!'

'As best as I can to...er...impress (is that right?')...

'No! It is not right!'

Robbie smiled once more and gave a faint shrug of his shoulders and a nod of the head in her direction. 'Not right?'

'No! It is not right that you wander on in this way, disturbing my horse...'

'Does that matter when I have something important...'

She replied quickly. 'Yes! It does matter, and whatever you have to say, if it is important or not...is of no consequence to me...either now or in the future!'

'Excuse me for being so rude in surprising you!' he faltered.

She remained silent.

Robbie once more shrugged his shoulders. 'To whom was I speaking?' *(Ris an robh mi a' bruidhinn?)* he muttered. Then he gave a faint laugh, 'To a lady of manners or a horse?'

The remark stung the girl but only for a second.

Then she regained her composure. For a brief moment her blue eyes had closed in annoyance and once more a faint red blush suffused her cheeks. Still she said nothing more, the memory of the first blush still troubled and angered her.

'There is little point talking then?' he asked politely after a few seconds had elapsed.

'Little!'

'Oh!'

'You seem disappointed!'

'I am!' Robbie replied innocently.

'Are you really a cottar who can speak English?'

'I am a highlander from Sutherlandshire, my station is of no regard to you or your ilk.'

'Yesterday you were not so easily stung by the rebukes of my factor and his men but I see that tetchiness is here today.' It was her turn to face him with a long stare.

'*Tha cuimhn' agam air...*(I remember)...but I do not understand all you say, though I have no doubt that it be mostly true!' He spoke rapidly in Gaelic to irritate her and to give vent to his frustrations, fearing that his poor English would be so incomprehensible that his main aim to annoy her would be lost. In his anger he remained silent for a short while, both of them staring at each other like medieval combatants, neither wanting to give way. Then Robbie resumed speaking English. 'I thought you could help, that is all!'

She paused and looked at him keenly. She was impressed with the depth of strength and an overwhelming kindness in its eyes. Such a mixture of looks and emotions she had not observed in highland features before, men, she generally considered to be coarse and dull.

Robbie was unaware of any impression he was making, intent on asking the one question he had travelled so far to ask. He continued. 'I was wondering if you had heard anything about my friend, the blacksmith, Niall? I am so worried about him. I haven't heard from him for weeks, neither has anyone else.'

She stepped forward one pace and gathered her coat about her, 'Were you stealing the Great Laird's sheep?'

'Do you want me to tell a lie?' he retorted almost slipping back into Gaelic in his nervousness.

'No!'

'Then don't ask!' He said sharply.

'If it means so much to you and creates such ill-feeling, I will shut up! How can I answer your question without knowing the facts or the truth? How can I confide in you under such circumstances? No doubt,' she paused, 'I've lost you in what I'm saying!'

'You answer a question with a question, may be it's the way of the English, I do not know.'

'Yes! That about sums it up...you do not know...much or anything...and I am wasting my time!'

Robbie suddenly felt remorse. But his emotions were stifled by his irritation. He turned towards the horses. 'Good day to you!' (*Latha math dhuibh!*) His voice was directed towards the stallion, shining pure and white in the morning sun. 'And a good day to your mistress, whose beauty and temper are as fragile as a spider's web in the morning dew!'

Whether the remark had any effect on the girl, he did know, for she flounced out of the field in rapid strides.

'The others in the glen can come if they wish,' he thought. 'But knowing of the Laird, the factor and the girl...it would not be worth their while! *(Cha b'fhiach dhaibh tighinn!)*' he muttered.

Giving the horse a final stroke on the neck, he jumped over the wall, and followed the way he had come.

Within twenty minutes Robbie had climbed the hill into the next glen, and, as is the nature of his race, was enjoying the autumn sun - having put all worries and extraneous thoughts out of his mind.

Coig deug (fifteen)

Robbie Sutherland made his way quickly towards Alasdair and Mairead's small thatched cottage in Rogart. His day was never too full or his time too pressing to cause any inclination to worry or fret over matters beyond his control. God interfered in worldly affairs in mysterious ways, was his recurring conclusion whenever life threw up a puzzling chance or an extraordinary happening. If the girl wondered as she fed the horse the next morning as to what profound effect she had had on the highlander, she would have been surprised by his jaunty walk and disappointed by the broad grin as he approached his brother's house.

The journey had taken him just over three hours.

From a small byre close by came the answering call from Mairead. Within moments she appeared in the small doorway and waved in pleasure at seeing her brother-in-law. She smiled broadly and flung her arms round his neck, warming his cheek against hers.

'Back so soon, Robbie. How did it all go then?'

Robbie laughed. 'Oh! If anything...badly I suppose! Although I should not laugh!'

'Why badly?'

'Well, I have a smarting shoulder for my pains from a blow, no news of aught in my head and little chance of finding employ in the Laird's household or anywhere else. I have little doubt that our trembling cousin will see to that! For he's afraid of the Laird's shadow and perhaps even his own!'

Mairead let go for a moment, then impulsively reached up, and kissed him. 'It's always wonderful to see you Robbie. You bring a sort of cheerfulness wherever you go in that strange manner of talk'.

Robbie gave a slight blush in his confusion; then instinctively seized her face and held her close for a second. But it was all over in a moment and each emotion returned to the normal plain.

Then she spoke. 'I've been thinking, Robbie, we must fight these wicked people, fur the Highland's are doomed if we don't. There'll no be a single township left. I feel it in my soul!'

'D' you no think that I have given it much thought?'

'Aye, I do!'

'But fighting's a long and dangerous game, Mairead, and many a man will die, as I have said before.'

'Aye, many will die...even without fighting, as I have often said before! For hunger and pestilence will see them off!'

Robbie paused for a minute as they walked towards the house. 'Aye, you may well be right, that I must admit!'

'I am right!' exclaimed the girl, her voice rising with the emotion; then more softly she said, 'if ye take to the hills Robbie I will come with ye. I would like to do that!' *(Bu toil leam sin a dheanamh!)*

Mairead spoke in such a matter of fact voice that although he felt surprised and flustered for an instant, he accepted the request as a matter of course. He looked into her eyes and saw the earnestness there. He knew she had made up her mind. 'Will you! Even if Alasdair stays behind?'

'Aye, I will, and never has a truer word been spoken.'

They walked into the house in silence and both sat down on small stools placed at either side of the fire. She picked up his left hand, stroked it gently then abruptly let it go. 'Oh, bother the peat...it burns but at a snail's pace, for it's soaked up some of the summer's rains and not yet fully dry,' apologised Mairead. Then she reached over to hold Robbie's hand once more. 'Alasdair will fight, I'm sure o'that!' She paused and reflected, gazing at the thin tendrils of smoke. 'But if he fails me, then I will come alone. I like ye enuf fur that!'

The man shrugged his shoulders. 'Och! My brother'll no fail us! When I was a wee boy he taught me all I ken...about the mountains, the livestock....'

'And courage?' The girl asked eagerly.

'Aye, that too!'

'Well then, speak to him Robbie as a brother and a friend. Convince him that to resist is right, God's way!'

'I know not whether it is God's way, Mairead. But it may be mine...the only way, I fear!'

'Doth the Lord sleep while a' this happens? Tell me that! Fur we have no had guidance from the ministers o' the Kirk.'

'You'll no hear from most of them, I would like to bet!' He shook his head solemnly.

There was a short silence.

Mairead surveyed her brother-in-law, observing the serious expression and smiled. 'In some ways I luv' you mair each time I see ye, Robbie.'

He looked at her for a few moments but did not speak. He felt her slim fingers resting on his hand. 'More?'

'Aye, mair than anyone but Alasdair and mair than when we first met.' She reached up to kiss him but Robbie swayed back on his stool and laughed.

'I can but say there is naught but beauty in thy face and pleasure in your manner, Mairead. But to kiss you for the second time, and not out of friendship's greeting, would be against the Holy Scriptures...be that not so?'

She smiled. ''Tis so! But if the Lord is no watching over this land, as I think, then no one would ken but ye and me.'

'But I would know, and that would sore trouble me and...' He stopped and laughed.

'And?'

'And may tempt me more and more.'

'That's good,' she replied in a matter of fact way. 'But enough o' this blathering for I must get back to milking the cow, for such a commodity is scarce at present.'

With a final gentle kiss on the man's cheek, she hurried out, smoothing the folds of her black dress, leaving Robbie to contemplate the fire and the complexities of life, and love, in general.

Sia deug (sixteen)

Hardly had one November storm abated than another flew in on the northerly gales. And in the morning there blew a bitter wintry wind and a burst of hail drummed the pastures. In an arctic blast of ferocious intensity the wind returned, more malevolent than at first. Thus frost held the high grounds in one glacial sheet, rock hard and treacherous; while snow invaded the glens, densely packed and impenetrable in places. The red deer wandered down from the higher reaches and foraged with the sheep and cattle - and winter's grasp was unrelenting.

The nights were frosty, the ground smelted hard; the sun was no sooner up than it was held in check by the mists so that only the top inch of the ice could thaw before it gave up and set hard once more. There were no scents or perfumes in this land, and all wild life was mute in an environment deserted.

By noon in this harsh landscape and, with an easy walk, Robbie set off to his parent's home close to the shore of Loch Shin, immersed in thought - at conflict with his normal nonchalance. His mind raced between glorious and heroic escapades, to being involved in steady, rational arguments with the Chief and the local families. He hoped that reasoned discussion would prevail in uniting the undecided factions. Robbie had a feeling of destiny that he had never felt before, a purpose in life; but he still had no distinct plan. In such a stream of thought, and heated with the exertions, he hurried on in silence. For the outpouring of the waterfalls and burns was stilled by the icy grip. Sometimes he would pause as if he heard a voice but it was only the breeze picking up for a moment and sighing in the cracks and crevices of the rocks. The illusion was one of uniform whiteness with only the black perspective of the mountain peaks behind him, but they were ghostly fragments as the mist smoothed their contours with long, wispy tendrils.

Robbie's spirits rose as he approached his home, and his footsteps quickened.

The peat fire smouldered, the small windows were shuttered with thick woollen cloths, and the partially warped wooden doors were forced shut as tightly as they could be.

Still the cold draughts managed to make their mark in the small rooms.

Robbie's father sat at a broad yet crudely carved table, slicing away at a thick oatcake and cutting fine strips of dried venison with his knife. It was a larger room than most in the neighbourhood and the furniture was of superior design being handed down from several generations. He looked up as the door rattled in the wind and what he thought was the sound of approaching footsteps. Before he had time to consider the situation, the door had opened and his youngest son walked in, with hair frosted white and cheeks chaffed red by the icy blast. Robbie nodded towards his father and reaching forward took a small piece of oatcake, uttering a brief 'thank you' as he did.

'By the will o' the Lord, this cauld blast may break soon,' his father remarked at length, 'it's a trifle early to be called winter, but it has taken on the mantle.' Other than this remark his voice gave no hint of being surprised, nor was there a tone of reprimand at the long absence. He was dressed in a rough dark coat and trousers, his beard hung grey, ragged and dishevelled. But the brown eyes behind were still alert and kind, especially as he focussed on his son. 'Thy hair is as white as mine, Robbie lad, and as your mother always says, you look like me a fair deal especially in my middle years.'

The young man laughed. 'Well, I see what is to come in that way then,' he replied taking another slice of meat at the father's bidding.

'Aye, such matters are no hard to predict.'

Robbie gave a brief sigh.

'But other things,' the elder man continued somewhat gravely, slowly chewing the tough brown meat, 'are more difficult to see, yet by my word, the omens are no so guid.' For a few minutes the man rolled the venison round his mouth and, finally satisfied with its softness, swallowed the coarse fibres in a long gulp. Then he put a glass of milk to his lips and another long draught encouraged the silence even more.

'In what way, father?' Robbie asked at length, his hunger interfering with the proceedings as he helped himself to more food.

'Oh! In all manner o' ways! There's a hush over the glens, the silence that comes before the storms. We've fought many a storm in the past your mother and me...but from what I hear of the Highland townships, many a man and his wife and family have been driven out.'

Robbie nodded.

'Yet, such evil has not come this way and may not yet do so!' The father continued hopefully.

'You mean the factors...'

'No, there's never been a factor or sheriff who would venture onto this land, for it's the Clan Chief's by birthright and given o'er to me as his direct blood-relative...even the auld Laird kens that!'

Robbie laughed. 'Well, that is what I thought but it is good to hear such confirmation from your own lips, father.'

'Aye, my brother's a guid man and will stand by me! It's in the Sutherland manner that brothers are so close that a sword blade cannot come between them.'

'You've heard of the Minister's death, no doubt?'

'Aye, I did!'

'Aud Domhnall was with me when we found him. But there was never a mark on the man, which was a puzzle. Not so the sister, she had perished in the flames and burnt to a cinder. There's no greater wickedness in mankind than that!'

His father nodded and went silent for a few moments. Looking up he asked, 'Are you well son and not in danger?'

'Fit and well father, and hungry to boot!'

The door rattled once more. Robbie looked up as his mother entered.

She was as tall as her husband, almost six feet in height and well proportioned from hard physical labour over the thirty-five years of marriage. Her face was also marked by a gently kind but firm expression.

'How are you Robbie?' she asked, 'I have no seen you for a few weeks? I heard your last remark...I've never known ye man and boy when ye were not waiting for something to eat'

He hurried towards her and, putting his arms around her, softly kissed her. '*Tha gu math, tapadh leat!* (Fine thanks!), mother! How are you?'

The woman blushed at the warm embrace. 'Away with such nonsense Robbie,' she cried laughing yet hugging her son.

'I have been in a mind to come for some while, but I must say, that I have been lingering in the eastern Glens a little too long for my own good,' was the cheerful reply.

'In the Glens!' His father gave a wry smile. 'What good is there in those glens?'

His mother hurried over to put the kettle above the glowing embers.

The father continued. 'What good can we get from such happenings in these times. Perhaps it is the will o'the Lord! And we take comfort fro' that!'

''Tis surely a strange will, Ross,' replied his wife reaching up into a small cupboard.

'Aye, many a Christian people hav' suffered in times gone by. The guid book says so! No man is pleased with the manner o'events in the glens and the mountains. But we must get on with them as best we can, at least for the time being!' His father emphasised the last remark by a sharp rap of his dirk against the wooden tabletop.

'That's true father,' Robbie replied at length. 'But perhaps...'

'Perhaps what, my son?' said the man looking up.

'Oh! Perhaps there should be more determination, more spirit against such changes.'

His mother sat down on the small stool next to the table. 'You mean resist them, Robbie,' she said dubiously, 'with force and killing.'

'Aye! Resist them!'

'Insurrection is your goal then?' his father spoke slowly and with purpose.

Robbie paused for a few seconds and looked fixedly at the tabletop as if for reassurance. 'Aye, in a word, that's what I mean!'

'But Robbie, think what it means to the Highlanders...' his mother began to ask.

'I have thought, and there seems little else our folks can do. Mairead agrees too!'

'And what about Alasdair?' His father stared at his son for a moment, 'Is he tain with such thoughts?'

Robbie paused.

His mother noticing the slight hesitation resumed. 'Alasdair was always a silent, peaceful lad. I canna believe...' then her voice tailed away as she noticed her husband's sour look.

'I always thought that he would be the strong one Robbie, but it turned out not to be that way!' The man shook his head gravely. 'But his wife has spirit to match her auburn hair, that is no in doubt!'

Robbie smiled. 'Aye, she has too!'

His mother shook her head. ''Tis always fighting talk amongst ye men, never one of discussion and compromise. I dislike a' that conceit, men puffed up with what they're about to do, hinting at valour they but rarely have. If they had the bairns to bring up there'd be less time for such idle boasts.'

The father and son listened to her in silence.

Robbie gave a sigh. 'Perhaps there can be no compromise Mother. I don't wish to hurt you, but things have gone too far in my way of thinking.' He tried to disguise the firmness and anger in his voice but it was not lost on his mother

His father slowly nodded in agreement.

But his wife stood her ground. 'I don't understand!' (*Chan eil mi gur tuigsinn!*) I just can't stand here and listen to such foolish talk. The King's battalions will rage in the Glens and all will be death and destruction like forty-five (*1745 The Jacobite rebellion). You have oft heard me talk o' those sad times. And how do we ken what manner o'suffering there was and what hunger and pestilence? By word of mouth that was handed down by our ancestors and passed on through the tongues of generations. That's how the picture is still so vivid in our minds and buried so deep in our hearts. Look at the great battles of the past! Look who has suffered! Not the rich...but the poor and unarmed such as we...Robbie...such as we!'

Her son reached out and took hold of her hand. He started to say, 'Mother...if you wish...I'll stay'. *(ma thogras tu....fuirichidh mise)*, but she got up swiftly to leave the cottage.

'I still have some animals to feed,' she remarked as she closed the door.

The men sat silently for a few seconds.

His father spoke first. 'There are many faces to a mountain and many paths to climb it by. But if the route is clear...go by the direct path, Robbie. Straight to the top! Do I make myself plain!'

'Aye, you do father!'

'Women can be the strongest creatures on earth, Robbie, and oft have to suffer the more when their menfolk are lost - whether it be in wars, seas or skirmishes. But they can be stubborn and at times too gentle in their ways, especially when a firm grasp o' the sword is needed.'

His son nodded in agreement and reaching forward threw another log onto the fire, which hissed with the dampness.

Silence then reigned for a short while as the flames took hold. The glow outlined the seriousness in their faces.

Robbie sighed. 'I'll speak one more time to Alasdair and some of the others and see what I can do!'

His father laughed. 'Tak' Mairead with you, for she will be as good as any man!'

His son laughed. But recalling their last conversation, he suddenly cut short his laugher and pulled a wry face away from his father's gaze.

'Aye, she's a beautiful girl, and no one cud wish for a better daughter-in-law by her manner and ways.' His father smiled and looked at his son.

Robbie smiled. '*Tha!* She is very beautiful, I'll grant you that!'

There were a few more moments of silence as the man went on eating his food, still slicing the venison into short strips and transfixing several pieces on the dirk.

But Robbie's mind had wandered. He thought of the girl on horseback and his new sister, comparing their beauty and out-spokenness. Such was his preoccupation that little more was said until his mother returned.

Her face was cheerful when she opened the door and she sat down beside them warming her icy fingers before the flames. Robbie loved her expression of contentment and good humour; proudly he reached over and held her hand for a moment.

'I think I'll partake of a wee dram, Robbie. How about you?' His father moved to get up.

'Fine father, I'll not be saying no!' his son replied.

'Away with ye both,' interrupted his mother, 'I'll be getting the whisky and three glasses,' she emphasised the last words, and they all laughed.

Thus with several draughts of whisky and warm water they beguiled the evening's soft fire glow in good humour. And they discussed the glories of the wedding and events, good and ill, that had befallen them since they last met; although some things Robbie kept to himself.

*****

The troubles, anxieties and wrongs were recurring thoughts to the young Highlander.

How could he improve on his failed mission, indeed how could he seek revenge and address some of the terrible events that had befallen the people of the Glens?

The night passed fitfully, as one thought after another came tumbling into his consciousness, collided and were lost in a web of indecision. The moon was full and cast a long silver shadow across the moors cutting the frosted parts into ribbons of light and darkness, where the trees and rocks impeded its rays. A log fire smouldered in the corner of his room, his mother had seen to that, worried by the possibility that her son may be harbouring some illness after weeks of living rough. He liked to inhale the pine odour as it slowly filled the room, and the occasional flickering ember gave a reassuring brightness of comfort and home. For the time being he was at home and curiously a child again wrapped in the cloak of welcome security.

Still sleep would not come, his mind racing to one possible solution after another, and yet, at times, he felt strangely detached from it all, as if it was a bad dream. Then his mind would race again, 'Why on earth should anyone listen to me?' These worries subsided and he was addressing a crowd, but their taunts echoed. "You're far tae young and without a scrap o'experience in these matters. Go home! Go home! Go home!" He sat up in bed. The draughts whistled their melody in the eaves and the thatch seemed to swell with the gale.

He settled back. Mairead was his only ally! Not Alasdair, and none in the Glens so far had rallied to any cause. Life went on regardless...or so it seemed. The Highlanders stuck to their old ways...aye that they did...regardless! His thoughts raced and the chill air swirled about his face. He pulled the coarse blanket higher and, curling up, turned on his side.

Then the other side, and the blanket came adrift once more!

Finally after what seemed hours of mental turmoil he fell into a deep sleep and was only roused by the licking of the collie dog, which had sneaked into the house and bounded onto the bed.

Robbie ruffled the long black and white hair and smoothed the animal's cheek. 'Well, Samhradh, you have no forgotten to rouse me up with the dawnings, have you not! It would be far better', *(bhioda e fada na b'ghearr)* he continued laughing, 'to let me lie in, for I have little to do on such a wintry day an' enough time to do it in!'

'Aye, it's almost seven o' the clock and as black as Hades outside!' His father entered the room with a small bowl of gruel in which the honey and cream had been swirled. 'Your mother always seems to find a little extra for you, Robbie, whenever you come. The honey is frae the hillside yonder where the gorse and flowers cluster all summer long.' Satisfied with the details, he sat on the edge of the bed.

His son took the wooden bowl in his hands and began to drink the thick liquid in delicate mouthfuls, for the food was piping hot.

His father waited. Then spoke. '*Seadh,* (Aye) we had a fair guid crack last night, but when I got t' bed I began to think that maybe your mother is right.'

'About what?' Robbie had stopped drinking for a moment.

'About the clearances...and the futility o' fighting. It means bloodshed in the long run...and, well...your mother may be right.'

The young man paused and licked the honey that stuck to his lips and relished the taste. After a moment's contemplation he went on drinking until he had finished. Then he muttered, 'You really think that's so!'

'*Tha!*'

'Yes, you say! They will no wait for us! (*Chan fhuirich iad ruinn!)*

His father paused. 'Who will no wait?'

'The Laird and his men! They will no allow us to change our ways, to give us time to restock our animals, to let us take new employment. They cannot wait! They must harry 'n' drive! You and I know of scores, no hundreds, who ha'e been forced off their land...aye... their land of a right, without recompense. Not one silver shilling, not even one penny piece, has come their way.'

'That is what I thought Robbie until I spoke with your mother. She says that the Laird and his wife are honourable people, and the word is that many o' the people driven out o' their homes hav' been given a guid share o' land in another valley'

'Where has she heard that?' asked his son in an incredulous voice.

'From none other than Minister MacCaoig!'

'I don't even trust the Ministers,' Robbie replied quickly.

'Oh! Robbie, how can y'say that! Yourself baptised!'

The young man reflected for a moment. 'Well...perhaps it is a bit hasty to condemn them all! But,' he continued slightly raising his voice, 'there is talk that several o' the smaller holdings have been taken by these men of the cloth while the rightful tenants have been moved on.'

His father went silent. 'Tain by the Ministers themselves!' he said in surprise.

'Aye! 'Tis shameful right enough!' But Robbie seeing it was futile to continue the conversation, threw back the bedclothes and clambered out of bed.

'There's enough warm water for the ewer,' the elder man spoke also getting up and stretching.

'That's good,' was the frank reply, and grabbing a rough towel from in front of the fireplace, he hurried outside clutching a boiling kettle. The dog followed subserviently behind, wagging his tail.

The air was heavy with an icy mist that caught his breath and hung tantalisingly about his dark, curling hair now much longer than in summer. The beard had gone and the skin's tan had faded so that his skin had a uniform colour, even where the beard had been. Without it his face was much more handsome, with a cleft just visible in the chin, and dimples in his cheeks when he smiled that caught the attention.

Robbie washed quickly, but still had time to splash the warm water over the dog that responded with repeated barking for more. He dressed, put on a dark woollen overcoat that reached down to his stout boots, and having eaten a hearty breakfast set off on his mission with a great deal of cheerfulness manifest by hearty whistling and a jaunty gait.

In the morning air the mountains were invisible, as were the hills that crouched before them. There was a stifling stillness only broken by his steady steps on the frozen road. He walked with care avoiding the iced-over burns and broad stones, treacherously smooth.

Setting out just after eight he had walked the eight miles towards his brother's croft before the sun was shimmering and full above the horizon, such is the shortness of the Highland day. His breath trailed the journey above and behind him, but there was no wind.

He paused at the side of the hill, resting on a fallen stunted oak, whose branches had rotted over the last three years since a great storm had felled it unmercifully. He wondered how Mairead would greet him and felt a pang of disquiet. He hoped it would not be as familiar or intimate as last time – and he pondered over her attitude for a while – before rising and setting off across the hillside.

After another two hours the house came into view, compact amongst a small group of eight cottages, each with a faint thread of smoke reaching into the dampness.

He hurried up, knocked and opened the door. Mairead had just begun to prepare the oatmeal gruel and half-a-dozen heavily salted rashers of venison while some small pieces of mountain hare were gently sizzling in a broad based frying pan. The fire hissed and crackled as the sticks glowed and flared capriciously about the pan. The girl looked up.

'Ciamar a tha thu, Robbie?'

'It is very cold, very cold.' (*Tha I fuar, gle fhuar*)

She smiled and resumed her cooking. 'Come and sit next to the fire and warm yerself then!'

As Robbie approached she suddenly got up and pointed to the stool. 'Here you can hav' this and I will sit on the floor beside you.'

The young man sat down and the girl settled on the floor beside him, still watching the pan and turning the cooking meat with a broad fork. She put her arms about her knees as she thought for a minute.

In a brief moment and to her own consternation she felt the finality of marriage, as if a great void had opened up between Alasdair and herself; a void that could not be breached at any price. Suddenly, in her momentary desperation, she asked, 'Are ye well?' to calm her strange panic. Then, as the shadow of conscience passed, she glanced his way.

'Yes! By and large!' he appeared unmoved by her proximity that was the disconsolate factor that irritated her like a swarm of May midges.

Mairead was undaunted and unabashed. She rested her auburn hair against his side as she leant back, supporting her body with his right thigh. She felt that sooner or later he would be obliged to take notice.

The meat sizzled and crisped in a delicious aroma.

'Have y' thought any mair about what I said the other day,' she asked in a matter of fact way.

'About taking strong measures to combat the factors and their followers?' Robbie said with a short laugh. 'Is that what you mean?'

'It is of no laughing matter, Robbie,' she replied, nevertheless smiling and turning her face towards him for a few seconds. She caught her skirt against a button on his long coat and a thin thread pulled out as she struggled to free it. He reached down and gently examined the thread in such a curiously serious manner that she burst out laughing and said, 'Give me that!' And in a minute the wool was snapped and she suddenly stood up free from entanglement.

Robbie laughed too as she lifted up her skirt above her knees to examine the tear. He watched her for a moment before replying, 'Aye, you're right there, Mairead, it is a serious matter. But man must have the odd laugh in the face of adversity...'tis the Highland way.'

The girl nodded. She remained silent for a short while. 'Have ye also thought mair aboot what I said? About me joining you! Even if Alasdair remains behind and tends the farm.'

'No! I must confess I have not!'

'Not thought about it once! Y' mean to tell me Robbie Sutherland that you have not given me one thought since you saw me last!'

'I did not say that!'

'Well, what did ye say?'

Robbie smiled as she sat down next to him again. He put his hand on her shoulder and she leaned back pressing her head against his chest for a few moments. 'Y' dinna mind me sitting like this?' she asked with an impulsive smile and a shake of her auburn hair.

'*Chan eil!* I like it a lot. *(Tha i a'cordadh rium glan)*

She then sat up, reached out with the fork that had lain by her side, and turned the meat over. 'See ye distract me now and thus guid food will go to waste if I'm no too careful.' She spoke softly, almost afraid to break the curious silent bond that had suddenly sprung up between them. Yet she still watched his every expression and felt a spontaneity she had not experienced for months.

'I did not want to distract you from the cooking, Mairead, for the cold and the walk has sharpened my appetite.'

'Well then, answer my question...and you shall have some food.'

'I have forgotten the question with all the blathering.'

She laughed and turned again to face him.

This time her gaze was met by his smiling eyes; for a brief moment nothing was said. Mairead had a strong urge to kiss him but his lips were just out of reach. Something seemed to flow between them. She thought he said, 'I could have married you!' but his lips did not move, his arms remained motionless, and she knew it was all fantasy.

In a second the urge had passed.

She wondered if he had noticed, or even felt, the same compulsion.

But his mood was still one of light-hearted banter. 'Of course I have thought of you, but as an accomplice in the manner of such dangerous schemes, I have my doubts! For what would Alasdair say...?'

'Och! What can he say!'

'Plenty!'

She laughed, 'Well, that's true enough, for he has the gift o' the gab when he wants to!'

Robbie took the long fork from the side of the fire and speared a rasher, letting the fat drip and sizzle on the flames for a few seconds. Waiting for a moment until the food had cooled a little, he gently placed the end of the venison strip against her lips. It was warm, breath warm, and Mairead responded with a polite smile and bit the rasher in two. His expression was one of juvenile pleasure, that facet of silly incongruity that marks those years of spontaneous laughter.

After a short silence she laughed and taking the other half forced it into the young man's mouth. He gently bit her finger in mock anger and she laughed some more.

Still laughing she said, 'There's something else Alasdair can get mad aboot, for he's one rasher less and without a by-your-leave fro' his ain brother.'

Robbie laughed. ''Twill not be the first time, I'll be thinking, that I hav' pinched a bit o' his food.'

'Did you ever take anything else?'

'Aye!' (*Seadh!*)

'Such as...?' Then she laughed again. 'One of his girls?'

Robbie shook his head. 'Alasdair was far too canny for that, and anyway I was far too young, that no one would have fancied me!'

'To me you're not too young!'

'Perhaps not!' He smiled, 'Anyway, one way or another, this conversation is no so good, I'll be thinking!'

Mairead reached up to stroke his cheek. 'And why may I ask?'

'You may ask!'

'Then why?'

'For you're letting the meat and oatmeal burn to a cinder with all this idle talk!'

The girl hastily stood up. 'Oh! Bother! Now look what ye hav' made me do!'

'What o' this earth have I made you do?'

'Burn the oatmeal! Quickly, get me a wooden spoon so that I can skim the best off into this pot. Honey will do the rest and Alasdair will never ken!'

'*Seadh!*' (Aye!) Robbie thought to himself, 'He would never know!'

The girl took the pan off the fire and placed it on the hearthstones. Then walking to the door she called her husband's name several times.

Within a few moments there was a banging on the door and the dog arrived shaking the dampness off his shaggy coat. 'Damnations!' muttered Mairead shooing the animal to one side, 'there'll be filth and mud in the gruel, to add t' the taste!' She laughed again and as she shook her head the long auburn hair waved about her shoulders.

Alasdair opened the door fully.

He greeted his brother warmly. 'How are father and mother?'

Robbie smiled! 'As good as ever!'

'I suppose they hav' a great concern about the happenings in the Glens?' he asked sitting down on the stool and accepting a metal bowl filled with gruel. 'I'm fair famished with the work, the weather so bleak on the hills that I've brought our score of highland ewes and a couple of rams down to the sheltered fields. They're in with the neighbours, but well marked, and there'll be no mistake.'

'You asked about our parent's views on the troubles...' He stopped as Mairead pointed to the pan and shook his head and smiled. 'I've had more than enough to eat for the present!' he continued breaking off the conversation and winking at the girl.

'Aye, go on!'

Robbie continued. 'Mother worries about the Great Laird's men and got it into her head that hundreds of soldiers will be used against us.'

'Soldiers!' Alasdair pulled a face, 'used against us!'

'Oh! It only a whim o'fancy on her part! You know what Mother's like...always taken with worries and bad omens.'

'And Father!'

Robbie paused. 'Father's like a stag looking both ways to see how the land lies and where the dangers are coming from. He's no so sure as he makes out! He seems ready to defend his lands but gets comfort from the fact that he's the auld chief's half-brother. Except this man - our uncle,' he said with disgust, 'with a birthright handed down through the generations, is no more than a lackey of the Great Laird, that Sassenach, who assumes the Chieftainship by marriage. So whatever the auld Chief says, it means naught!'

Alasdair ate on for a moment. 'There's naught new in that! The chiefs have been lackeys to the lowland lords since Culloden, and only rule to do their bidding. Still they have their pride!'

Mairead handed him a plate smothered in meat. 'What pride?'

Alasdair was irritated. 'Pride in the clan!'

'Nonsense!'

'Away with you both,' interjected Robbie, 'stop the bickering. It seems like the last time I was here that there was naught but arguments, I'll be thinking!'

'Well, the chiefs have no mair pride than a worm. By any reckoning there's been at least twa hundred souls taken from the land and herded elsewhere...who kens... and at least a dozen deaths frae cold and hunger ...and the winter not yet set in.' Mairead stared defiantly at them both.

'Is that so?' inquired Robbie looking earnestly at the girl. 'I heard of three deaths but...'

'Aye! That's the truth!' Alasdair nodded. 'But what can be done about it!'

'Oh!' said his wife in exasperation, 'how oft have I heard that said!'

Robbie ignored the remark. 'My plan is to raise a group of men to watch over the glens and confront the tacks men, factors or their ilk as they go about their evil business. From what I heard there is only a handful of them in the pay of the Lord Stafford and with some stout resistance we can harry and drive the sheep and these villains from our lands.'

'But at what cost?' the brother replied.

'Who knows!'

Mairead shook her head. 'Aye, there'll be a cost, we've all said that before! But the Laird is not one for confrontation, they say he's a sickly man who cannot cope with the Highland life. That's why he lives warm and comfortable in the city o' London. And guid riddance too! For it's a total disgrace!' (*Dearg naire*)

Robbie smiled 'If every man had your spirit, Mairead, the job would be over and done by now!

'*Tha!*' She continued, 'but any plan must be thorough and well-thought out… and the support strong!'

Alasdair sat contemplating for a short while eagerly watched by his brother. He sighed. 'That worries me...the support. There are few men enough for the husbandry in each township, never mind the patrolling o' the valley. I fear few… if any… will leave.' He stopped to consider for a moment. 'Take this township and the surrounding area, there are but eleven men of an age to travel, and if need be, fight. Even I would have difficulty in leaving the animals at this time of year....'

'Then I could leave!' Mairead spoke quickly.

There was a stunned silence as her husband pondered her words.

'You!' he exclaimed.

'Yes, I have said it before. What is it about men's memory that women have to keep repeating themselves, time and again? I could be away for but a few days at a time, and it would be a great help talking to the womenfolk, for their's is often the final say in such matters, despite what the men may think!'

Robbie laughed. 'Aye, you could be right there!'

But her husband looked serious. 'What ye say could be true! And it has a vein of commonsense in it! He thought for a moment. 'But walking and living in the Glens with the December storms almost upon us will be hard.'

However, Robbie and Mairead ignored this last remark.

'That's fine then and settled,' said the younger brother smiling. 'It is a bold plan but when the auld Laird sees our resistance, and with the help o' the Ministers of the kirk that we can trust…and the guid Lord beside them, we shall win through.'

In that optimistic mood he took the last rasher from Alasdair's plate and flung it to the dog. *'Slainte!'* (Good health!) And may God be with us!'

Seachd deug (seventeen)

At sunrise the Marquess was pleasantly aroused from his contentment, the Marchioness likewise and the butler and maid displayed all the reverential humility that was deemed necessary in servants.

Yawning with lifeless eyes and a dissipated look, the pinched Marquess ate breakfast in bed, dressed in warm and elegant surroundings, considered the meal from the night before, rinsed his mouth with fresh water to reline his tongue furred from the champagne which had not been of the very best krug...and generally felt life was acceptable.

London was in full cry, November's greyness and ineptitude delightfully subdued, if not banished, by the brightness within the fashionable buildings of the fashionable squares and the fashionable clothes.

He waited in silence for the maid to clear the breakfast trays, chose his clothes for a relaxing day, and wondered which of the many invitations they were to accept over the next two weeks.

Scotland was far from his mind.

It was not, in truth, a place worth considering when in England.

He would ride out to his lunch venue in the City and called for the horses to be ready by eleven.

Impatiently he waited to wash and dress. The mail had arrived and the courier just departed. The Marquess surveyed the bundle and was in the process of tossing them aside when two marked 'posted in Scotland' arrested his attention.

He rubbed his temples in agitation as he read. The recent blizzards had been terrible - drifts everywhere, Sellar had written, and the sheep destined for the Highlands had been delayed. It would be April or May before they were pasturing in the Glens, many would be heavy with lamb by that time, and the expected numbers could be severely reduced.

The Marquess pondered this fact and sucked on his lower lip in exasperation. Time was passing and the sheep had to be moved on!

He wondered how the reclamations were proceeding, what resistance was manifest. He had reassured his wife so many times that the movement of the populations, the destruction and conversion of dwellings, were a necessary prerequisite to a new prosperity in that far north.

Perhaps she did not always believe him. The thought of any hardship amongst the crofters depressed her, although she was always the first to acknowledge the squalid conditions they lived in, and their resistance to change.

He had always considered their seclusion behind the great Glen a blessing, at first blithely unaware that the lands up there would be so richly endowed with hundreds of square miles of grazing.

Now that he had formed his master plan to more riches by importing sheep, it was important to speed up the clearances. He knew that in his heart-of –hearts…and he had every trust in McBain, Sellar, Loch and the rest. Even the Ministers of the kirk, the sheriffs and other lairds, would fall into line when the land and the pickings were to be shared out.

Then he turned to another letter, one more from the Highlands. How wearisome was bad news before lunch. He began to read:

My Lord Stafford,

I conceive it a duty I owe to you Lordship, to address you upon the present occasion, and a more distressing task I have seldom had to perform.

During the last year 1809 in the parishes of Dornoch, Rogart, Loth, Clyne and Golspie, an extensive removal took place; several hundred families were turned out, but under circumstances of great severity Every means was used to discourage the people, and to persuade them to give up their holdings quietly, and quit the country. And to those who could not be induced to do so, scraps of moor, and bog lands, were offered in Dornoch moor, and

Brora links, on which it was next to impossible to exist, in order that they may be scared into going entirely away.

At this time, the estate was under the management of Mr. Young, a corn-dealer, as chief, and Mr. Patrick Sellar, a writer, as under factor - the latter will make a conspicuous figure in the future communications. These gentlemen were both from Morayshire.

A new era of depopulation commenced; summonses of removal were served on large portions of the inhabitants. The lands were divided into extensive lots, and advertised to be let for sheep farms. Strangers were daily traversing the country, viewing these lots.

The houses had all been built not by the landlords as in the low country, but by the tenants or by their ancestors, and, consequently, were their property by right, if not by law. They were timbered with bog fir, which makes excellent roofing but is very inflammable.

About two months after they had received summonses of removal, a commencement was made to pull down and set fire to the houses. The old people, women and others then began to try and preserve the timber, which they were entitled to consider their own. But the devastators proceeded with the greatest celerity, demolishing all before them, and when they had overthrown the houses in a large tract of country, they ultimately set fire to the wreck.

These proceedings were carried out with the greatest rapidity as well as with most reckless cruelty. The cries of the victims, the confusion, the despair and horror painted on the countenances of the one party, and the exulting ferocity of the other, beggar all description. In these scenes Mr. Sellar was present ordering and directing the whole.

Many deaths ensued from alarm, from fatigue, and cold; the people being instantly deprived of shelter, and left to the mercy of the elements. Some old men took to the woods and precipices, wandering about in a state approaching to, or of absolute insanity, and several of them, in this situation, lived only a few days.

In such a scene of devastation it is almost useless to particularize the cases of individuals. I shall, however, just notice a very few of the extreme cases which occur to my recollection, to most of which I was an eye-witness. John MacKay's wife in attempting to pull down her house, in the absence of her husband, to preserve the timber, fell through the roof. Donald Munro, lying in a fever, was turned out of his house and exposed to the elements, Donald MacBeath, an infirm and bed-ridden old man, had the house unroofed over him, and was, in that state, exposed to the wind and rain till death put a period to his sufferings. I was present at the pulling down and burning of the house of the family of William Chisholm in which was lying his wife's mother, an old woman of near a hundred years. I informed the persons about to fire to the house of this circumstance, and prevailed on them to wait till Mr. Sellar came. On his arrival I told him of the poor old woman being in a condition unfit for removal. He replied. 'Damn her, the old witch, she has lived too long; let her burn.' Fire was immediately set to the house, and the blankets in which she was to be carried were in flames before she could be got out.

Your Lordship knows that a humble petition, subscribed by a number of tenants on Mr. Sellar's sheep farm was presented to Lady Stafford, complaining of various acts of injury, cruelty and oppression, alleged to have been committed upon their persons and property by Mr. Sellar.

To this complaint her Ladyship was graciously pleased to return an answer in writing.

In it her Ladyship, with her usual candour and justice, with much propriety observes, "That if any person on the estate shall receive any illegal treatment, she will never consider it as hostile to her if they have recourse to legal redress, as a most secure way to receive the justice, which she always desires they should have on every occasion."

Her ladyship also intimates, "That she had communicated the complaint to Mr. Sellar, that he may make proper inquiry and answer to her."

It would appear, however, that Mr. Sellar still refuses or delays to afford that redress.

In consequence of these proceedings, on an express injunction from his Majesty's advocate-depute, and a similar one from the sheriff-depute, I was compelled to enter upon an investigation.

I examined the facts and it is with the deepest regret, I have to inform you, that such an individual has seldom disgraced any country, or sullied the pages of a precognition in Scotland as Mr Sellar.

This being the case, the laws of the country imperiously call upon me to order Mr. Sellar to be arrested and incarcerated, in order for trial, and before this reaches your Lordship this preparatory legal step must be put in execution.

No person can more sincerely regret the cause, nor more frequently lament the effect, than I do.

I have the honour to be, &c.

Robt MacKid.

The Marquess pondered over the letter for a full five minutes, decided not to inform his wife, for the time being, took a long draught of sherry to settle his nerves, barked at the servant for the carriage and, within a couple of hours, was dining right royally on quail and pheasant, the unpleasantness of the morning completely forgotten.

*****

At first, the people of Sutherland had believed that the Sheriff, Mr. Cranstoun, would bring factor Sellar to justice. But this did not happen!

The Sheriff proceeded with utmost caution, stating that 'if the tenants mean to take a precognition immediately it will proceed before the Sheriff-Substitute, Mr. Robert MacKid, as my engagements will not permit me to be in Sutherland until the month of July'.

Thus with a deft feint he handed it over to Mr. MacKid, who decided to actively investigate the matter.

So the letter was written to the Marquess. Sellar was held in the Tolbooth at Dornoch, and so far as MacKid was concerned, there was no reason to grant him bail until the trial.

But this was not to be! For the Court of Judiciary in Edinburgh granted him bail and his release.

Full of confidence and vengeance, the factor determined to continue the clearance of the highlands, seeking no mercy and giving none in return. Now it was a mind suffused with hatred.

H-ochd deug (eighteen)

Whatever plans had been hatched by Alasdair, Robbie and Mairead Sutherland, their implementation was to prove difficult.

The December storms broke with unmitigated fury and high winds lashed the hills and mountains. Even the deer crept closer and closer to the townships, but many a hind was found frozen in the snow, and the poor dug them out and shared the fresh meat in jubilation.

Sheep and cattle were corralled behind crude fences or crowded into barns, timbered chiefly with bog fir. There they eked out a meagre existence and as the days drew shorter and colder, many animals suffered. For the beasts began to weaken as the supply of fodder dwindled, so the futility of keeping so many alive became a constant worry. After much soul searching and, with anguish, many were slaughtered although sorely needed for breeding the next season.

With such worries and fears compounded, the Highlanders anxiously awaited their fate!

Ross Sutherland looked up from his task in the byre.

He had been sawing some logs in the corner, out of the icy blast. He stretched his back that ached from the constant heavy exertion.

The sound of horses came steadily nearer.

He counted the steps and instinctively noted the different rhythm.

Three!

His first thoughts were to dismiss the sounds as idle fancy.

'Why would any living soul be venturing out on a day like this?'

But the sounds grew steadily nearer.

Putting down his saw and pushing the pine trunk to one side, he shook the sawdust off his stout leather boots and walked to the half-open door.

Gazing over the low portion he beheld three men approaching, cutting a straight line through an area of fell where the winds had whipped the surface almost clear of snow.

He waited and watched.

'Hallo!' someone shouted.

He answered the call.

The riders looked up and seeing him in the doorway hastened towards the byre.

'Ross Sutherland, I believe?' It was the second rider who spoke from behind a broad scarf wrapped round the lower half of his face.

'Aye!'

'You dwell here, is that not right?'

'Aye, I do...and my wife.' He noted that the three had lined up before him.

'There be no sons then?'

'Aye, there be!'

'Answer man, how many?'

The father still held his gaze, slowly looking from one face to another. *'Deug!'* (Two!)

'Aye, that I've heard tell,' said the man still speaking from behind the scarf. 'Would one be called after your ancestors, Robbie?'

Ross agreed with a nod of the head.

'And where could he be now!'

'Somewhere! (*Aiteigin!*),' said the man with a faint smile, 'in the Highlands that's for sure, but he seeks employment awa' fro' this glens in recent months, and where his wandering tak him', only the Guid Lord kens!'

'That might be true,' said a burly man turning to the first speaker, 'there's not much to do in this strath, but nobody will persuade me that his whereabouts be not known.'

The leader nodded. 'That's a pity! But we will find him and weasel him out, never fear!' Turning to Ross he said, 'You will know me right enough when I bring that laddie to the Procurator-Fiscal. My name's Sellar, bye the bye, and it's in your best interests to remember what I say!'

Ross's wife appeared in the yard, her black shawl pulled tightly around her shoulders. 'Remember you, how could a body forget! Awa with the mealy-mouthed lot of you! I'd rather eat worms and vermin than pander to the Sassenach cause as you do! You're no fit to wander the lowlands of our native land, never mind this country of ours. As for finding the lad, he's done no wrong, the Lord knows that! And so would you if there was an ounce of compassion and religion between the three of you!'

Sellar laughed and produced a small flask. Taking a swift draught of whisky he handed it to one of the others. 'Well, the devil makes the mistake of putting the pair of you in our ways. The air has a fair nip in it and the blood was cold until a moment back. But you, woman, and the whisky, have put some warmth into the meeting.' He laughed again. 'We will take the lad before the first lambs are born and you will have to fend for yourself the summer through!'

Ross stepped forward. 'What has been said by my wife is true! There is no evil in our boy and no wrongdoings can be laid at his feet.' He stopped for a moment. 'But I'll swing for the man who lays a hand on him.' Taking out his dirk he swiftly nicked the palm of his left hand. A faint trickle of blood dripped onto the snow, its very redness accentuated by the pure white around it.

The men watched in curiosity tinged with alarm.

'Aye, by this blood which is also the blood of my boys, I'll swing for the first man that harms them.'

Sellar pulled back his horse. 'A family hanging is a thing to be witnessed,' he muttered to himself.

Ross, his anger rising, reached forward to grasp the bridle, splashing a faint smear of blood on the animal's cold neck.

At this point his wife rushed forward. 'Spare us the bloodshed until it be needed!' Turning to the men she said quietly. 'The mair you do, the mair the Highlanders will despise you and the masters...but mark my word...there is not a man, woman and child who will no rise up against you if the clearances go on. Not a man, woman or child!'

Sellar motioned the other two away. 'Aye, you are full of yourself now, woman, and you cottar, for that's what you'll become when I'm done with you! This house will go to the devil and the land too, when the time comes. And the bodies will hang until the flesh has been taken by every witch about, and the skulls used to drink of the water from a Holy Well!'

Before there was time for a reply, the three spurred their horses into a solemn gallop, leaving Ross and his wife to stare solemnly after them, before going indoors.

*****

The old man, Domhnall and his wife Ealasaid also sat solemnly staring at the peat fire in their remote cottage, tucked away up a small glen and sheltered by a clump of pine trees to make it almost invisible from the main valley.

A third person sat on a small stool opposite, gently twining his fingers.

'They said they would no come back again next year'. (*'Thuirt iad gun tigeadh iad ais an ath bhliadhna'*). Domhnall spoke in a voice quavering with fear.

The other man reached out and took hold of his thin, shaking hand. 'Never fear Domhnall, Factor Sellar and his men are fair and good minded people. They say they mean no harm!'

The old man glanced towards his wife. 'What thinks you, Ealasaid?'

She looked at her husband for a brief moment. 'They're up to mischief.' (*'Tha iad ri mi-mhodh'*)

'Aye, that's what I gleaned, Ealasaid!' replied her husband slowly. Then turning to the man he said nervously. 'But ye gave us a fright, Minister! Like the witches themselves do on a winter's night, appearing as the Lord himself, risen from the dead!'

His wife repeated his final words and held her hands as if in prayer.

'What's bothering you?' (*De tha a' cur ort*) the man asked.

'We thought you were dead Minister, fur we saw your body buried, as clear as a loch on a summer day.'

As the firelight flickered on the man's face the features of the Minister McBain were clearly seen, his body thinner than before but still solemnly clothed in black. 'You were wrong, Domhnall. Clearly wrong! You feel the warmth of the fire in my hands do you not, there's no chill of death about these fingers.'

Ealasaid laughed, a shy noise that seemed to emanate from deep within her frail body.

Domhnall smiled in agreement.

'So you were wrong, the pair of you! Weren't you! It was my brother, if the truth be known before the Lord!'

'Aye, we were!' the old man replied with a suspicious smile. 'Minister McBain, a friend, and a guid one at that, to the Highland poor folks. *Tha,* but it's a terrible life at times and a struggle that the Lord hath sent to test us, poor souls that we are!'

It was his wife's turn to smile in agreement.

The Minister rubbed his hands before the fire, and frictioned some warmth for the log was slumbering and the flames were slowly ebbing away. 'What brings me here, a Man of the cloth, on such a day?' Without waiting to be asked he continued in a hushed tone. 'I seek a transgressor, a young man whose ways have not found favour with the God Almighty.'

The old man shrugged his bony shoulders. 'In what way can we help, Minister McBain?'

'Well, it's like this! The poor folk of the Highlands have suffered enough, and the men who own these lands...'(here he paused and surveyed the couple's faces), such as the Great Laird of Sutherland, have found favour in the eyes of many a subject by taking him to new lands - fresh glens, green pastures and fertile acres. You will no doubt have heard of all of the clearances?'

'*Tha*! We have that!' replied Domhnall somewhat discomforted.

His wife looked alarmed and the Minster noticing the change in mood thrust a long branch into the fire and stirred the ashes. Within moments the branch had flared and the heat and light seemed to defuse the situation.

'I have to say that there are some among my flock, Domhnall, that have taken it upon themselves to rant and rave, and through civil strife and disobedience risk the wrath of those I have spoken about!'

Domhnall went very quiet for a moment and then, slowly raising his gaze to face the Minister, said softly and in a deferential voice. 'I have no heard of the likes o' that, only some of the wrangs that hav' been served upon us...'

'Chan eil, Domhnall!' (No, Domhnall!) The man interrupted brusquely.

Ealasaid looked in amazement. *'Tha!* (Yes) sir!'

But the Minister, faced flushed with irritation at being contradicted, continued. 'I look for two men and two men only!'

'And who be they?' asked the Shepherd in a faltering voice.

'A blacksmith by the name of Niall McIomhair.'

'I know him only by name!' The old man replied. 'And the other?'

'Robbie Sutherland, youngest son of Ross!'

Ealasaid gave a short cry of alarm and then corrected herself.

The Minister fidgeted with the burning stick, pushing it to and fro in the fire.

At length he said, 'So, where is he?'

There was another pause. Domhnall was about to speak when his wife interrupted. 'We never ken where he'll be, the last time I set eyes upon him was at the wedding of his brother to Mairead, our kin!'

'Is that so!'

'But ye were there, Minister,' continued the woman.

The man corrected himself and said quickly, *'Tha,* that is right!'

'And we ken no mair!' said the old man abruptly.

'He may be with his family,' ventured his wife noting the anger in the Minster's eyes.

'Chan eil! I have been to both his brother's cottage and the father's. What say you if we think a bit more!'

'About what?' the old man asked in alarm.

'About where the boy could hide...say in a shepherd's hut in the mountains! You must know of such places!'

'Aye! I do!

'Well speak man, and tell me! Where is the warmest, safest haven in these hills. A secure place tucked away in some valley that you know of!'

There was a silence.

'I ken of many places but not that could weather the mountain storms. For my liking he may hav' gone anywhere.'

'It is not of your liking, my friend, that I ask! But of the truth before God! Where is the boy?'

'I ken not!' cried Domhnall in anguish. 'And if I did...I wud no tell ye!'

There were no further words spoken. The Minister grasping the branch brandished it before the startled faces of the old couple so that the flames singed some of their sparse hair. Then with a cry of despair he hurled it against the far wall producing a shower of sparks.

The old man puts his arms about his wife to comfort her as the Minister strode out of the room, slamming the door so the black latch rattled and fell.

The stunned silence was broken by a faint sob from the woman.

'No damage has been done to the house!' said Domhnall, still comforting the old woman. 'We buried Minister McBain and he rose from the dead, but only as his brother. He'll no fool us, whatever he thinks!'

He wife kissed him on the cheek and smoothed the wrinkled features. 'It's good! (*Tha e math*!) You're still as sharp as an eagle's claws with eyes to match that bird, my husband (*mo cheile*). He's a rare fool himself if he thinks we'll be so easily tain! If we had no seen the body ourselves...it wud hav' been a near thing!'

'Aye near, but that's never enough! I must tak myself to the mountain hut by the morrow. For Robbie lies hiding there and who kens what that factor, Murdo, will do next!'

*****

The landscape was pure white as Robbie made his way through the snow, which had set so hard as to make a smooth highway for a couple of miles. The snow had erased all the customary rocks, tufts of coarse grass and knotted heather that generally impedes progress in this harsh land.

His tall figure moved gracefully, without stumble or mishap, like one of the feral goats that had in generations past taken refuge in the crags and peaks.

Out of his solitary existence grew a natural fortitude, an absolute precision of movement and action, and a curious self-confidence that was part of indomitable Highland spirit. The iron discipline and bravery that had so distinguished itself within the British army (and was to do so to an even higher degree in future) was a feature of his inheritance. Come rain or shine, life had to go on, and if that meant a new course of action, so be it, he reasoned. The strict demands of justice spurred him forward, and he became stronger as the steep mountain pass approached.

It was at this confluence of the glens that he paused to study a small township not half a mile away.

It took only a glance to see the ruined shell, the heaped stones by the gaunt remains of the houses, the absent roof timbers.

He was becoming immune to the suffering and devastation, but one feature arrested his attention and propelled him down the white slope at such speed that for the first time he momentarily fell.

Picking himself up and brushing the snow off his coat, he hurried on.

By the side of the cornfield sat two women, a child and one of the husbands.

The greater part of the pasture and fences had gone – part demolished, part charred from the fire.

'I see that all is not well here,' said Robbie breathlessly as he arrived, 'if there's aught I can do to help, I'll be only too willing.'

The man spoke, 'It wud be guid if ye cud mend the walls o'the dwellings with us, but if we did, they say they'd be down agin in a week.'

His wife now cradling the seven year old boy continued, 'It's mair than we can manage to keep the Laird's sheep oot of the pastures and cornfields. But if we cannot…what then?'

Robbie gazed at the meagre plot, the upper shoots just visible through the snow, which had been blown thin in the winds that swept that side of the valley.

'Frost and snows, hail and rain, we'tain them all over the years, but without a home, what can we do? We'll live here as long as we can, but as the Laird's sheep get mair and mair ravenous it teks a' our time, day and night, to keep them awa'.' The man spoke without a trace of rancour in his voice and his wife's sister sighed.

It was her turn to speak. 'My husband's gone to Kildonan to get some help from our relatives, but it's a fool's mission, for they have naught to gee us.'

Robbie asked simply, 'What are you eating?'

The child's eyes looked alert for a moment.

The man gave a coarse laugh followed by a shrug of the shoulders. 'Aught we can find, mostly potatoes, but they're feet down in snow and hard earth…the odd hare that's trapped and …' his voice tailed away.

'A sheep or two?' Robbie inquired.

The man winked, 'Perhaps…when times get bad.'

'There're enough of the four-footed clansmen about,' joked the young Highlander.

The women laughed.

'I'm Robbie Sutherland, son of Ross. There's no need to worry, for any secret's safe with me.' Suddenly he regretted giving his name, fearing that his enemies might return this way and obtain his whereabouts by force or threat.

'I didna hear the name, and I would no ken it anyhow!' remarked the man noting Robbie's moment of hesitation.

'Thank you friends! Perhaps we'll meet another time in better circumstances.' Robbie shook hands then slowly made his way back to the path, leaving the small group in their torn and inadequate clothing. 'By the Lord,' he thought, 'for how long can they face these bitterly cold nights. God give them strength!'

Naoi deug (nineteen)

The wind that swung to the south and came off the drier warmer lands heralded one of those strange climatic interludes so common to that part of Scotland.

The ice warped, cracked and seemed to cry out in strange agonies on the smaller lochs; icicles crashed like pointed cymbals from the rock faces while the snow sloshed and squelched about the animals feet, producing deeper and deeper imprints of their random tread.

So in relatively warm sunshine Robbie Sutherland reached his new intended destination, a place of refuge, and a place where he felt his persecutors would look last. He had taken the warning to heart and thanked Domhnall profusely.

He climbed into the stable roof, sat with legs idly swinging on a main oak beam, and waited.

He listened to the trickling water in the gully outside, saw the horse turn restlessly in his presence, compacting the straw into tighter and tighter layers, and smelled the stale odour of animal and wet hay.

Round and round went the horse, occasionally looking towards the beam.

It was nearly nine o'clock by Robbie's reckoning when the first footsteps were heard.

It was the measured tread of a groom.

Robbie scrambled across the beam and dropped noiselessly onto a broad piece of flooring that served as a storage area above half of the stable. He settled down in the hay.

Curiously he picked up a small handful and ground the strands into a fine dust. He was surprised at the smell. 'Poor quality, for one so proud!' He thought and smiled. 'Worse than any feed we give!'

The groom did not interest him other than he wondered if the man might climb the ladder into this loft space.

But the groom was a round-backed, whiskered man with a curiously bowed appearance right down to his legs in brown leather breeches; so that the young man smiled, and tried hard not to laugh as he watched him waddle to and fro. ''Tis a strange place overall and not one where money is spent for quality!'

The groom fussed the horse and saddled it up.

The horse shied and ground its front hoof against the stone floor. Then reconciled with its duty, it stood as still as a statue.

The groom shuffled off leaving the barred door ajar, but the animal did not move. With its dark eyes fixed towards the wall, it stood solemnly.

Robbie watched through a crack in the boards, he lay and waited. Neither of them showed any impatience, neither man nor beast!

He must have waited about ten minutes before a figure appeared and reached out to grasp the bridle. It was the cue! Robbie sprung onto the ladder and was standing beside the girl in a moment.

She had not heard him and only realised his presence by the falling strands of hay and the dull thud of his landing. She started and let out a suppressed scream; then suddenly regained her composure as she recognised the face and figure.

'Hallo!' Robbie smiled in her direction. 'I hope I have not startled you?'

'No more than last time!'

Catriona surveyed him with slight disgust. She brushed her fair hair back nervously but there was defiance in her eyes.

'Good!'

She wheeled the horse round. 'What are you doing here?' she asked at length.

'I could say I was looking for you, and that would be half correct!'

'Would it?'

'Yes! It would!'

She held the horse still for a moment.

'And what would be the other half?'

'To hide here!'

'Here?' she asked in amazement.

'Aye, I said "here"!' Robbie replied frankly and without a hint of remorse, which surprised the girl.

'And who gave you permission, the Marquess, The Marchioness, the Factor, the Bailie, the groom or even myself?' She ended in a note of exasperation.

'Aye, all o'them!'

'All of them!'

He laughed. 'You could put it that way, if you liked!'

She shook her head. 'Is there anyone more contrary or perhaps downright foolish as you in the Highlands?' Catriona gave a slight snort.

'Probably, those who serve the Laird without seeing the wickedness of his ways!'

'You are impudent about my relations, and will suffer for your impudence in a few minutes...when I call for help!'

'Well, a few minutes can be a long time in this world, if need be.' replied Robbie with another smile.

'We will see then!'

'Aye, we'll see!'

'Have you no home to go to,' she asked.

'I have that!'

'And where is this elusive dwelling, may I enquire.' Catriona tinged her voice with sarcasm, which the man ignored in his usual bland way.

'Here and hereabouts! And do you have a home in England?'

'I do!'

'A big house?'

'Not as big as this! Although the Lord Stafford has a huge mansion in Lilleshall, in England, I sometimes stay there. Anyway what's it got to do with you and hiding here?'

Robbie smiled, 'Nothing, I suppose, I just wanted to know a little bit more about you, if you don't mind. They say the girls in England are as pretty as the rose that the land takes as its national flower. Is that true...I suppose it is!' He looked into the girl's face, which made her frown.

'And what about the thistle, you can hardly say that the women of Scotland take after that!'

He laughed. 'No, but the men do, with their tam-o-shanters and their bristly legs. Aye, and if you stand on a Scotsman's toes he'll make you fair yelp with pain.'

For once Catriona laughed so uproariously that the horse stepped to one side in its confusion. Then she collected herself, 'Why do you put your life at risk like this?' Her voice had suddenly become serious for the first time. His strange vulnerability attracted her. She looked at him intently and for the first time smiled, an expressive, warm smile and Robbie's emotions responded instantly.

'Because of the Clearances and those that suffer and die.'

'Do many die?'

'Aye, scores and scores! From starvation, disease and a broken spirit. People who have loved this land and cherished this land and held on to every blade of grass for a thousand years or more. Aye, they'll die, rather than be driven to the coasts and mountains where there is no food and no shelter. Ask auld Morag?'

'Ask who?' She listened attentively while the horse stood statuesque.

'Morag. An auld lady who lived her life in a township near Rogart.' Robbie spoke with feeling.

'Tush! What could an old Highland crone say to me to convince me that what you state is true?' It was Catriona's time to laugh, but it was a nervous sound.

'She could tell you more now she's dead than a thousand words when she was alive!'

'Dead!'

'Aye, dead! If you could have seen her twisted limbs and body charred like hide from the finest ox. Hair cropped to the scalp by the flames, and eyes burnt from their sockets as if a flock of corbies (crows) had suddenly appeared from hell.'

The girl remained silent.

'That was the factor's men. Brave men with brave hearts against a palsied auld woman! Aye brave men, of the lowland stock!' Robbie spat out the last few words, lapsing into the Gaelic tongue in his anger.

'I cannot believe what you say!'

'Well that's to be expected! But I have come to tell you - and I know not why - but I'll fight to the death, and many brave souls with me. And factor Murdo McBain, he will go with me if I go, and Sellar and all the others as well! That I swear by the spirit of my ancestors and the will of God!'

She looked earnestly into his eyes. 'What's your name?'

'Robbie Sutherland'

'And you?'

'Catriona'

He waited.

She began softly. 'Robbie, there are too many forces ranged against you. Not just the Laird and his family, nor even the servants. But many people you would not expect to help.'

He listened, head bowed.

'Many of the chiefs and tacks men are for the Clearances. They see prosperity in wool and meat. Yes, Robbie! Your own kith and kin are behind the Laird!'

'I do not believe that!'

'I suppose it would take more than this Sassenach voice for you to believe that!'

Robbie smiled. 'You're sometimes one for repeating yourself!'

'Aye! I am! And I will repeat, that many in the glens have secretly sided with the Authorities. Ministers of the Kirk have been given lands, so that their wealth has increased a score-fold in the last few years.'

'I knew there were ministers among them!'

She nodded. 'I have heard them at dinner, Robbie, wheeling and dealing with tenants lands in return for preaching "forgiveness", "humility", "deference", and "obedience". Words I have heard quoted and used a thousand times. Believe me!' Can you understand! There are those that are determined to strip the land of every small township and farm. They are the majority of power, they cannot be resisted!'

There was a silence as the girl patiently waited for his reply.

Robbie's eyes misted over for a moment and then returned to their normal intense gaze. 'I understand most of what you say, but I'm no pleased to hear it, that I can tell you honestly.'

Catriona wanted to reach out and touch him but held back and took refuge in grasping the bridle once more.

Robbie collected himself. 'If what you say is true, then the Will of the Almighty is set again us! But there must be some hope, some hope somewhere! And wherever it is, well, let us pray that it can be found! But it's a dangerous folly to resist, in your opinion.'

'Yes, it is!'

'But it must be done, or the Sutherland Clan will be driven from their true homeland.'

She nodded and turning the horse led it out of the stable.

Robbie ran after her. 'Wait...where can I stay?'

She looked at him intently for a few moments and then shook her head.

'What say you?' he asked somewhat impatiently.

Catriona stopped for a moment. 'There is too much for me to comprehend just now...too much to fathom out! If what you say is true, then right will be on your side in the long run. But if it's what the Laird's men say, then you are a sheep-thief and a rabble rouser and fit to be transported from these lands.'

'You did not answer what I said!'

'What were your plans in coming here?'

'To seek refuge, perhaps hide in one of the empty cottages or barns on the far side of the park.'

'Under the very gaze of the Laird's factors and servants?'

Robbie paused. 'Aye! The very place they would no think of looking!'

'And who would feed you?'

'I was kind of hoping you would!'

'Me? Feed you! And why should I do that! Tell me! Why would I not betray you?' She looked earnestly into his face and let go of the reins for a moment.

'Because you would not dare!'

'And why not?'

'For the sake of hurting the one you love best.'

She laughed. 'You don't know me and my emotions...if you think so, you are a fool and sadly mistaken.'

Robbie's face suffused with anger for a moment. 'No, not me!' He paused to consider his next remark.

Impatiently Catriona interrupted. 'Who then?'

'The horse!' Robbie's brown eyes looked determinedly in her face. He saw her pupils dilate in anger, and the blueness diminished into black.

'You have the nerve...the effrontery to threaten me by injuring my horse!' Her voice rose to a crescendo.

'Aye. Aught to save my skin and those that depend on me! It's a fair price!'

'Anyway, there was no plan to hurt him, only hide him away for some while until matters settled.'

'I am dumbfounded by your impudence,' she paused, 'and you have precisely five minutes to leave this stable before I call the factor's men!'

Robbie looked over her shoulder. 'You have but little hollering to do. See! They're coming now from the Great House!

Catriona turned.

But in that moment the reins had been snatched and the horse mounted. With a cry Robbie leapt the gate and was across the field in an instant. 'I'll bring it back in an hour if you meet me by the old well on the low road to the loch,' he called triumphantly.

Then he was gone over the brow of the hill, leaving Catriona to wonder what he was all about, and what should she do next.

Fichead (twenty)

February gave way to March, and the storms whipped in by the wind and snow splattered across the frozen lochs.

As the weather warmed and spring showed in its infancy with the occasional green shoot amongst the dead bracken and the odd creeping tendril from the bramble, the stark Highland landscape began the change into spring glory.

A cluster of sparrows disturbed the hens around Domhnall's door and, while the old man hewed wood, his wife filled the pitcher from the well a hundred yards on.

The metal bucket clattered into the natural chasm filling with clear spring water, then Ealasaid pulled it back on a coarse rope.

The noise had extinguished all other sounds.

So she jumped with surprise as a figure laid a hand on her shoulder. 'Ah! Mairead, it is ye! How are ye? (*Ciamar a tha thu?*) But y' gave me a fair fright dear, by the Almighty!'

The girl reached forward and kissed the old woman's cheek. 'Fine!' (*'Tha gu math, tapadh leat!*') *Ciamar a tha thu, seanmhair?* (How are you, grandmother?) I'm sorry if I did scare ye, but it is the clattering of the bucket I'll be thinking and your waning ears that are the cause of the alarm. Never fear, it's only me!' She laughed.

'I'll never fear aught that has such a bonny smile and a warm heart. But these are bad times in the glens and much is t'be feared And I'm tired!'(*Agus tha mi sgith!*)'

'Aye, that is so! Where is *seanair* (grandfather)?'

But Mairead did not wait for an answer, seeing the old man walking towards her with outstretched arms she returned the embrace with a long laugh. 'Why grandfather, ye be as hail and hearty as ever, like a spring lamb.'

He laughed. 'Mairead, it is a blessing (*Mairead, tha I beannachd*) and good for my eyes to see...and even better for my soul.'

'Aye, and mine also, for the pair of ye are strong and well and that's all that can be asked.'

'How is Alasdair, Mairead?' The old woman smiled taking the girls hand and leading her into the cottage.

'Oh! He's fine!'

'Any other news y' be bringing to cheer me up?' Ealasaid looked hopefully towards the girl and her stomach.

'None as yet!'

'Well, the Lord will provide when the times are right!' The old woman spoke with emphasis.

'Aye, He will!'

There was a short silence as they entered the cottage and into the warmth. A couple of hens scampered out, through the half open door, and the old man closed it behind him.

'I'll be making a cup of hot elderberry wine, which is as warming as anything one could wish for on such a spring day.' Domhnall busied himself looking in a small cupboard, producing three metal cups and a bottle of wine. He poured the contents into a large pot and hung it over the fire. The flames curled around the pot, and he sighed with satisfaction. Then he looked up. 'What says Alasdair about the clearances?'

Mairead's pause was not lost on the old couple. Her hesitation spoke volumes to their still sharp minds.

'He seems to wander along the same tracks, to and fro, sometimes willing to defend the land...and at other times, well, he seems right glad to accept any change in situation, anything the factors' offer...in return for our moving.' She wrung her hands in a short expressive, yet resigned, manner.

Ealasaid spoke softly, she was aware of the girl's dilemma. 'Is everything fine with you twa?'

Mairead gazed at the fire.

'The wine is mostly warmed by now,' Domhnall said mechanically, discomforted by the sudden turn of the conversation.

'Hush, my husband! Let the girl answer!'

'Things are no so good grandmother, no so good!' She waited for a brief moment. 'I dinna ken why! It seems that he is different now, but perhaps it's me that's changed. I dinna ken! I honestly dinna ken!'

'If ye dinna ken my loved one, who does? But it has been so little time! Between you and me (*Eadar mi fhin's tu fhein*)... have you tried to be a good and loving wife? *Chan eil*! Don't answer me, Mairead, I ken you have and shouldn't have asked.'

'You hav' a right Grandmother! As no one else! For Mother being dead and father not willing to listen…even if I asked…which I probably wouldn't! I will always try to love and obey, as the good book says, and all will be well in time. But the last few months have been bad for us all, with the uncertainties and all that! I'm fed up (*Tha mi eachd searbh!*) and, well, it is no the time fur children, and that's aboot the truth o' it!'

The old woman gazed at the flames and their glow reddened her pale features and showed purple and bright on the dark blue of her dress. 'That's a pity!' (*'S bochd sin!*)

Mairead continued. 'If I hurt anyone, it's myself most of all.'

'That be a selfish thought, Mairead!' Domhnall reached out and poured the warmed wine into the cups. He handed one to the girl who took it mechanically.

'Aye, perhaps it be! But it's the truth! And pains me all the mair, for a' that!'

Domhnall nodded and sipped the wine, which felt acidic against his tongue.

'I do not believe that ye've reached a fair sorry state as yet,' his wife said solemnly also drinking from her cup. 'We toasted you both on your wedding day and we'll toast ye both now…guid health and may happiness return, both to you, and a' the Highland folk!'

Her husband repeated her words.

Mairead smiled but the questioning continued.

'There's nobody else then, although it's but a short time fur that to happen?' Ealasaid consoled herself with the final words.

'Grandmother, no one else!'

'Ye are sure now!'

'Aye, I'm sure!'

The old woman stared hard at the girl for a moment and then looked away. 'Well, Alasdair's a fine man, and'll make you proud and happy in the long run, that's fur sure! So be patient, my dear!'

Once again Domhnall repeated the last remark.

'That's one thing I'll need, patience and I don't mind waiting!' Mairead said the words so softly that the couple did not hear them as they went on drinking their wine.

'It seems a long few months, grandmother, is marriage always so slow at the start?'

'It can be and it can't! Sometimes it takes a bit o'time to get used to each other's ways. As well as love there has to be a sort of respect and mutual confidence which like the heather grows mightily slowly at first,' Ealasaid laughed and pointed at her husband, 'we'll be getting there one o'these fine days!'

Domhnall nodded in agreement and smiled. 'With all the upset of recent months it will tek time, but I dinna ken if Alasdair has my staying power.' He smiled broadly at his granddaughter. Ealasaid gave a mockingly reproachful look, then they all laughed.

'You make me feel better, sae much better.' Mairead was so touched that a lump arose in her throat. 'I'm pleased y' both understand.'

'Aye, we do that!' replied her grandmother.

'Of course we do,' emphasised her husband taking a long draught of the wine, surveying the empty glass and then pouring another. Mairead reached out with her glass and her grandmother followed. 'This is a guid as we'll get fro' the elderflower, in my experience,' muttered Domhnall reflectively, thinking back to the last autumn's rich crop. He continued, 'There were a fair few nettles and thistles aboot in the hedge backs last October, and the wine was bought with a price in weals.'

Mairead had suddenly begun thinking about her husband and the troubles once more and did not reply. The alcohol had strengthened her resolve to do something…although it did not resolve into any firm course of action, as yet.

*****

Mairead closed her eyes for a moment and let the incessant hum of voices be the background to her thoughts.

The coarse brown Hessian flapped at the windows and entrance, the wind just picking up on an early March evening. Yet the barn was warm with the thirty or so people huddled within, some sitting on rough wooden stools, the others lounging on the floor. A dozen children either sat or ran amongst them, being called to sit down and be still whenever their noise drowned the speakers.

For arranged on the platform of piled straw at the end of the barn was a small table. There stood, facing the audience, three of the township - two sturdy, younger men (one being Alasdair) plus old Domhnall. He was the only person present who was not from the township and who did not farm there. But his cottar's duties extending over a wide range of husbandry, his knowledge being recognised by all, and his wisdom never in doubt, he was the principal speaker at this meeting in the barn.

As he began to talk Mairead opened her eyes.

The evening sunlight was warm and golden in the oak rafters, and the faint wisps of dust accentuated the rays, which struck thinly through the gaps of the planked, wooden walls.

' *Uill* (Well), if we fight, man to man and hand to hand,' said Domhnall gravely, 'most of us will die. I hav' no fear o' dying but that is an auld man's blessing. But you, you have bairns and wives to look after. Believe me,I hav' thought about this predicament many a thousand times…aye even more…and I canna but think that we will hav' to accept their terms!'

Here a murmur ran round the barn, and there were muffled cries of "*Cha toil!*"(No!)

Domhnall raised his right hand. 'Pray listen, brother Highlanders. 'Firstly (*An toiseach*)…we barely eke a living frae this land, it's a barren, harsh land as we all ken...but we love this land with as much fervour as any other man's loves his native heath. Aye...and perhaps mair fur we have to battle with our loved one, subdue and cajole.'

He paused and collected his breath.

'Aye, subdue by God's Will and be grateful for a' we get! But the Laird and his men, aye and the ministers too, are all fur us moving on. Ministers of the cloth, men of integrity and learning; these men say from the pulpits..."Move on to better pastures! Take your ox and sheep and goats there...where the land is guid and wholesome and no covered with bracken and ling. Right then! (*Ceart ma tha!*) Let the sheep have these lands, they say, and you go forth and multiply your goods elsewhere." '

Again he stopped and his old face looked pinched and strained, with the semblance of tears in his eyes. He shook his head once more. 'I hav' talked with Eanraig here, and Alasdair, and the other young men o' the farm, and with the elders who have worked here, aye... and the local Clan Chief. We can see no other way but to do the Laird's bidding. I repeat, no other! Listen to me! There'll be money to hand, it'll settle you into your new township, and you can take your timbers with you as had been done for centuries and all can be settled into the new abodes by summer. Now, I am done! What say you?'

There was a general murmur of agreement.

'In time it will be all right, things will settle down.' Mairead could see the speaker and did not turn round to look at him, but she knew the voice and the vacillation within. Alasdair was holding forth.

She had an impulse to speak but held her breath, anger welling within. She could not believe her ears. Everyone seemed obsessed with their own lives, there was no prospective plan only the retrospective preoccupation with small and smaller plots of land being given and then subdivided even more and more by the lairds and the factors. People had gossiped, whispered and planned furtively but nothing had been brought out into the open during the last few weeks of turmoil. She felt frustrated and impatient. Now she wondered what the next speaker might say, what ineffectual plans might be envisaged. She was surprised when she saw the next speaker rise from his seat.

It was Eanraig's father, who was partially blind and lame. He struggled to stand and grasped the back of the wooden chair before propping himself on his stick. 'What you say has reason, Domhnall, and a fairer man never drew breath in these glens. I have been proud to ken ye and Ealasaid fur many a long year and I hope many mair. But let us think! If we move now...how do we sow our summer crops, and what is this wonderful new land like? If men be there, and I suppose there'll be a few if the land is sae guid, what will they say when we take some off them. Will there be mair strife, banter and bloodshed amang our kith and kin?'

Domhnall replied firmly and with understanding. 'Angus, I ken thee well and that has been a pleasure to me o'er the years. But there is guid authority that the land is new and green and you will be given mair than enough to settle on and build your homes.'

The lame speaker steadied himself with a stick. 'True...if all be true! But what if those that fill our mind with dreams, falter and go back on their word. We'll hav' taken down our buildings, moved the beasts and livestock and be left with naught or little better than naught!'

Alasdair spoke. 'My neighbour Eanraig and I hav' talked at length and feel a new start in a new place would be the right and proper thing to do! So think our wives! So thinks my wife's father!'

Mairead bit her lip in frustration and felt the iron taste in her mouth. Her first impulse was to stand up and disagree, but not wanting to be disloyal she hid her frustration and listened in anger.

'If that be so, and the younger ones amang us think sae, then who am I - an auld man, feeble beyond my years, to say otherwise. But caution bids me speak, fur the word of a lowlander and Sassenach oft has a double edge to it, and like the sword can inflict a savage wound from both sides. Think y' all on that! So I'll hold my peace!' The lame man sat down with a fixed expression and said no more during the proceedings.

There was a general half-hearted discussion, with only one or two dissenting voices and little support for any resistance. In just under an hour the meeting broke up.

Mairead waited for Alasdair to finish his general banter with Domhnall, then they crossed the common pasture towards their cottage.

Half a dozen cattle lay in a sheltered doze by the stone wall, where the shoots of blackthorn and elder appeared contrastingly fresh and alive amongst the lichened, rough grey stones.

They walked in silence.

No words were spoken until they reached the cottage. Alasdair opened the door and pushed in, showing no regard for Mairead who was three steps behind. With a sigh, he sat down on a stool and gazed at the fire. The dog nuzzled up to him but was not noticed and gave up after a couple of minutes. It sought consolation in the corner of the room and gnawed at a sheep's thighbone, the rasping noise irritating the man.

'So we must leave?' Mairead broke the oppressive silence between them.

'Aye!'

There was another long pause as she busied herself washing the pots in a small alcove, the water rushing out of the jug into the stone basin being the only noise that broke the gloom. For the dog had paused to watch them conscious of some impending storm.

'Is that all you can say, "Aye"?' she asked, her voice full of irritation.

'What mair can a man say when he is forced to move all to another place, to give up the land he has worked for!' Alasdair's voice rose as he spoke.

'What land? This land was nurtured by the sweat of my ancestors and given to us by my grandfather's and father's goodwill. If my mother could hear you whimper she'd be fair ashamed, I can tell you. Your land is the land we will get from your parents, and that's some time off!' She spoke bitterly.

'Does all the work a man has done here in the last few months mean for nought in your eyes?'

'In the scale of events, aye!'

'And me, how do I stand - in the scale of events?'

There was another pause as she stacked the pots.

'There is much to be said in your silence!' It was Alasdair's turn to speak bitterly.

Mairead considered her words. 'Think as ye will, Alasdair! These are strange times and my considered opinion is to resist, and not take their scraps and morsels as if it were God's bounty!'

'Ye speak like Robbie!'

'Aye, I do!'

'Maybe you should join him wherever he be!'

'Maybe!'

Alasdair gave a feigned laugh. 'What can a woman do in such circumstance, I ask you?'

'Perhaps as much as some spiritless men, who cackle and fly about like grouse! But I'll say no mair. I'm away to bed and guid night to you!'

Alasdair continued to stare at the fire. He tried to bolster his convictions by thinking about what the others had said, but deep down there was a nagging unease which tortured his soul; and, as for Mairead, she suddenly felt that their union was cursed by the evil spirits of the Glens. She was his companion, and little else. Yet strangely, she did not care!

Aon air fhichead (twenty one)

One month later saw the real birth of the summer season. The rains had passed and the heath and moorland were beginning to dry out.

In the Highlands the May weather reigns supreme, dull and gloomy winds from the east are thwarted by the high pressure of the bulk of the mountains, and the days can be hot and sunny.

Banks, damp meadows and inlets become tinted a primrose yellow by flowers, massed in profusion. The insects teased by their colours hover pollen-seeking and familiar. The air has a freshness and warmth that encourages the heavy scents and perfumes of the glens.

While the mountain passes and cart tracks stay dry and firm.

It was on such a day, cuckoo-called and with larks overhead, that all the sounds of summer were blended with the heavy rattling of cart wheels as they bumped and bounced over innumerable ruts on the steep incline of the mountain track which eventually led towards the coast.

A dark, sturdy horse toiled up the hill pulling a wagon loaded with timbers, chattels and goods, the animal's back steaming in the heat of the midday sun. Behind trailed a brown collie and with it a dozen highland sheep, scrawny in appearance and fearful in nature. Occasionally the dog barked but the sheep seemed to follow the wagon by instinct, and their uncertainty was solely due to the strangeness of their surroundings.

The man leading the horse was clearly discernable as Alasdair Sutherland and the auburn haired woman walking two paces behind him was his wife. She would stop and gaze at the surroundings but offered no words of reassurance to her husband. He seemed to plod on as mechanically as the horse.

She watched the sun's reflection on the innumerable small lochs in the valley disappear as they rounded a steep bend in the track. She wiped the perspiration from her brow, using the broad sleeve of her green dress. The dog trotted at her heels for a moment and then wandered off into the coarse heather to chase a rabbit or stoat. The girl laughed for a moment at the forlorn chase and then resumed her steady gait.

To Mairead this was a day of destiny.

A week before, Alasdair had surveyed the new land some five miles from the coast beyond Brora and considered it good. There were just over two-dozen acres, a small river and an area of flat pasture where they could construct a dwelling and extra barns.

Divided between five families the land would be more self-sufficient than the farm they had just left.

'Anyway,' she thought, 'if the place canna support us all, we will leave fur the coast and the fishing there!'

Mairead knew the consequences of failure.

Her marriage seemed doomed in her mind, and any further impediments would simply force her to abandon her new life and take her back to her ancestor's town, Wick, and the occupation of the generations before her - in the herring industry.

The sudden necessity to move on had been forced upon her by her husband and others, accepted without a fight or a word of resistance; and now, if necessary, she was determined to fashion her own future, whatever the consequences.

The thought that her own destiny lay in her own hands excited her and she looked at the solemn face of Alasdair and wondered what thoughts were running through his mind.

The brow of the hill was tediously approached and conquered; Alasdair allowing the horse to drink its fill from a small burn while the dog lolled on the grass, still keeping a wary eye on the sheep.

'Far to go?' She asked mechanically.

'*Chan eil!* About two miles!'

There would have little else said had it not been for a loud call that echoed and hung in the mountains.

Mairead looked up.

Racing down the hill was Robbie, leaping the heather. He was soon splashing through the stream, scattering the sheep and causing the horse to push back the cart, for an instant. 'I am tired, I be thinking, of racing after you two! The devil take the day, for the air's like an inferno and the sun's not yet full high.'

He took the girl in his arms and swung her round. 'How are you both?'

Alasdair was delighted and wrung his brother's hands. 'Robbie, I couldna wish for a better sight than you coming thro' the heather! Fur I hav a fair bit of work to do before the month's through and you're the man to help me!'

'*Tha!* I heard ye were going from the township, auld Domhnall told me. But I've been keeping low for I did a foolish thing and I'm a mind to repent it now!'

'Aye, we heard!' said Mairead smiling.

'Well, I took the horse for a wee gallop and then let it go but they do not know a good joke when they see one, and to tell the truth, I do not see a bad joke when I make one! The factors Murdo and Sellar were no so pleased!' he laughed. 'But the girl, I bet she enjoyed it, for she has a strange way of humour about her!'

'Did ye hear the outcome?' Mairead asked.

'Of what?' Robbie took a long drink of water from his brother's flask.

'From the girl!'

'No, I've no spoken to her since! But she's a bonnie thing, there's no doubting that!'

Mairead looked annoyed but tried to disguise her feelings with a laugh, while the brother's continued pleasure was plain to see.

'You will be able to stay and help us Robbie?' asked Alasdair breaking into the conversation.

'Aye! I see the time has come for you and the beasts to move on!' There was a solemn note in Robbie's voice. 'How is the fodder from last year, bleak as it was?'

'No guid!'

'Not good, brother! How can you afford to move at this time?'

Mairead replied. 'It is none o' our choosing, Robbie. None at all! For if this summer is ag'in us then most of the animals will have to be slaughtered. Eanraig is bringing up the black cattle, and they're in sorry need of good pasture after this lean winter.'

'Aye, 'tis so!' ventured Alasdair. 'And if we have to slaughter them, well the market's no sae guid, fur the prices have fallen.'

Robbie looked perturbed. 'There's smoke rising from yonder glen of yours!' he exclaimed.

'What manner of trouble is it now, mair homes destroyed,' exclaimed the girl with a cry.

'No, Mairead,' said Robbie trying to reassure her in case it was their old home that was in flames, ' they'll be burning the pasture and bracken behind us, then the sheep can be moved in, for the auld barns 'll give them shelter whether they're charred or no! But it's the dead heather and cotton grass that will be put to the flame...to make a richer grazing for the flocks.'

Alasdair sighed. 'It's no right and Godly that places where families have lived for centuries should fall to the devil's will so readily.'

Mairead nodded in agreement. 'Aye, and they say that auld shepherd Dryden carries the torch that puts the land to fire. The right hand of Sellar and therefore by design the right hand of the devil, himsel'.'

'Only God knows what those raw-boned beasts will eat!' Robbie gazed at the animals around him his voice tinged with despair. He looked at Alasdair and noticed his drawn weary face. Mairead seemed on the surface her usual self but he noticed the puffiness beneath her eyes and the occasional lapses into brooding.

'I hav' heard that the pasture's guid, Robbie, in the place we've been given!' His brother seemed cheerful.

'Is that so?'

'Aye, it's so!'

'And who might be telling you that tale if it wasn't the factors or one of their men, or even a minister or two?' Robbie gave a derisory laugh. Then he worried that he might have upset his brother by this hasty reply, but Alasdair looked solemn and Mairead did not acknowledge his comments. She walked on ahead with a fixed expression that Robbie felt boded ill for the future.

'Och! Yer always calling the ministers!' was Alasdair's eventual reply, trying to make light of the criticism.

'Aye, brother, and with good reason! Their whining voices are a fallacy before the Kirk, that I firmly believe; aye, and before the archangels in heaven. For I have heard that several have been about with the factors and acting as pious translators with the Gaelic - fooling the poor people with their mealy-mouthed promises.'

'I wouldn't doubt that for a minute!' Mairead spoke more to herself than the two brothers.

Robbie strained to hear what she had said and quickened his pace to be by her side. 'They've been talking earnestly to the poor tenants and saying that compensation as well as good grazing and shelter will come their way, but I doubt if any of it is true!' Robbie gave a bitter laugh. He had caught Mairead up and was a few paces ahead of Alasdair who walked by the side of the horse.

There was little more said during the next two hours. Each person had their own thoughts and fears, and kept them to themselves –Alasdair confident in his new life, Robbie eager to help and defuse the situation whenever possible, but Mairead introspectively determined that there was much more to be gained from life than she had experienced so far, although in what way it could be experienced, she had not the faintest idea. The day wore on and the journey under the warm blue sky seemed to last forever. However, by mid-afternoon they had reached their destination.

*****

A square shaped man with rough hands and a grey beard approached them; watched by his wife and three children. 'Will you be Alasdair Sutherland and his wife,' he asked addressing Robbie.

He smiled. 'No, this is Alasdair, I'm Robbie...his brother!'

The man shook hands with the couple and then the brother. 'I'm Fearchar! You are welcome to what we have to share, which is not much, by the Grace o' God! Anyway, come in and sup with us, the bairns have been wondering if ye have any wee ones.'

'No! There's none!' replied Mairead.

'Oh! That's a pity! Never mind, in time...' He gave a deep, guttural laugh and walked indoors.

His wife greeted them warmly.

'We have put aside a barn for ye and that'll be thy dwelling for now. There's straw and a clean area for the furniture. The thatching is a bit worn and leaks in part but naught that a willing hand canna put right in a day,' she said cheerfully.

'We are most grateful for aught we can get at present,' Mairead replied once more noticing her husband's silence.

'There'll be three other families coming then,' the man continued. 'That makes five in all! But we're a new township, yet with the burning of the bracken and heather, and some honest toil, we can make the strath a fertile place.'

'I ken my neighbours but who is the other family,' asked Alasdair cutting through the man's introduction. His heart had sank for the township looked poorer than he remembered from his last visit and its surroundings were beginning to become rank with weeds, thistles and ragwort.

'Ian and his wife Mairi with their one bairn, and the other twa families from your township who follow you.'

'Aye, there's Eanraig and his Anna, and Uisdean and Sine from our township who will be coming here. They have no bairns as yet, although Sine is due right soon!'

Alasdair spoke in a disinterested way that was not lost on Mairead. She also shared the disappointment in the surroundings, but in a curious way it pleased her for she felt she had been justified all along in not wanting to come.

The other man smiled. 'Guid, we'll be a group o'the hardest workers in Sutherland and they're be nae one to stop us!'

Mairead gave a rueful smile that Robbie spotted and he smiled back, trying to raise her spirits.

Fearchar waved his hand towards the small thatched cottage. There was no doubting his enthusiasm. 'Come and have a wee dram of whisky from Pulteney , and my wife Ailios will provide something good and filling.'

Alasdair smiled but Mairead hesitated.

'I'm a trifle fatigued by the journey, Fearchar. I would just like to sit and rest at the side of the wagon for a minute. Robbie, would you uncouple the horse, and let it roam by the roadside for a while.'

Robbie did as he was bidden and, after removing the trappings of harness and the bit, he let the animal free to wander and eat at will. He settled beside the girl, who reclined against a broad wheel. Alasdair walked off with the man in earnest discussion.

'They sound like bees in a hive,' Robbie said, inclining his head to the hum of voices emanating from the tiny cottage. He sighed, 'Well Mairead, what think you?'

'No much Robbie...no so much!'

There was a brief silence.

She continued. 'I still fear for the future, mine and Alasdair's.'

'You speak as if they were separate things, your life and his!'

'That may be so! I'm all in a muddle with things at present, but I see one thing clearly - that my future is no with Alasdair, as well ye know! But it is a union before God! That I will acknowledge...and all witnessed by the clan. Yet, there is no love between us, Robbie, it seemed to have evaporated so quickly and without reason...perhaps it is because I do not respect him or his opinions...and he cannot bear me or mine!'

'Why speak you so, Mairead, that cannot be true!'

'I keep believing that it is not true, but my heart says that it is!'

'So what will become of you then?' Robbie looked earnestly at her and tenderly brushed her hair from the side of her face.

'I dinna know! Maybe, as I said, I could return to my mother's birthplace near Wick and seek work in the fishing business. She's been dead a few years but a sister and a brother live there in the same house, although the man's too keen on the spirits to rely on. He works only when he sees fit, and barely has enough to feed him and his family...even in the best o' times. But my aunt...she's always been kindly disposed and my salvation almost certainly lies in her hands. I think I'll go there for a while and see how things turn out. If you want to wander that way with me, to see me safe, ye can.'

'Have you spoken to Alasdair about this?'

'No, but he kens right enough! And the silences between us says mair than words.'

'Would you like me to speak to him and see if there's aught can be done?'

'Robbie, you're gentle and kind, and someone I could have loved. But the Lord's will was agin me in this matter. Say naught, for it might turn brother agin brother, as in the scriptures.'

Robbie shook his head. 'No, naught can come between us! Alasdair kens that! Anyway, it would only be a gentle inquiry and easily put aside.'

Mairead gave a short laugh. 'I'd rather speak for myself if y' dinna mind! When the time comes ...I'll just go...perhaps without a word to yourself, knowing the way you disappear out of my life so easily.'

Robbie laughed. 'Well, there are occasions when a long absence is the correct thing to do, especially with the Laird's men breathing down my neck half of the time.'

At that moment Fearchar called. 'The food is a' ready now, cum ye in.'

The pair got up.

Mairead took hold of his hand. 'Do not forget to contact me when I've gone...I rely on you Robbie...so much!'

Dha air fhichead (twenty-two)

A smile played about the firm broad mouth of Robbie Sutherland and his brown hair hung forward over his brow as he tugged a piece of dead heather from the side of the meadow. It was June and two weeks had gone by since he had helped his brother settle into his new home and finally finished the conversion and fencing.

Mairead had left early one morning, almost three weeks ago, without any regrets. She had told Alasdair about the intention of visiting her relatives in Caithness and spending some time there. He had not replied for some moments, as if studying her statement, turning the consequences over and over in his mind, analysing the implications. Then with a resigned shrug of the shoulders, he had simply said, 'So be it, if that's your wish!' He had not waited for any further reply, nor begun any discussion or reasoning. There was no animosity between them, no recriminations, just a controlled silence that unnerved them both for the rest of the night.

Now the tension had gone. Initially, she had fretted and with a strange agitated feeling tried to subdue her guilt. But after a few days in Caithness, she had discovered an overwhelming release of happiness. Robbie had found her as if by instinct, like the winter moth that scans the darkness of the heath, and she sat watching him tug and heave. At first the heather would not move and small pieces of last year's flowers flew off and it stuck to his face like fine grey down.

Two dozen or so girls and boys watched with interest and chided him on.

Mairead laughed most. 'Come on, Robbie, where's thy brawn?'

With the biggest pull he could muster, a huge clump of heather left its peat stronghold and at the same time Robbie sat down with an almighty bump.

'See what you have made me do,' he joked, 'tear my breeches before the night's begun!'

'Oh, awa with your old black trews,' called out a girl from amongst the throng, and more merriment ensued.

'I heard that, Fhiona MacDonald and no doubt that would please you fine!' Robbie called back in a teasing manner.

'Aye, it wud, Robbie Sutherland, right fine at that!'

'You have other things to do, Robbie,' reminded Mairead breaking into the banter deliberately, 'so light the heather and let the festivities begin.'

The young man walked over to a small pile of hot peat and gently blowing on the grey ash soon kindled a small flame.

Holding one corner of the dead heather against the flame he soon produced a flurry of sparks and the makeshift torch was lit.

'Well, Robbie what are you waiting for now?' asked the plumply vivacious Fhiona with pursed lips.

'Do you ever stop asking a man questions, Fhiona MacDonald?'

She giggled. 'Aye I do, but only when I get to the right answers!'

Another of the men shouted, 'Come on Robbie, the flame'll be deed in a few minutes, dinna delay man!'

Mairead added her voice to the multitude of calls. 'Get running, Robbie! St John's Eve will no last forever!' (*June 24th).

Robbie set off at a steady pace watching the flames fall back as his run quickened.

'Steady, Robbie, or the whole thing'll blow out!' A woman called after him.

'I'm doing my best, but it's a tricky business.'

'Do not worry,' responded Mairead, directing her voice over her shoulder towards the laughing woman, 'he's done it before!'

'Has he now?' laughed Fhiona to the amusement of all around her. 'So pray tell us mair!'

'I'll tell ye mair when there's mair to tell...perhaps in the morning!' replied Mairead.

The group laughed, and cheered on the runner with a series of whoops and yells.

Robbie turned at the far end of the green meadow grass about four hundred yards away and ran back. The flames had begun to die.

'Come on, hurry Robbie,' yelled Mairead.

Someone shouted, 'Dinna bring us bad luck for the harvest season!'

And another cried, 'We dinna want meagre crops in Caithness!'

Panting, and with the last flame almost extinguished Robbie threw the smouldering mass to the ground in front of them. 'Quick, all of you,' he said between deep breaths, '...jump through the embers to be blessed!'

'Well, jump yourself, Robbie!' yelled Mairead grasping his hand and pulling him forward.

They both jumped together and the smoke swirled for a second around the hem of her green dress.

Laughing, they sat down on the grass.

Hardly had the merriment subsided when two fiddlers appeared from Wick - narrow shouldered men, with a lively bounce in their step. Each carried a flagon of ale as well as the instruments. Next came forty or so young men and girls, mostly from nearby fishing villages. One man who carried an accordion let it swing lazily at times so that it emitted a wheezing sound. He joined the other two musicians.

Within half an hour they were joined by a similar number of Caithness fishermen and their womenfolk who were equally vociferous, with jocularity enhanced by the ale and spirits.

Mairead ran and greeted two of her relations. "So y'r on y'way to Wick then?' asked the women.

Mairead nodded and hugged her. After the hugging had ceased the woman said 'Come on!' and Mairead hurried off with both of them to unpack a basket of food stored near the high wall of a sheepfold. Broth, chickens, hams, oatcakes and potatoes were unpacked amid much merriment. The boys hung round in groups and pretended to grab the food while the girls held them back with much tugging and shoving and tangling of arms.

Within the hour the warm night air was a dazzling array of music, laughter and happy voices, with the new grass being trampled in one corner of the field by scores of dancing feet. Songs, spontaneous and with the soft Gaelic intonations drifted through the night air, added a special atmosphere to the scene in the half-darkness of the night.

The full moon rose, clear and large in an indigo sky, yet there was still the luminescence of day, which lingered on and on towards the dawn. It was an endless Highland summer day; where light never became true darkness and the sun hardly set before rising once more.

Crickets basked in the warmth, and added their shrill sounds to the music. Countless small gnats and midges swarmed as myriads of black specks round the outreach of the trees but when they drifted towards the dancers in small dark clouds they were repelled by the burning branches, lit from the clumps of heather. But the flames were only a pale imitation of themselves within the continued brightness of this time of year.

Mairead and Robbie danced and sang; tankards of ale were passed to and fro, often whirling with the dancers until the swirling froth spilled to the ground. No sooner did the music cease, than the fiddles had struck up again, a jig or a reel, while the musicians dripped sweat and smiles in the humid air. Mairead was happy to be near her own folks if only for a short while, and temporarily freed of Alasdair's moods.

Between dancers the revellers ate, throwing the odd scraps to the magpies and crows that hung around and chattered in the highest boughs.

The sounds and laughter brought back memories of former times, but Mairead chided Robbie for his thoughtfulness and he laughed and pulled her closer and said 'How pretty you are!' in a whisper which was just loud enough to hear. Then he brushed his lips softly across her neck to gently define the hidden emotion.

She lifted her eyes and then closed them for a moment as she felt the warmth of his lips. Then she gave a half-smile followed by a laugh. And Robbie laughed with pleasure too! She picked up a white flower, examined the yellow stamens, then shook the pollen into the palm of her hand. Plucking the petals she formed a small pyramid. Robbie watched and smiled, then just as she was finished and the stem was stiff and bare, he blew the small white and yellow spray onto her arm, and it hung there like the petals on her wedding day. She laughed and decided to leave it there for a few moments, gazing at the man with undisguised pleasure. 'You're a brae man Robbie Sutherland,' she thought. She leaned forward and taking some pollen onto the tip of her forefinger she marked a yellow stripe across his cheekbones. 'There, you're like the Sun God, Robbie, arising from the East.' She put her hand inside his shirt and the other around his neck, stroking it, but in abstract way.

'What are you thinking Mairead? About home I'll be bound.'

'Nay, about nothing in particular, other than this is a lovely night, one I'll never forget.'

Robbie did not reply, content in the reverie until she stopped stroking his neck.

'Only the night, you say?' he asked so blandly that Mairead felt mildly irritated.

Noticing her scowl of annoyance he hastily added, 'I thought you were thinking about me! But, it's a wonderful night, I'll grant you that!' His laughter pleased her. 'What else are you thinking, Mairead?'

She suddenly smiled and pointed upwards.

For the moon hung like a huge golden lantern above the trees. However, a dance or two later it seemed to have broken free and sped towards the vaults of heaven, as if it was unfettered, freed from the usual restrictions of the night.

'See, it's a full moon tonight and that bodes well on St John's Eve!' Mairead pointed skyward as she lay down on the grass behind the fire, her face flushed against the auburn hair, which had tumbled down during the dancing. From time to time she shook the curls. For not only had the moisture darkened the colour, it held fine wisps against her neck and shoulders.

Robbie lay down beside her. 'Aye, but I do not fully ken...'

The girl put her arm through his and turning, rested her head on his shoulder. 'Dinana ken what?'

'What the superstitions say!'

'About what?' She laughed.

'Oh! About a man kissing a girl before the full moon...or is it the new moon?' Robbie smiled and glanced away for a second.

Mairead brushed the hair from his brow and noticed how it also clung in fine strands with the moisture. She gazed into his eyes for a moment and said as firmly as she could in her nervousness. 'Robbie Sutherland...y'ken full well what the saying is...so dinna tease me! If y're going to do aught, just kiss me and be done with it!'

'In front o' the fire?'

'Aye, forget about St Bride (* the Celtic goddess of fire and also of marriage). If she is looking, which I doubt it! She'll no hold ye to anythin'!' Mairead replied.

As the flames flickered slightly Robbie kissed her softly on the cheek and then the lips, feeling a warmth of affection he had not experienced before. The dancing went on for many minutes but the sounds seemed blurred as he kissed the girl time and time again.

Finally he spoke. 'Are you happy here?'

'In Caithness? Aye! I am!' she replied without hesitation.

'You wouldn't return to Sutherlandshire with me?'

She paused. 'How could I, Robbie?'

'Aye, how could you! I forget my brother when I'm with you, Mairead. It's sinful, that I know, but I cannot help it, and that is the truth before God and St Bride!' He kissed her again. 'But I don't feel ashamed...at least tonight.'

'Why should ye! Alasdair has nae hold o'er me now!'

'Aye, he has Mairead! In both Holy and Common Law!'

She laughed once more and kissed him on the cheeks and held back his brown hair, surveying his features with pleasure. 'There're no laws in the Highlands now, but the laws we make.'

Robbie shrugged his shoulders. 'Well, whatever the right o'wrongs, we are together tonight...and who knows...for many a night to come!'

'Aye...perhaps!'

Before he could say more there was a firm push on his shoulder. Looking up he saw the plump, smiling face of Fhiona MacDonald. 'Robbie Sutherland, will you no be dancing with anyone else?' she asked sitting down beside them.

Mairead was just about to speak, when Robbie spoke, 'Fhiona MacDonald, I will!'

'With whom then?' She said laughing.

'Perhaps you!'

'Well, what keeps you idling here?' Fhiona had risen unsteadily to her feet, her long dark curls swaying about her shoulders.

'Me, I think!' answered Mairead.

'Tush, you're his sister, and hav' nae hold o'er him!'

Mairead bit her lip and said nothing more.

With a long laugh Robbie was dragged to the dance floor and plunged into a reel, which lasted a dozen minutes or more.

When he returned, amid sundry wild protestations from Fhiona, he found Mairead gazing at the flames.

He sat down and kissed her on the cheek in a comforting gesture.

He waited for a moment before speaking, 'Is aught wrong?'

She looked up and laughed. 'No! Nothing! For a minute I was thinking aboot being your sister and then about your brother and then aboot all the strange events that hav' led us here. But it's the will o'providence!'

'So you don't mind me dancing with the second prettiest girl at the feast?' He adopted a reproachful tone.

'*Chan eil!* Not at all!'

'Be that true?'

'In a manner of speaking "yes"!'
'Why?'
'Because I will lose ye someday, one way or another! And where could we travel to be a common-law man and wife?'

Robbie thought for a moment. 'The problem's too vexing for such a beautiful night as this, and moonlight gives a shine to your auburn hair which takes my breath away.'

'Robbie Sutherland...may the Holy Water cleanse your mouth after such an untruth!' But she laughed as she teased; then kissed him after she said it.

He did not reply, contented to press his body close to her in the deep bracken.

Mairead felt her heart race, she had exchanged her longing for reality, as she lay back in the deep foliage, she knew she had never felt so in love. There was no need to resist!

Tri air fhichead (twenty three)

The July sun broke hot and comforting, the grass was tinder dry and the glen lost in a shimmering haze by early morning. The deer hung around the north mountain faces, cooled in the shadows, and the eagle called plaintively over a land seemingly devoid of life.

For the township where Alasdair and Mairead had once lived was almost deserted.

The burn was cracked dry, and a few black cattle lay panting in the shade of the wall-backs.

Occasionally a wisp of air swirled in the heat, throwing up a fine whirlwind of dust two or three feet high that drifted onto the parched tufted grass.

The dusk carried a respite and the cool night air, still bright as day, was welcomed by the families who rested within.

Sleep was difficult that summer's day and Eanraig and his wife Anna rested uneasily within the cottage. But even more uneasy were the man's thoughts!

Still undecided, he had not hurried to follow Alasdair and Mairead to the new township, content to linger with Uisdean and Sine in their home of the last three years.

Yet their neighbours had a more pressing need to remain. Sine was almost at term, and the heat added to her discomfort. Their first born to-be was large and lying low, so that she bulged uncomfortably and waddled awkwardly around the cottage.

Both had prayed for the child to be born before the journey, but a week had passed and there was still no sign. Under the pretext of staying on to help their friends, Eanraig and Anna, had found themselves becoming even more determined to stay in the place that had belonged to their family for generations.

The stone of the cottage walls and the narrowness of the windows cooled the room and Sine, not yet twenty-four, sat up in bed. She was finding it difficult to lie down for her stomach was uncomfortably tight! She looked at Uisdean sleeping beside her, smiled and gently kissed him and pondered the future. Still, she reasoned, Mairead had faced the uncertainties of starting afresh and she would have to be equally determined. She looked forward to meeting her best friend.

A faint whining of mosquitoes broke the silence.

Then a distant, almost ethereal, sound of horses' hooves.

For a moment she thought the stillness of the night was playing tricks, carrying voices from afar.

Sine listened intently.

But the noise became more defined.

The hum of human voices grew nearer, and then there was another silence.

More silence and suddenly a dull knocking on the door.

It was a suppressed, echoing vibration. She gently eased herself out of bed without disturbing her husband and furtively looked out of the window. What she saw alarmed her.

A broad man, with a white pony by his side, stood with his hands on the door of the cottage opposite - Eanraig's door.

Five other men, still mounted, were behind him.

'Open up in the name o' the Laird!'

For a few seconds Sine watched through her window, transfixed.

'Open up!'

'Who are ye?' Eanraig's voice was clearly heard from his narrow window.

'Factor Sellar!'

'I thought ye were held in the Tolbooth in Dornoch, man! What do you want of me and my wife at this ungodly hour o' night on a summer's eve?'

'There's no law and no tolbooth that binds me, if that answers your impudence. Aye! That fool MacKid may try to prosecute me but he's a poor specimen of a Sheriff and a man too! But there's a law that binds you! And that law wants you and your kin out of this dwelling!'

There was a pause and the door opened.

Eanraig appeared, looking bewildered. 'What now man... you're jesting to be sure!'

Factor Sellar motioned to three men to dismount and unbuckle their pistols. 'We'll joke with these guns if you do not make haste, and that's the long and short of it!'

'But giv'us time factor please, till morn!'

'You have had time enough! It's almost a full moon since you were warned to go. All have left but for the pair of you...and those yonder.' Sine drew back quickly as she saw the speaker turn and look towards their cottage.

But in that glance Sine saw the danger it foretold. She hurried over and shook her husband. 'Uisdean, Uisdean! Wake up for God's sake...there is trouble afoot...in Eanraig's!'

Her husband looked bewildered for a moment and then jumped up. He quickly began to dress.

Now they heard Anna's voice, pleading gently. 'Please Factor Sellar, we'll go soon but give us mair time to gather our things.'

But factor's men had already pushed past Eanaraig and soon their meagre possessions were being dragged to the door and hurled outside. They stood helpless and bewildered. Sine and Uisdean watched in fear and amazement, glancing nervously through the narrow window, not daring to go outside, hoping that they would not be noticed and not involved in any way. Sine trembled violently, her pregnant frame shook with fear.

'Please Factor...' they heard Anna's voice, almost a whisper.

But Sellar cut her short. 'Stop blathering woman or we'll torch the whole place with all inside.'

'Y're no going to destroy the cottage before the furniture and timbers are saved?' pleaded Eanraig.

'You've had time a plenty! And this doing rests at your foolish door, no mine!' was the factor's reply.

At that moment Uisdean appeared in his doorway, breathless and agitated. 'What manner o' wrang is this, Factor?'

'Aye, I thought we'd soon rouse you from your slumbers. You had better be sharp too, for your house'll burn next!'

'But think o' my wife, Factor Sellar!'

'What aboot her man?'

'She's with child and the bairn cud be born at any time!' His voice rose in anguish.

'That's none of my business, but your misfortune! It seems every thing is laid at my door, whether I have aught to do with it or not.'

Sine appeared in the doorway, her face white with fear.

'Surely you have compassion on such a young lass?' Anna had overcome her initial anxiety and spoke in anger. She stepped forward and waved her fist at the Factor. 'Have pity upon the girl,' she screamed, ' have pity upon the puir wee baby, I beg o' ye! Or you'll burn in Hell!'

There was no reply.

The contents of the house began to appear. As they were thrown in haste, Eanraig and Anna saw their belongings crumple and break. Into an untidy heap were thrown a snapped chair leg, a cabinet full of utensils, bed linen, sheets, rugs, towels and clothes of every description; mostly poor but precious in their way, the best of their possessions, the best they would ever have. Higher and higher the pile grew until it took a life of its own as it suddenly slid sideway across the dry ground. The four could only watch and wait, fearful and subdued.

Then one of the factor's men appeared from within Eanraig house, kicking a stool to one side that had been dropped in the doorway. He suddenly disappeared around the side of the building. But was back in a minute. In horror the four saw what he held in his hand - a piece of burning heather.

Anna gripped Eanraig's arm. His face was suffused purple with anger and hate. He looked towards the Factor, and in that moment he felt an overwhelming desire to kill. This hatred took over his reasoning, his whole frame.

But Factor Sellar was his usual calm self. He nodded towards the man. Purposively he held the flames against the corner of the overhanging thatch. They heard the familiar crackling as the red energy suffused forth.

A grey plume of smoke drifted upwards.

Suddenly the tension snapped and Eanraig let go of Anna. In a giant bound he grabbed hold of the man with the flaming torch.

It only took a second for Uisdean to join in. He swung wildly into the man's face. Blood spurted from a broken nose and the burning torch fell to the ground in a shower of sparks which flew as orange and red flecks towards the Factor's horse. Startled, the animal leapt back almost dislodging its rider.

For a moment there was confusion, a melee of humans and horses bound in a cacophony of sound - a screaming of voices and a clattering of hooves.

Then a shot rang out.

Sellar had taken aim.

Uisdean fell to the ground bleeding from a wound above the ear, his scalp partly torn from his skull.

Sine rushed forward and cradled her husband's head against her pregnant abdomen, blood cascading onto her exposed skin.

Anna caught hold of them both and weeping comforted them as one.

But the five men rushed forward. It took only a moment to pin Eanraig against a wall, his face a mask of hatred.

'Tak care, mun!' said one, 'The factor's is no mood to argue and the pistol's still in his hand!'

But the Factor surveyed the scene only for a second and, without looking back, rode off.

The group's attention was suddenly directed towards Sine. For in her distress she suddenly gave an anguished cry of pain.

They watched as she staggered towards some bushes towards the side of the house. But before reaching them, she fell to the ground as if in a faint.

Now through her whole being came the agony of contractions, wave upon wave upon wave.

Motionless with fear she lay still. Then came the tears, slowly at first, then more rapidly as she realised her predicament.

Then the pains increased, as the convulsions overwhelmed her.

Turning first one way, then the other, the pain reached a crescendo within twenty minutes.

Anna acted quickly, putting aside the horror before her. Anxious, instinctively willing to do what she could, she was helpless in her ignorance. She tried her best, wiping the sweat from the Sine's brow. She kissed the young girl repeatedly and gave reassurance as best she could, in whispers against her cheeks, in soothing words, in tones and gestures as she used to comfort a child. 'It's all right precious one,' twill soon be all over!' She kept repeating the words softly, and over and over again, stroking the girl's face as it contorted with each contraction.

Meanwhile the men had stopped the torching and, not sure what to do, had backed slowly away. Even to such hardened individuals the superstitions of the Highlands made them cross themselves and shake in fear at what had been done before the Lord.

But their repentance did nothing to stop the smoke as it poured from the thatch, and hung in low plumes about the two young women, giving them an acrid blue cloak of modesty.

Eanraig suddenly collected himself and ran for a blanket to cover Sine. But flames whirled and hissed from the windows and doors and there was no way in. Repulsed by the flames, he could only hold his head in despair. Never in his life had he felt so helpless and gripped by despair.

Sine gave one long scream.

The child twisted its way into an alien world.

It was all over in a short while.

The baby boy was as mute as his dead father.

The sobbing girl kissed the blue cheeks for minutes on end, until Anna gently released her grasp.

The heat of the burning cottages crimsoned her cheeks and painted a terrifying inferno of blood-red to the pupils of her eyes as she gazed vacantly into the flames.

Within the hour Eanraig had buried the father and son together.

He set out to see the bailie at the first light of dawn.

Ceithir air fhichead (twenty four)

The courtroom at Inverness was crowded to capacity, and at ten o'clock in the morning Patrick Sellar appeared before the Circuit court and before the Lord Commissioner of Justice, Lord Pitmilly. As was the custom of the day the trail proceeded without a break until one o'clock the following morning.

Lord Pitmilly deigned to adjudicate in his own inimitable way, not letting reason, honesty and fair arguments sway his judicial opinion.

The indictment charged Mr Sellar with culpable homicide, fire-raising, throwing down and demolishing houses, barns, mills, kilns and sheep-cots etc. The length of the charge was emphasized by the fact that the Advocate-depute, Mr Home Drummond, was nearly two hours reading it.

In the dock stood the confident young advocate, Patrick Sellar, a man who once detested sheep farming but under the guidance of William Young had become, in his own words, 'converted to the principle that the populace should be employed in securing the natural riches of the sea-coast, that the mildew of the interior should be allowed to fall upon grass and not upon corn, and that the several hundred miles of alpine plants flourishing in these districts in curious succession at all seasons, should be converted into wool and mutton for the English manufacture.'

From the dock he looked with contempt at the humble highlanders. They squirmed and shuffled uneasily under his gaze, fearful as to their fate if he should get off.

None were more afraid than the forty witnesses who had been carefully questioned by MacKid. However, as circumstance would have it, only fifteen were called for the Crown to press the prosecutions case.

Nine men, stout in their opinion and confident of their rewards were called for the defence. For these men were heavy with bias, being the Sheriff-officers and faithful servants who had accompanied Sellar.

And Sellar had other irons in the fire of injustice. There were the glowing testimonies from the Laird and sundry gentlemen; the fulsome letters of praise from distinguished professional people of the county.

The Judge listened to a Minister's response that 'Mr Sellar was incapable of any cruel or oppressive action,' another landowner described him as 'a person of the strictest integrity', another as 'a most respected character,' and so on. The Judge was always impressed by any gentleman's intelligent, reasoned and lucid opinion. That is what he believed and left the jury in no doubt on this matter.

The Highland witnesses fared badly.

'Speak up man!' The Judge's voice was crisp and harsh and in clipped lowland English.

'I'm speaking as well as I can, Sir!' The shepherd Gunn nodded towards the Judge.

'What does he say?'

'He say's he's talking as loudly as he can, your Honour, but his voice is weak at present,' replied the translator, a middle-aged Minister.

'Damn the man and the others, can none speak English? This infernal trial will last for days at this rate!' The translator shuffled and replied, 'Not many, Sir!'

'What can one do with such a situation!' The Judge glared from beneath his wig, through pebble glasses and put down his pen in exasperation. He had a very red, round face, with dark, expressionless eyes and a pinched, bent nose. His whole being was one of resolute squatness. 'Help him as best you can, Minister!'

'I will, your Honour!'

'Good!' The judge took up his pen and held it poised in an erudite fashion. 'Well...'

The shepherd looked up for a moment and then quickly cast down his eyes. He wore a threadbare jacket and grey trousers that must have seen a generation or two.

The Minister took up the cause. 'Speak up man!' he demanded in Gaelic.

'I wud if a kenned what the Judge is aboot.'

'He's aboot what ye saw when Factor Sellar visited that township where you were shepherding.'

The Judge waited.

'I saw nothing, I ken nothing.'

'Hush man! The Judge'll hav ye fur contempt of court.'

'What's that!' asked the bewildered Gunn.

The Judge interjected impatiently. 'What on earth is the fool saying now, Minister?'

The churchman hesitated. He brushed back the long lock of hair that covered his bald brow and said firmly. 'You were there, tending to a flock near the township early on the morning in question and witnessed the proceedings, did you not?'

'Aye! To a point!'

'He did have a good view of the proceedings, your honour,' the minister translated.

'Is that so, Shepherd?' The Judge inclined his head and stared at the old man.

The Minister spoke calmly. 'You saw Factor Sellar, did you not and the attack by Uisdean?'

'Aye, I did that!'

'You saw the Factor defend himself?'

'I didna say that, Minister, or the Lord strike me down, in consequence!'

'But y'saw the gun being fired in self-defence?'

'Aye, I saw the gun being fired...'

The Minister held up his hand to silence the perplexed man. 'He says he saw the Factor speaking civilly to the two men and the deceased - the man named Uisdean- impulsively rushed forward to attack the Factor.' Turning towards the bench the translator smiled. 'He confirms what has been said, your Honour, as true.' A murmur of amazement and disgust went round the court.

The Judge nodded and wrote something down. 'You may stand down shepherd Gunn. Next witness!'

Alasdair stood before the court, looking strangely subdued in his black jacket and trousers, with no tartan about his person.

The Judge was in no hurry to ask a question but surveyed him for a few moments before saying sharply, 'Do you speak English?'

Alasdair nodded.

'Much!'

'Aye, a fair bit!'

'Your Honour,' retorted the Judge.

Alasdair paused and, as he glanced towards the back of the room, he had an uneasy feeling that Mairead was standing there, -watching, disapproving. He scanned the anxious faces. There was only one woman with her head covered by a green shawl and her face was in shadow. His concentration, temporarily distracted, was brought back to reality with a firm admonition. He said mechanically, 'Your Honour'.

'I'll have no disrespect for the Court here! One more impertinence and I will make you step down, testimony heard or not! Do you understand?'

'Aye, I do!' replied Alasdair calmly and with conviction.

'Where were you on the morning in question?' The judge spoke slowly and deliberately.

'About my business, your honour.'

'And what business was that may I ask?'

'Aye, ye may,' replied Alasdair respectfully.

The judge retorted, 'Have you not been warned about being insolent!'

Alasdair went silent for a moment and replied, 'I had left the township some while back and had visited it the night before this terrible event, being on my way to see my parents near Loch Shin.'

'But it is your testimony that Factor Sellar shot the man in cold blood, without provocation.'

'Aye, that is what I heard from Sine and before God…that is the truth!'

'But it is not what Shepherd Gunn witnessed, and he stated on oath that he was telling the truth.' The Judge stared from beneath his black bushy eyebrows, his dark eyes even colder than before.

'It's not what the Shepherd said...'

The Judge slapped the gavel hard on the bench top. 'Do not contradict me Sir, do not contradict! It is written before me, translated by a man of the cloth. A man who speaks perfect English and understands perfect English which is a rare an animal as one can find in the Highlands.' At the end of this reprimand he looked around the court. The stern gaze left Alasdair in no doubt as to not pursue the argument and he waited for the next question.

But it did not come!

To his amazement he was asked to step down.

'But your Honour, I haven't told you all that I know...'

The Judge banged his gavel again. 'You have said enough Sir, for this court! Stand down or I will have you committed!'

Alasdair hung his head for a moment and when he looked up the figure wearing the green shawl had left the room. But he knew it was not Mairead, she would have waited, he reasoned.

He pushed his way through the crowd and went outside.

The air was misty and chill, and he stood with his back against the building, the roughly hewn stone magnifying the chill.

He stood there contemplating the future for a half an hour or so, while three other witnesses -two being employees of the Marquess- waxed eloquent about the generous nature, hard work and fairness of the Factor.

Eanraig was also given a brief moment.

But perplexed by having to speak some of the time in English, which he barely knew, and questioned in all directions, he felt even more angry and violent as he sat down beside his wife. She had hardly understood a word!

By the time Alasdair returned to court, the Judge had already closed his mind on the case.

When Lord Pitmilly came to sum up in a clear voice that contrasted starkly with the hesitant and at times almost incoherent shyness of the local men, he told the jury that it was unnecessary for them to consider any of the charges except relating to one burning to death, of an old woman; he pointed out that the evidence of her son-in-law, a tinker called William Chisholm, although corroborated by other witnesses had to be considered against that given by the defence, and if the jury found it difficult to match and strike a balance, then they must take into account the character of the accused and the testimonies relating to Mr Sellar already given.

As to other matters and related to the death of a crofter, the sworn testimony of the blatant attack by the man, the lack of credible evidence against Mr Sellar - that in this case the balance was poised in favour of the accused.

The crowded room was hushed in amazement at the summing up and Alasdair and his friends feared the worst. They realised that in the first case, the heinous crime of burning a frail woman to death had been damaged by the testimony of her son, who was dismissed as a tinker, a bigamist and a thief. In the second case, the murder of an innocent man, the minister's inaccurate and unfair translation, Alasdair's second-hand testimony coupled with the agitation and incoherence of Eanraig, would be the deciding factors.

When the jury retired the highlanders had only to wait fifteen minutes, barely enough time for the jury to settle into their deliberations.

The Factor was found not guilty and acquitted on all charges.

The man was innocent, a verdict the judge happily shared. 'Mr Sellar, it is now my duty to dismiss you from the bar; and you have the satisfaction of thinking that you are discharged by the unanimous opinion of the Jury and the Court. I am sure that although your feelings must have been agitated, you cannot regret that the trial took place; and I am hopeful it will have the same reassuring effect on the minds of the people of this country, who have been so much and so improperly agitated.

So the Highland men crept home in subdued silence knowing that the law would allow such men to proceed with even more cruelty, and perfect immunity.

None feared more for his safety and family's well-being than Sheriff MacKid.

*****

If exhaustion had proved the key to her trouble, Mrs MacKid would have slept very soundly that third night; more so her husband. Sleep had been fitful the previous days. She had watched the moon's first quarter in the southern sky trace a sickle across the window, and in between short bursts of deep slumber, which lasted only a few minutes or a half-an hour at the most, she would note its position, sigh, and long for the dawn.

And the light of the east soon brushed across the hills and cast rays against the old oak dresser that had seen many dawns in its humble lifetime.

She would tremble with anxiety and the movement, however suppressed, would wake her husband. Then they would talk in a hushed whisper so as not to waken the seven other children in the adjoining rooms. For the Sheriff's house was more amply proportioned than most in the town.

Their spirits would sometimes rise in the faint hope that the trouble of recent months would settle without recriminations; but the gravity of the verdict hung heavily on their shoulders. They could, and did, go over the trial in great detail, minute by minute. However, with each analysis of the facts the more incomprehensible was the verdict. And their conversation would meander without purpose, and without reaching a definite conclusion. It was a discussion made even more dispirited by the obvious conclusion- a conclusion they could not admit to, even in the most pessimistic of times.

Occasionally an optimism, not really based on reality, would lighten their moods. It was in one such moment that his wife spoke. 'He will not show his face here!'

Her voice was adamant.

But after a moment of defiance, her husband's somber voice replied 'I'm not so sure.'

There was another pause. Then he continued slowly, 'We must not dwell on this matter any more, and if we have to leave...so be it, my dear. We will go with precious little, I'm afraid!' He said the last few words quietly and with gravity.

'Whatever we take, you'll leave with your honour and propriety intact.'

'I would have found it fairer if the Great Laird or some of the Ministers and Sheriffs around had spoken on my behalf...but it was not to be. To them my honour and propriety meant so very little...if anything at all!'

He remained silent and his wife took his hand placing it on top of the grey sheet and giving it an affectionate squeeze. 'Do not suffer any penitence for what you have done, in the eyes of the Highlanders, you were right and a man of principles, seeking true justice.'

'Not in the eyes of the Judge...' But his wife cut him short.

'Forgive me for speaking so harshly about any man, but that Judge was as prejudiced, garrulous and as wicked as any man or woman we have met in our life. There's not one good word been said on his behalf since the trial ended.'

'I feel that in time we will be forgotten; and the risk I took in writing to Lord Stafford, and the incarceration of Sellar in Dornoch, will have proved to be a risk not worth taking. We have led a steady, blameless and God-fearing life...but it all seems to no avail...I feel it in my soul.'

She pondered on his statement for a short while as the light just began to show in the East.

He continued, 'That man Sellar has so high a reputation of himself, that his conceit blinds others to his failings. His excitation with greed and cruelty is as unnatural a personality as can be ever envisaged in man. And yet, those around him are also so warped with greed themselves that they couch their opinions in flattery, the art of honest speech has passed them by.'

She turned and whispered, 'Those men cannot read much in his countenance, that I believe, for his eyes are made only to express his own feelings about himself.

Never has such wickedness gone unpunished in this land.' As if they had suddenly confronted the iniquity for the first time, they went silent and lay still, hardly conscious of each other.

Sellar was indeed a man of reputation who never sullied that reputation good or bad by any alteration in his character.

As the mid-morning wind shook the oaks around the house free of any trembling, capriciously clasped leaves, so the couple waited in the drawing room for the inevitable sound of the horses hooves on the cobbled path and the sharp, staccato rap on the door.

And the time came! For once Sellar had dismounted and stood framed in the archway - broad, sallow and unbending. His eyes, doubly cold, were curiously illuminated with a fitful expression as if he was about to break out into laughter at some private joke. His manner was relaxed but in its very ease even more threatening.

Mr MacKid stood nervously before him, his wife trembling violently by his side with her arms around the two youngest children. 'You are welcome within Mr Sellar, we will not show any incivility here.'

The factor nodded but said not one word as he walked in. He made himself comfortable in a chair by the window. 'It's a fine house you have here, Sheriff,' he said gazing around and rubbing his palm on the rough texture of the stone wall. 'A fine house, I'll be thinking.'

'Aye, that's true enough!' MacKid replied cautiously.

'Better than any prison, Mr MacKid, that you'll grant as well, no doubt.'

The man stood silently before the factor not even daring to sit down in his own chair.

There was an uneasy silence, only broken by his wife ushering the children into a backroom.

'You have not discovered the pleasures of one of your own jails, Mr MacKid, have you?'

The man continued in his stubborn silence.

'Anyway, it has struck me that in view of the trial you so recklessly brought about, and the damage you have done to my name and reputation... that you would be pleased that we never set eyes on each other again.' Sellar gave another fitful smile.

The Sheriff sighed, 'I suppose it would be the best for all concerned.'

'Aye...it would!'

'There's little justice in this world when you make the wrong decisions, Sheriff, all manner of things can go against you...don't you think?'

The man lapsed into silence and glanced at his wife, who with fear dare not speak.

The Factor continued, 'I have had several days to think about the matter, that you will realise...and perhaps more at the beginning in the Tolbooth. Have you aught to say man?' The suddenness of the command aroused the Sheriff from his contemplations.

'I might have been a bit hasty, that I'll admit, factor; and could have proceeded with more caution for the truth and your welfare.' His voice quavered.

'Aye, you could!' The factor said benignly but with a long stare at the wife. 'Aye you could that!'

'Perhaps I did not estimate the effect....', but the Factor cut him short with a hollow laugh.

'You have for all intents and purposes gone from Sutherland, Sheriff. You are here only in form and feature!'

'I can only apologize, Mr Sellar and ask for forgiveness,' the man replied humbly and hesitantly.

'Think nothing of it, Mr and Mrs MacKid. You did your duty as you saw it, fit and proper. A man can only do what he thinks and do it to the best of his ability.'

For the first time the couple relaxed a little and the woman moved closer to her husband.

'Which brings me to my next point! You have but two weeks to take your effects from this house, as fine as it is, and leave the county.' The factor laughed uproariously, noting the couple's terrified countenance.

'You do not mean to say that we must leave at once. I have my livelihood here and as Sheriff....'

Sellar laughed even more boisterously than before. 'You have no job here, MacKid, I am here to tell you that you have been dismissed.'

With that final remark, and not waiting for any response, he left the couple and their large family pondering their injustice and their future.

Thus Patrick Sellar rode away with his two companions, still pleased with the effect he had produced.

There was no other option. With no income and with as many belongings as they could quickly transport, the MacKid family prepared to leave for Caithness.

*****

From Robert MacKid,
To Mr P Sellar,
Dear Sir,

Appertaining the matters as were discussed without a full resolution and satisfaction to both parties, I would humbly beg that you consider the following before resorting to any hasty judgments, which would be against your honest and benevolent character.

After much thought and turmoil regarding the matters that have arisen and the discomfitures, and indeed turmoil, they have occasioned, I submit the following: I give credit to those misstatements of which now I am thoroughly ashamed and which I now most sincerely and deeply regret. I allow that you are entitled to exemplary damages but would plead with you not to prosecute. I shall not only acknowledge it as a most important obligation conferred on me and on my innocent family, if you will have the goodness to drop your lawsuit against me, but I shall also pay the expense of that suit.

I will also pay any further sum in compensation.

Finally, and one important point, you may make whatever use you need to, with this letter. I would sincerely ask that it is not published in a newspaper. I am forever mindful of the misguided faith that the people have placed in me, and would not wish to hurt them; I would also like, I must acknowledge, to retain some public respect.

I am,

Robert MacKid.

Mr Sellar was more than pleased. In addition he demanded two hundred pounds over and above the expenses; this compensation being the ruin of the little man. He left Sutherland with his semi-destitute family, as quickly as he could, never to return.

Coig air fhichead (twenty five)

But the trial was not the end of the matter.

It was Alasdair who went out one blustery day, when the first summer leaves were spinning down from the trees as the uppermost branches foundered in the gale, and the bracken was so flattened by the storm that it looked limp and dead. For fifteen minutes or more he sheltered as the wind, unusual in its intensity for July, gusted from the east and the rain hung almost as a huge curtain that divided the glen into two distinct halves- one sun and one rain. He pondered on his marriage that seemed as divisive as the scene before him.

It was at his mother's request that Alasdair was on a mission, namely to locate the whereabouts of his half cousin and the family, displaced by the Clearances.

Only a short while before he had been busy mending the roof on an old barn to make a more comfortable home in what was left of the new township. And the work was tedious, sawing out the rotten timbers and replacing them with roughly hewn pine. He had used the horse to drag two stout saplings, some ten years into their growth, from the upper slopes of the hill, across the pasture that as the bulrushes knew full well was more than sodden in its lower quarter. There the stumps caused deep furrows in the soft ground and the horse heaved and strained, flanked with sweat while Alasdair pulled and heaved with all his might

It was in this state of exhaustion, feeling fed up with circumstances, that he remembered Mairead's request to visit her family. Suddenly, he had an urge to speak to her. Yet he felt afraid! In a strangely subdued frame of mind he donned his thick black coat, buttoned it up to the chin and with a heavy heart bent head-down into the wind. For some reason it seemed the most natural thing to do, to ease some of his frustrations.

The journey was only seventeen miles but the going was tedious and the young farmer had time to reflect on his changing fortunes since his marriage.

It had not quite been as he had expected.

Mairead was still visiting her relatives in Caithness, what she was doing barely perturbed his equanimity. He had no real doubts that she would return. He had turned this question over and over in his mind, usually as he lay alone at night. Then the wind would whistle and the trees would spread their whispered response into the darkness, and he would try to rationalize and fail. He knew that Mairead always read more into simple situations, ones he considered unimportant. But she always analysed each point, argued each point and corrected him when she thought fit – which was often. He had felt lucky to have married her at first, then worried as many small facets of their existence together had become irritating, compounded by the intransigence of his authority. He felt puzzled, idiotic at times, unable to express himself as Robbie would have done, yet he felt a total loyalty to their vows, an obedience before his family and God. Sometimes there were long arguments about the way they could change their fortunes and how the sudden hardships of the Highlands could be stopped – he always sought a firm but peaceful direction, Mairead was blunt in her defiance and willingness to fight, shed as much blood as was possible. She had no sentimental regrets about servitude and obeying the Lairds, she belonged foursquare in a new order of highland women.

He had lost some of his old self-confidence, in that irreconcilable antagonism. At times everything in her speech and manner seemed to contradict him. The sworn oaths of obedience had vanished, so had his idea of an idyllic family life. That worried him and he was puzzled as to what to do next.

With such gloom and indecision Alasdair ploughed on, still seeking an answer but resolving nothing.

The fact that he had been a disappointment, or that she had expected more from him than was reasonable, did not enter his mind.

If pressed by the elements, he would have simply replied that he was doing his best.

But the elements had other thoughts on their minds that day. It was to shake the foundations of the mountains, rock that had existed since the very origins of his world, everyone's world. The tapestries of the lochs and grazing lands were before him, with small lattices of planted trees to break the gales and segment the poor vegetable and grain plots. But the solid ground controlled their destiny.

When he crossed the outermost plantation, through all the tumult and the commotion in the rushing air, Alasdair came in view of a small stone house and three ancient outbuildings, in themselves no bigger or taller than the main building, but more dilapidated in every way - with cracked walls that seemed to stagger in the storm. For at that moment a lashing of hail beat down. So that in the blackest of skies what weak sunlight had watched the farmer's course now gave up its inquisitiveness and abandoned the land to its fates.

Even in the gloom Alasdair noted that the there was no smoke issuing from the roof of the house.

He hurried up to the door and called, 'Shepherd Gunn!'

There was no answer.

Alasdair paused and held his breath.

The windows and main door were boarded up, fixed by a multitude of nails, some still bent and protruding in their hasty insertion.

He pulled at one large piece of wood, waist high at the main entrance. But it held fast. He tried another and a third. But to no avail!

He recoursed to a violent kick inwards, then a second, then a third and suddenly the wood gave and the door flew open!

The room was bare.

Where the crude table, chairs, stools and bed had once stood was now vacated to hard brown earth.

Alasdair puzzled for a minute and turning abruptly headed for the main barn.

As he opened the door he was suddenly aware of the dank smell of humans, a smell as rich as a ripe fruit but fetid at the same time and repugnant.

Against the straw huddled George Gunn and his wife, with a baby at her breast. Seven other children sat silently beside them on a mound of damp straw covered in rags, old clothes, bracken and hay. He was astonished at such suffering.

In the corner lay the shepherd's ninety-year old grandmother.

Alasdair thought he never seen such wretchedness in all his life.

'What by the Lord…'

George put up his hand to silence him and pointed to the old woman.

Alasdair went silent for a moment.

'The Laird and the factor hav' had their revenge, Alasdair and on my bairns and an aud woman, that's what its come tae! We had our hopes and our sufferings in the past, by the Lord Almighty, but naught as bad as this! All my life's work has come to this! Highland folks that have defeated armies by the broadsword, turned barren land into good are defeated by the factors, pompous aud judges and the lairds.'

The old woman pulled herself up by her thin arms. ''Tis ye Alasdair Sutherland! Did thou bring any food?'

Alasdair noted the livid blue of her arms and the shaking fingers.

'No!'

'Will you be long?' (*Am bi sibh fada?*)

'No! (*Cha bhi!*) I'll be back on the morrow with some! First let me kindle a fire and get some blood into those limbs. Forget that snivelling company of judges and the like for the moment and we will mend the damage that's done in time. But ye canna stay in this damp pit any longer! You're no so well as a' that! Do you remember what happened?' (*A bheil cuimhn' agad mar a thachair?*)

'Of course! I'm not so weak in mind as to forget the present!' she replied with a smile, 'even at ninety years and mair!'

Alasdair laughed too. He turned towards the door.

The hail had stopped beating on the corrugated roof and the shabby building felt eerily silent.

'If we go back in there (Shepherd Gunn pointed towards the house) we'll pay for it, the factor has thrown us oot with naught but the rags we stand up in! We need patience but that will not quell the pangs o'the stomach, especially in the bairns. They've gone as mute as a hare hiding in the heather.'

Alasdair took hold of him by the shoulder. 'To the Devil with the factor and his men! Where are they now! I tell you! They'll be in the inns with bellies as full as any barrel and twice as round, I'll be bound! They'll no come back for many a day! We'll get a braw fire blazing and I'll take myself home for the food. It no so easy walkin' in this weather but it'll break as these summer storms always do. I'll be back on the morrow and then we'll mek plans to get you accommodation for a fair while until we decide on the future. But we must consider how we will deal with these corrupt men. For they'll linger around the Glens like a bad mist until our last-breath is gone! That I heed! But we can move on, reclaim some other lands, far from the evil that surrounds us.'

The old woman sighed. 'To move on at my age cannot be the will o' the Lord! I've paid rent and rent through seventy summers, never one pound, never one shilling not even a farthing, owed. And now I'm out in the cold, destitute and as poor as the day I was born! Aye, the pitcher's full o'grief but not sae full that even at my age I still intend to empty it. Mourn? Aye, one day I'll mourn but proud like a Highlander and braided in freedom!'

George raised his head from his subdued contemplations. 'We may be poor, Grandmother, but we have one another have we not? There's no sorrow that last forever, take a comfort in that!'

His wife did not speak but shifted the suckling baby to the other breast.

'Aye,' replied the old lady solemnly between coughing bouts, 'we have each other, but they have the rights and what law there is…is on their side; we have the starvation and they willna gi' us a morsel to eat. A' their finery and lace! I'll never live to see their disgrace on Earth but I'll be in heaven to witness their disgrace before God…and that gives me the greatest comfort of all!'

Sia air fhichead (twenty six)

Whatever Robbie Sutherland felt about his relationship with Mairead, there was no hint of guilt. In his mind her marriage to his brother was over and, in the curious turmoil that had overtaken the Highlands, such a thing was of little consequence.

Not that he was afraid of God and the consequences!

If he thought deeply about the situation, he realised that there may be some retribution to pay later, but his mind was fixed on other matters that would probably overshadow this affair on the Day of Judgement.

He was determined to wreak vengeance on the Factors McBain and Sellar and all others connected with him.

He was also able to bide his time and two full moons had passed.

He had heard nothing more about the blacksmith MacIomhair despite inquiries in many of the villages he had passed through on the way to Caithness. There was no doubting, in his mind, that his friend had perished at the hands of the Laird's men.

Yes, he would seek his vengeance one day, and that thought drove him on and occupied his thoughts, even to the exclusion of his feelings for Mairead.

Yet there was a perplexity before him, a deep longing to return to Sutherland that ran counter-current to his desire to stay and work in Caithness. Herring fishing was not to his liking, overall, but would provide a steady income for months to come.

His lodgings in an Inn at Wick were near to Mairead's relatives and provided adequate food and ample whisky day upon day.

He looked out over the harbour and watched the small fishing boats bobbing on the restless sea, with the sound of washed shingle and rock-broken waves before him.

There was the one simple decision to be made - when to return...and what to say when he met Alasdair.

He took further comfort knowing that his brother rarely ventured to these parts, and that the chances of him hearing anything outside the area around his new township, were fairly remote.

Whether to tell him one day as to what had gone on…was another matter!

Robbie shrugged his shoulders and watched the lazy flight of the gulls, seemingly toying and teasing the waves to bring them down, to sweep them into the ebbing tide.

Like the majority of Highlanders he left unpalatable decisions to fathom their own solution, little bothered by the complexity of it all. So he relaxed and waited.

He dozed in the sun until a movement attracted his attention, and he sat up and smiled as he watched Mairead climb the sharply etched stone steps from the village. He acknowledged her with a wave and another cheerful smile.

'It is a lovely day,' (*Tha I breag,an diu*) she called.
'*Tha!*'

She laboured up the steps, pausing just before the top, the wind slightly dishevelling her auburn hair, her eyes bright with happiness.

'I did not think I would see you today, Mairead.'

'And why not, Master Robbie?' she replied in mock reprimanding tones.

'Because I was setting off to see the harbour master about finding a job at sea!'

'Had not you better be going then!'

'Aye, I should! But not before we spend a wee while together, for the view's fair fine here and the air is good and fresh. It livens the soul.'

'Does it now!' she laughed as she sprawled beside him on the grass. 'You'll no be for kissing me on this beautiful morning then?'

He laughed. 'I might at that, but it will take a second bidding for I haven't been asked to kiss someone for quite some time and I'm out of courage, one might say, and need some prompting in that manner....'

'Whist man, it's only been a day as you full well know, so dinna tease me Robbie Sutherland!' she said firmly and kissed him. 'That'll shut thy gabbling fur awhile.'

Robbie held her close and felt her soft hair against his cheek. 'How can I leave you Mairead when you are so much to me?'

She picked up the melancholy whisper and kissed him again. 'I will never leave you, Robbie. But then, by your words, it'll be you that'll be leaving me.'

He paused. 'I cannot tell!'

Mairead waited for him to continue and after a short while said. 'You canna tell what, Robbie?'

'Where to go and what to do!'

She picked up a small flower and rolled it round in her hand for a moment, as if to conjure up those emotions of their first evening together. She crushed the petals. 'You hav' always been o' one mind, unlike...' She hesitated.

'Unlike Alasdair?'

She threw down the distorted flower and watched it drift a few yards in the gentle breeze. 'Aye, unlike him!' She sighed. 'It's not that I did not love him at first, Robbie, nobody could have loved her man mair. But he was so short of spirit, or courage you may call it, that I began to loose interest, although I've never despised him as being weak, just acknowledged the fact that he's different in temperament from you and me!' She smiled and continued, 'Because...you always seem so set in your resolves to stop all the injustices and inequities that hav' fallen on our people.'

He looked into her face and smiled. 'I can tell you one thing, Mairead! I'm pleased in some ways that you've left Alasdair, for there would be no happiness or comfort in being together day after day with all that anger and discontentment. And you being with me has not soured the feelings sworn before God. Aye, I ken his manner, and although he sometimes appears weak and indecisive, he can be strong although it is often of a stubborn kind.'

'Are you pleased that we met here...in Caithness, Robbie?'

He took hold of her hand. 'I'm right pleased, Mairead. And you?'

'Right pleased too!

She took up another flower and held it still for a moment. 'So, you don't think I should go back to my husband, Robbie?' She talked almost abstractly as if directing the question to someone elese, yet still seeking confirmation for what had been said a moment before. She added with resignation, 'Even if it's too late.'

He studied the scene for a moment. A light breeze drifted in from the sea, and wandered disconsolately through the long grass that swayed in its freshness. The blood red poppies on the fringes shook off the bumblebees as if in annoyance, but their persistence paid off, and with a summer-hum they settled back to their labours. The gulls still criss-crossed the waves in their endless mission, crying in anguish to the boats whose triangles of white sail rose and fell with the eternal drift of the sea.

To Mairead it seemed that the reply would never come.

'By the laws o' the Church, you should! By the laws of decency also! But there's all manner of laws in this world...and some are made to be broken...at some time or another, I suppose. And it's difficult enough to find true happiness in this life and as I said, you cannot make him or yourself happy now. So do what your heart tells you, Mairead, for only you know what emotions lie locked and troubled within.'

The girl lay on her side and gazed across the cropped grass stretching in gentle undulations towards the hills, the green yellow-splashed with buttercups but it was the bright, delicately petalled poppies that arrested her attention and the breeze smelt salty and fresh. On the shore were a variety of fishing boats, some drawn high on the shingle for inspection, repair and recaulking. Others were half-built with men and their wives eagerly anticipating the day they would bring in the silver, squirming pyramids of herrings. If she inclined her head to one side the mountains were thrown into an indistinct backcloth to their lives, somewhat less grand, more insignificant in the haze of morning. Yet those mountains lay in Sutherland and for a brief moment Mairead felt homesick and a curious longing to return swept over her.

Robbie waited in silence.

Raucous were the birds overhead now, rooks, cliff jackdaws and gulls, a swirling mass. Voices rose from the harbour as a small crowd hurried down the hill to welcome two fishing boats to the harbour. The boats made not a sound to disturb that avian cacophony, the aroma of hundreds of dead and dying fish teased and tormented the birds to their sudden plunging and mischievous snatching of fish from the decks. The men beat their arms to ward them off, specks of men standing rigidly at the helm and stern, with sails strung taught and true in the sea wind and spray. There was an order and, in an instant, activity as the sails were trimmed and then lowered so that the boat, as if by choice and familiarity scuddered up the flat beach to rasp the shingle and reach safety from the grasping, restless waves

Robbie's thoughts became lost in the contemplation of a life at sea. Then, in an instant and without truly recognising why, he decided to abandon this scheme and journey south and home.

'What in the world has taken me such time, Mairead, to come to a conclusion.'

'What do you mean, Robbie?'

'I have an urge to return once more, to see my own folks! What d'you think?'

'I was just thinking about what used to be and the wedding...that seemed a new beginning, Robbie, but in some ways it was an end.'

'Of what?'

'Of the auld life, which I knew and wud have been so happy in!'

'Perhaps so, Mairead...but surely there is still so much happiness for us to find, as young as we are, surely be!' He gave a half smile and then paused to watch other fishing boats turn and drift in the harbour. Suddenly small figures sprang to life and the crew's calls were answered by the men on the jetty. Ropes were thrown, and curled in the wind before bouncing on the rough stones, while the shore men hurried forward to secure the ship.

'So are you going home or no, Robbie?'

He put his face against her cheek. 'I think I'd better go, just this one time. It's been a fair while since I left.'

It was her turn to press herself against him.

'I'll no be asking when you will be returning, Robbie.'

'I cannot tell you at present, but it will be soon.' His voice was confident and she smiled.

'Ah well! It is the will o'the Lord that my life be broken up in this way.'

'I have said before, Mairead, that such manner of awful events in the Highlands is no the Lord's way. It is the way of the Sassenachs, Lowlanders and infidels. There has been so much suffering in the year, and which of them have paid for it? None, as far as I know!'

He shrugged his shoulders and turned towards the girl.

She smiled and got up, dusting down her blue dress. 'Away with ye then, Robbie Sutherland, and the Almighty be with you.' She held his hand for a moment and gazed into his brown eyes. Reaching forward she smoothed the hair from his brow but the breeze pushed it back again. She laughed and departed.

Robbie lay on the grass and watched her descend the steps to the harbour.

She paused to speak to the fishermen, paused for the moment to shed a bitter tear, and then was gone

And Robbie Sutherland walked until the sun struck long, dark shadows as the man crossed the meadows towards the hills of home.

Seachd air fhichead (twenty seven)

The same hills cast a deep shadow into the long pasture of the township where Alasdair had been living on his own since his wife had travelled north.

The small loch occupied Alasdair's attention as a distraction from the speaker whose silhouette was in the depths of the peat-brown water. However, although the face was indistinct in the breeze-chopped water, the tall angular form and aquiline nose was so characteristic as to be the unmistakable form of Murdo McBain. He stood with arms folded as if in meditation and, when he spoke, his voice was almost the languid whisper of the pulpit.

Alasdair was surprised and apprehensive, even more disquieted by the man's eerily subdued approach.

Murdo spoke. 'So you have come to your senses at last.' The whisper raised its intonation emphasising the final word.

There was no response from Alasdair who surveyed Murdo with contempt.

'Tush man! We all recant our mistakes at some time or another. Now is your time! Would my own kin was here to hear it!' He smiled.

Alasdair nodded.

'I know full well that you're a man with property in the making, for you inherit your father's property, isn't that so?'

'Aye, I know that too!'

'An all you've done to besmirch the name of Factor Sellar in Court holds badly again you. You know that, too!'

Alasdair nodded once more.

'It would only take one word from me to turn this house to tinder and to take all the animals from this township, leaving you and what remains of your neighbours' properties with precious little, other than the clothes you walk in. For some it would be the second time, would it not? They would hate you for bringing such doom upon their heads yet again, I have little doubt.'

Murdo paced to and fro for a moment and the coarse whisper rose and fell as he turned and faced about. 'Precious little of your Sutherland holding would remain, probably none at all! And why would your wife return then, ask yourself man that simple question? She is in Wick, a town of many opportunities, men and women rich in accomplishments, far removed from this small strath!'

It was the degree of anger in Alasdair's eyes that took the factor by surprise for a moment.

'See, you like her still!'

'Aye, and what o'it?'

'Nothing man, nothing!' replied Murdo McBain hastily. 'So there is no choice in the matter! You tell me where your brother is to be found and we spare what's left of the township, your family and your wife.'

Alasdair still looked more at the shadow on the loch than into the speaker's face. ''Tis unnatural and agin the Lord's teaching to betray one's kin, is it not?'

Murdo turned and gave a brief smile. 'That you may say in most circumstances. But there are times when the choice is very stark. No shepherd likes to rest on the mountain when a blizzard is brewing hard and chill, but what are the consequences of him pushing on along the same route? He gambles with a catastrophe! A fall into an abyss, broken limbs, exposure, or a sudden death which would often be more merciful. Your choice has to be made, not just for yourself but for others...other members of your family will be betrayed, for the Laird is fair set on sheep grazing your father's pastures before the next spring.'

He waited for the man to look up.

'Hear what I say, man! Take heed! You're no good for anything without your land and neither is your father', McBain continued in a more kindly, coaxing tone, 'the Clearances will just go on and on, too many men of influence have their future vested in sheep, I warned everyone the first time I came to this glen, but who would listen.' He paused again. 'Sometimes I feel sorry for you all, there's so much ignorance; a resistance to change brought about through this ignorance and the adherence to old Highland ways. Surely you know that, you're a brighter man than most!'

'I hear full well, factor...and I heed full well. But what you ask me to do is nigh impossible.' Alasdair had listened impatiently to the long diatribe.

The factor sighed and began pacing to and fro again, stopping for a second or two to mutter to himself. 'You know where he lives...when he is about here and hiding in the hills. Some cave or shepherd's hut, no doubt! But you know, that I realise for a fact!'

The whisper stopped and the only sound was the soft lapping of the loch water against the rushy shore.

Murdo waited.

Then the voice hardened. 'It is known that he journey's home with insurrection on his mind. That much has come out of Caithness!'

Alasdair looked up in surprise. 'Caithness?'

'Aye, near Wick!'

Alasdair resumed looking at the water. Suddenly and instinctively he had an air of despondency about him.

'No relations up there to stay with, I suppose!'

'We have no relations there!' Alasdair paused. 'Mairead had fishing folk at Wick...'

'So has he taken a message to her on your behalf,' interjected the Factor.

Alasdair shook his head.

'So he has other friends there, has he?'

'I ken not!'

'Has he gone to see the girl then on his own free will?'

'I dinna know nor care!' The voice was tinged with anger and irritation.

Murdo dropped the whisper once more. 'You would care if that were the case, would ye not?'

There was another prolonged silence.

'I neither know nor care!' repeated Alasdair mechanically.

'If he was apprehended, and transported, it would take him away from bothering the girl, even if there's no romance between them. That would, in my honest opinion, be to your advantage, would it not?'

Alasdair had had enough. 'You have far to much to think on in recent weeks McBain, and when all the injustices are laid at your door…you'll have a good while to think about them rather than other people's private affairs. For if ever a man was certain to be hung, you're the man, I'll be bound.'

Murdo replied calmly. 'Listen man! You know where to find me. Think about what I've said and see sense. There is but one way out of the predicament. If you do not take it then your family and you are lost to the highlands. Your ancestors will have toiled and suffered in vain. And the brother, what does he care - cavorting about with someone else's wife. Bringing shame and disrepute to the family that fed him. Aye, think long and hard, man, long and hard!'

Alasdair clenched his fingers in anger so that the knuckles pained. 'There is no proof o'sich a thing! It is only said to annoy me!'

'I only say what crossed your mind a minute back when you heard where he was! But the seed is now sown and you will not settle until you set eyes on him and have it out. Anyway, I must tarry no longer.'

As he rode away Murdo made plans to finally erase the hamlet before the week was through.

*****

'How can I choose?'

Alasdair contemplated the complexities of the situation, his back hunched and hands clasped on either side of his face.

There was no inspiration in the lapping waters, no sense of guidance as he gazed at the bare mountain peaks. Only the eagle soared, black-dot against the blue and grey.

Footsteps approached and to his relief he saw it was Fearchar and Ian. The elder man had a brisk, heavy tread while the wiry neighbour kept up with a measured stride and a serious expression.

'Was that the factor?' Ian asked.

'Aye it was!'

'Factor McBain, the worst but one?' continued Ian.

Alasdair did not reply.

'What in heaven's name did he want with us?' Fearchar stopped and held up his hands in exasperation. 'There's little enough to be had on this sparse heath for even our beasts. God knows where the next meal will come frae!'

'He spoke ill,' said Alasdair rising from the rock on which he had been sitting since the factor left, 'and has snared me or my brother like a mountain hare in winter.'

'In what manner,' inquired Ian nervously, 'for I've got Mairi and the family to look after...'

'Hush! Let the man speak,' brusquely retorted Fearchar 'we've all got someone and something to hold precious.'

Alasdair did not want to proceed but after a moment's contemplation felt he must continue. 'I fear that they will destroy the township and all we have, unless...' He stopped short.

'Unless what man?' The elder man waved his hand impatiently.

'Unless...I tell them where my brother Robbie is!'

'What on earth has thy brother to do with us, Alasdair,' asked Ian.

'Oh! They say that he has supported insurrection and rebellion among the Highland folk and was sheep stealing from the Great Laird with the blacksmith MacIomhair, who has no been seen since.'

A solemn look came over Fearchar's face and the colour seemed to drain away from around the eyes, his greying beard emphasising the change. 'They'll hang him! No doubting that, if they can. Ye must stand firm!'

Ian's hands shook nervously, 'But they will throw us out of house and hame,' he said in desperation, 'I canna abide that...where will we go and what'll happen to the bairn.'

There was a long silence, the three facing each other, yet there seemed no close communication - only a slight hesitant reproach on all sides.

'For God's sake listen man,' said Fearchar looking at Ian, 'we can fight these men if need be. There's twa muskets in the loft and plenty o' shot.'

'Fight you say, ye old fool,' shouted Ian, 'we will be deed in minutes. I'll be no party t'this!'

'You'll be a party to whatever is decided, or I'll use the first shot on you, by the Lord I will!' responded Fearchar.

'What are we becoming?' said Alasdair holding the men apart. 'There is no use in such bickerin'. Give me time to think.'

He walked ahead of them for a few paces and then turned. 'I will set out to meet Robbie and tell him what ails us. Then on to the Factor to say that my brother is coming to see him, that will buy us mair time. For I know Robbie will have a plan to fool McBain, he's a cunning as a fox before a trap, when he likes!'

'What happens if he has no a plan?' asked Fearchar.

But Alasdair did not reply and walked on to his cottage, where he sat in a whisky-haze contemplation for hours on end.

*****

Ian scrambled through the heather and bracken, his thin frame taking great strides away from the sheep runs and paths.

It was late afternoon on the same day.

His dog was not with him.

He hurried on alone.

Down glen and up again, then down for three long miles, he strode barely looking up. The grouse and capercaillie cackled in flight before him. He waded through flocks of sheep that separated like the waters before Moses and then resumed their close-knit formation, nibbling the sparse grass to the roots and scratching up a fine cloud of dry earth. This earth spun in the air and settled onto the sparkling quartz rocks that had been free to the sun for aeons.

He turned from the path across the valley floor where the marshland was firm, and provided a welcome short cut towards the Factor's house. The dried out bulrushes, yellow and brown in the August heat, snapped beneath his measured tread.

Ian hurried up to the front door and knocked. The Great Laird's castle was just visible in the distance. The turrets bathed in the glow of afternoon sunshine. The sight of such a majestic building emphasised his feeling of doubt, and for a second he hesitated about knocking again. Then he rapped on the door a second time, not so impatiently, but more with respect.

Then he waited.

The door slowly opened and Factor Sellar stood framed in the archway, his shoulders bent, his expressionless eyes fixed on the man before him 'Who are you?'

'Ian, once from the township near Rogart and now from beyond Glen Loth.'

The Factor stared at him, 'I know you not! But have they not cleared that Glen? Anyway, what manner of business do you have with me and my wife?'

'Has Murdo McBain a house here?' (*Am bheil taigh aig Murdo McBain an-seo?*)

'Speak English man, I know but a little in Gaelic and don't want to know more. If you cannot...be on your way.'

Ian hesitated and stumbled out the words. 'I thought this was Factor McBain's dwelling!' he said, his voice quavering in an apologetic manner.

The Factor continued his long stare. 'Indeed! Supposing you did, what of it?'

'I have news fur Factor McBain!' Ian was beginning to get his breath back and felt slightly more composed.

'What news be that, laddie?'

'Of Robbie Sutherland, a man wanted by the law.'

The factor paused still blocking the doorway. He slowly rubbed his chin. 'I ken of that man, what more?'

'He stays in that small shepherd's hut close to Creagan Glas!'

'I see!' Sellar had enough wisdom to let the man hasten on in his anxiety.

'The one belonging to old Domhnall and Ealasaid!'

The Factor's face showed no expression but continued in his fixed, cold stare.

'You dinna believe me!'

'Aye, I do! But I was just thinking how do you know such information without being party to the man.'

Ian began to tremble slightly, realising the trap he had fallen into, and added hastily. 'I have never been party to the man...only his brother Alasdair.'

Sellar smiled slowly, 'We can check on that bye and bye, can we not?'

'It's the truth as God is my witness, Factor, believe me!'

'I do, I do believe you!' But he spoke with the half-smile still playing about his lips. 'Of course, it may cost you something!'

Ian hesitated once more. 'Cost me?'

'Aye, a few pounds, lad! For thy township has already been set down for burning...but a few pounds, can change the situation very quickly indeed.'

Ian looked at him in despair. 'I have no so much money, Factor Sellar, believe me!'

'Laddie, I believed you before, and I believe you now. But consider...his Lairdship has a flock or two that must graze up there...and if you all remain…it will put the great man out sorely...to loose money. A small payment to me will ensure a good word in his ear...and a guarantee for the future of you and your family.'

'But Factor...'

'No "ifs" nor "buts" between us! Twenty pounds...'

'Twenty pounds! Good God man, I've nought to my name, all I own would bring but a few pounds!'

The Factor smiled. 'Well then, there's little to be lost by burning the place, is there?'

Ian stood mute in his despair. 'I have tried to help you Factor, please help me!'

'You have helped me a great deal and what you have told me is most welcome and Godly. I will put in a good word with the Minister on Sunday for the righteous soul of thy family.' He gently patted the man on the back, whose very frame seemed to have visibly shrunk during the last few minutes of the conversation. Sellar continued, 'There is another way!'

Ian looked up. 'What's that?'

'If you bring me part of the money tomorrow and the rest within three months then all will be right with you.'

The frightened eyes still focused on the cold, expressionless face. 'What about the others, Factor? Must they pay too or can we split the twenty pounds between us?'

The Factor stroked his beard. 'For the three families it would cost you thirty pounds plus the man Robbie. Without him, let me see... it would be twenty apiece.'

'You drive a hard bargain, Mr Sellar!'

'No, not me! 'Tis the Laird that determines the price of land! I'm only here to collect...with a little due for myself, you might say, for the inconvenience and worry.'

With a hopeless shrug of despair Ian turned from the door. For a moment he hesitated, had a strong desire to turn round and begin the conversation again, but when he looked up the Factor had gone.

The journey back was in a slow, almost funereal, tread as Ian tried to figure out what to tell the other members of the township. How could he explain his meeting with the Factor, and he chewed over the facts to distraction - how he had managed to obtain such information about the impending payments and the capture of Alasdair's brother.

Ochd air fhichead (twenty eight)

As Robbie Sutherland hastened down the steep, rocky hillside onto the soft grassy areas, he adopted a more cautious manner.

Lying down in the long bracken he waited as patiently as a wild cat approaches its prey, content to be still and watch. Patience, slow stalking, more patience…only the supreme hunters knew the value of sitting still, straining every sense, every sinew.

In such an immobile pose he waited for twenty minutes before starting up once more. He listened; crossed a deep, swift running burn that soaked his shoes and the bottom few inches of his trousers and waited for a few minutes more. He had removed the plaid scarf from around his shoulders despite the evening air growing chill with the open sky. The tartan was too obvious against the vegetation, a marker for any bullet.

Across the burn he hurried; then up the short hillside opposite until a small spinney of pines and birch was reached. In their shaded security he settled down cat-like and watched, scanning the hillside for any movement. The valley was as clear as a crystal, the peat earth soft. So soft that he idly scratched his name on it with a twig as he lay and waited.

A red deer came and went on the horizon and the odd buzzard wheeled and swooped. The air was still, apart from the sound of the rushing water and the plaintiff pipits' calls from the stones amongst the heather. Sometimes the spray from the burn would drift his way on a small breeze, which had suddenly sprung up and, gathering courage, spun towards him as a miniature storm. The setting sun swept long golden fingers across the horizon, sinking yet deeper still with each moment and awakening the calls of night, one by one.

Still he lay as if expecting someone, yet he knew none would come; and if they did, it would be unwelcome.

For in the cover of the shadow in the next glen stood the small mountain hut of Domhnall, his point of refuge.

But Robbie's stealth was born of a Highland instinct, and still he watched and waited.

How long he would have sat there is difficult to know, but his patience was rewarded by a figure moving cautiously towards the far side of the building, the main part of his body concealed by a small mound of grass and some large rocky outcrops.

Robbie slipped forward, almost in a crouching run and, using the burn bottom, picked his way noiselessly towards the nearside of the hut, concealed by the narrow gorge.

On reaching a cleft in the overhang, he slid quietly behind a large rock and lay and waited.

During his approach the other figure had slipped into the hut unseen. But Robbie heard the door creak open and then close with a faint click, which easily carried to his heightened sense.

Pulling his dirk, he crept to the hut. Crouching, he stood on one side of the door, beneath the small cleft in the stonework that served as a window.

The vigil had begun.

The sun slipped behind the far peaks and the mountains coloured purple and reds.

A few birds winged in from the fells heading down the valley. The pipits' calls grew less and less frequent.

Robbie's muscles strained in the crouching position and his thighs ached. He listened intently but not a sound was heard. After what seemed like an hour, with the Highland summer light still brightening the night sky, he cautiously decided to look in. But, just as he was about to stand up, the door began to slowly open.

Robbie resumed his crouch, the muscle even more tensely coiled than before.

A figure stepped out and looked to the left.

Instantly Robbie leapt and clasped the thin figure around the throat pinning the neck against the wall with the point of the dirk. Blood trickled from a small vein that he inadvertently cut, onto to his clenched hand.

'Who are you?'

The wiry figure trembled, 'Ian from the settlement in the shadow o'Beinn Dhorain near Glen Loth! I ken thy brother Alasdair well!'

'What brings you here?' Robbie's voice was uncompromising and suspicious.

'To warn you, Robbie, and that's the truth!'

'Are you armed?'

'What me man, I've niver taken up arms in my life!'

Robbie relaxed his grip. 'Here's a cloth to wipe your neck. What ails you?'

Ian wiped his neck and held the small rag against the bleeding vein for a minute until it stopped. 'The Factor...Factor Sellar...kens y're coming here.'

'How knows he? For there's not one Highland man who would betray Robbie Sutherland...about here!'

Ian stood silently his back against the wall.' There is!'

'Who?'

'I told him!'

'You!'

'Aye, me! To save my family and Alasdair and others in the township! But it's to no avail. They'll burn us whether we help or not! That's one lesson I've learned!' Ian's voice shook with despair.

Robbie sighed. 'You're an honest man, Ian, and who can blame you! Still there must be a way out of this mess. Just give me time to think!'

*****

Robbie thought that it felt like home and the idea made him laugh. He perched high on the main beam and looked across the broad floor that stretched halfway across the stable.

He knew this was the biggest risk he had taken so far, but recognised deep down that it was the only way to save the township.

He had to play a strong hand against the Factors Sellar and McBain.

He also knew that to appeal to the Marquess was useless and to attack, kill or ransom any of the people involved would simply lead to further bloodshed from the troops that would inevitably be called in.

He needed to be in control of his exploits but not be controlled by circumstances.

Yet there was this one way he might succeed and it was worth the gamble and the wait.

As he sat on the beam Robbie thought, 'So, I have been here before but without the recent hatred against me. Now, I suppose, I risk hanging or transportation while the last time I only risked transportation or hanging. How times change!'

He laughed and dangled his legs above the empty stable.

Then he pulled himself up at the sudden approach of feet. The sounds were heavy and masculine.

This was the last thing he wanted, an intrusion.

The stable door creaked open and the groom's voice, humming cheerfully, drifted in.

Robbie watched in mute suspense.

The man did not enter.

A woman's voice called.

He breathed a sigh of relief but still pressed himself against the oak beam.

The groom turned and retraced his steps into the yard.

He could make out two voices, but they were indistinct and somewhat incomprehensible in the swiftness of the English words.

'Would they both come?' Robbie asked himself, 'or would it be the girl as before?'

The question was answered in a moment as Catriona rushed in and stopped in amazement.

Before she could utter a sound Robbie had leapt to the floor with such force that a pain shot up his legs. Collecting himself he quickly called, 'Do not scream, it is only me again!'

Seeing the look of terror change to anger he hastily added, 'The animal's fine!'

The girl rushed to the empty stall. 'Where is it? What have you done with it this time?' Aiming a swift blow with the riding whip she caught him across the neck and produced a red weal. However, before she could strike again Robbie caught hold of the whip and wrenched it out of her hand.

'*Uill*! We'll have no mair o'that! It would be better if you had some manners (*Bhiodha e fada na b'fhearrr*),' he said resorting to his native tongue for a moment, 'No more of that, so I'm telling you!'

Catriona looked defiantly at him and turned towards the half-open door.

Robbie raced forward and barred her way.

'Let me through! Or it will be the worse for you!'

'If I let you through it will certainly be the worst for me!'

She paused in her anger. 'What do you want?'

'I know that the last time I took the horse, it was a poor joke. This time I've left it at the cottage with my friend and he has it safe again and in good wind. It will always be safe, believe me!'

She did not reply but made for the door once more.

'I have told you before of the miseries in the Highlands. Starvation, disease, and death...all at the hands of thy kin folk or their servants. Two thousand people, save three, have been driven from their homes in the strath of Kildonan, uprooted, aye, and burnt out - so I hear! An old widow, whose husband fought in the war (*peninsular) pleaded to have her cottage and cow spared, but they told her to get out and she did - dragging outside, as best she could, her bed, stool and all her meagre possessions. But the wind blew the flames back on them and despite her efforts her only possessions were destroyed. And that's but part of it! This time it is my kinfolk who will suffer. For the Factors plan to burn the township of my brother and his friends and there is nothing they can do to persuade these men to leave well alone. Both Sellar and McBain have spoken. They have even tried bartering for one prize they seem to wish above others at present...me.'

The girl's subdued expression turned to one of surprise.

'Aye me! Would you believe it!' He laughed. 'But the rest's no joking matter!'

'So I have a little suggestion to make!'

'And what is that?' She spoke firmly now and looked him full in the face.

'You tell the Factors and their men that if they do not touch our dwellings and our animals...the horse is safe!'

'And if I do not!'

Robbie paused. 'It is not in your nature to betray anyone, including me, but especially the horse...an animal that has put its trust in you!'

She still looked angry and flushed. 'If I give you my word...how can you trust it?'

'I have just answered that question! But your words must also be your uncle's! If not, there is no bargain!'

Catriona took a deep breath. 'It may come as a surprise to someone as uneducated as yourself, but there are people of honour...'

'Even English?'

'Yes, even Englishmen and women. And I am not blind, nor deaf as I travel about this area? But the changes are meant to be for the better...even if it takes time and some readjustment means suffering!'

Robbie listened carefully. 'The meaning is clear although your words are sometimes too hard for me to fully understand. On my honour, and on those who have the animal, no harm will befall it if the township is spared. And my friend will bring it back again when the moon's quarter returns!'

'But what if the Factors change their minds when the horse is brought back?' This time she spoke earnestly and with sympathy for the man's plight.

'We will have to risk that for the time we've bought. And we will have shown that some of us have a will to resist which can only get stronger as time goes on. These men know their Highland rights and they will fight for them! And they know that I am willing to risk my life in coming here. Anyway,' he gave a brief laugh, 'I could always take the horse again, one, two, or three times or more- it's easy and matters naught to me! That's if you don't care? It would be nice meeting you in this way!'

'So you think!' She smiled at his effrontery.

'I have given it much thought, and I do. In fact, even when wandering the moors and glens, you have followed me, I'll confess to that…which is more than a highland man usually admits to woman, even as beautiful as yourself,' he said honestly.

She scrutinised his features for a moment, but did not reply.

Robbie waited and then felt obliged to continue. 'Aye, it would be something good to walk with you through the Glens…that it would.'

Catriona felt a curious warmth towards the simple expression of devotion, and almost reached out. Collecting herself, she replied, 'Perhaps it might be nice!' laughed and then lapsed into silence.

Robbie could comprehend her beauty, but her restrained emotions were completely alien to his world, and the girls he had known. He tried to fathom out her emotions, but after a few moments, smiled to himself. At least he was making some progress! There was no out and out rejection. Yet he wished she was as direct in her approach as Mairead and Fhiona. Perhaps it was the English way? He smiled again, said firmly 'Goodbye' and departed.

*****

The slight woman, in her thirties, and pretty in her own way, prim in dress and tidy in manner, bent low over the kettle, adjusted its position over the largest flames, straightened up and listened to the footsteps that approached the front door.

Curious as to who was approaching, she hurried to the window and looked out.

The young man was just visible through the rain-spattered window. She puzzled as to his identity and, having straightened her apron, walked to the door.

Standing, with his brown hair wet and waving with the morning rain was Robbie.

The woman stood in the open doorway waiting for him to speak. The man smiled. ' *Hallo!'Smise Robbie Sutherland!'*

The women looked surprised at being addressed in Gaelic. But she had enough command of the language to reply, 'Come in *Robbie, Ciamar a tha thusa*?'

'*Tha gu doigheil!*' (Fine!)

'What brings a body here on such a morning as this?' she spoke in precise English to emphasise her superiority, 'but sit down before the fire and warm yourself, Robbie.'

'Thank you, Mrs Sellar!'

'Have you eaten, for there's a rasher or two of bacon in the pan and my husband not yet returned from his morning's work.'

Robbie laughed. 'He may be some time yet, Mrs Sellar!'

The woman laughed and placed the flat pan on the fire, moving the kettle to one side. She turned the bacon with a regular rhythm using a long fork, filling the room with a delicious smell. Little was said during this interval.

'So you're Robbie Sutherland, son of Ross. I knew your Grandmother, Robbie. We worked together in Dornoch, in service in the Manse. I was younger than your mother, but your grandmother helped me whenever I did anything wrong...and saved me many a scolding. Then she moved away to the West Coast and I never heard from them again. Still it's good to know what you look like. You've your mother's shaped face and smile, there's no doubting that!' She laughed and went on turning the bacon.

'It's nice to know you too, Mrs Sellar, after all you've just said. My mother's still in good health and I'll tell her about this meeting.'

'Aye! Do that, Robbie! And your grandmother?'

'She died a few years back, so did Grandfather!'

'Well, I'm sorry to hear that! How are things with you?'

'Oh! Good in some ways and not in others!'

The woman forked the rashers out of the pan, letting the fat drip back, and laid them on a broad slice of bread. The aroma drifted the young man's way.

She handed him the plate. 'So I believe! That's why I sent for you. How Catriona knows about you I do not understand!'

Robbie ignored the question. 'Factor Sellar has spoken of me then?'

'Aye, of that there is no doubt!'

'Not good then!'

'Oh! I do not always listen to what is said! I have relatives all over the Highlands and have known hunger and suffering myself. So what I hear must be true! But being the factor's wife, and him not the most liked of men, keeps me from most of my old friends...more's the shame of it!'

Robbie ate and listened. 'You know what is happening then?' he said quietly, almost to himself. 'Her Ladyship has sent potatoes, meal and all that to some places. But the people walk many a long mile to be turned back with barely enough for a week's feed, and some go searching about for days to find a minister who'll give a certificate of relief. Walking a hundred miles and more in the hope of a few scraps of food! While the townships they've been given in the north near Ben Loyal are on poor land and far, far from their auld homes!'

'But there's little we can do about it, Robbie. Believe me! My husband has his orders and His Lord and Ladyship are firm in their opinions and ways. He dare not disobey them!'

'Not even on the odd occasion...under special circumstances?'

'No! Not even then! Is the bacon good?'

'Aye, real good, thank you! It was short of me in my manners not to say so, but I was taken up with the problems in hand.'

'Well, that's a blessing...the bacon's good,' she replied smiling, 'for your grandmother was always a stickler for the best!'

'Was she now?'

'Aye, she was! But to get back to the present! You say you know where the Factor is? That surprises me, for he generally keeps his routine secret, sometimes from me.'

Robbie laughed. 'I think at a guess I do, Mrs Sellar. In my way of reasoning he'll be at the shepherd's hut, lying in wait! I thought he would not be looking for me here! But did you no take a risk in having me in?'

The woman sighed. 'Not at all! From what I know of you I thought you would have some part of your grandmother in you, and, if I'm not mistaken, would be a young man of some spirit. Whether you have done right or wrong is of no consequence to me. But beware of the forces against you Robbie, that's all I can say!'

'I thank you for the warning Mrs Sellar, I do indeed!'

There was a brief pause.

Then the woman spoke. 'I can have a word with my husband, Robbie, he's not too proud or stubborn to listen to me. But you must not come back to the county, or if you do, do not be seen! For if the horse you have taken is returned within days, I'm sure that the search will be called off.'

'But that's not the real problem, Mrs Sellar. What about my brother's township and the beasts? They must be guaranteed safety and allowed to get on with their lives as best they can. If that's the understanding, I'll take the horse back by evening, that much is certain.'

'To whom, may I ask!'

Robbie was just about to say Catriona, his recent accomplice in all this subterfuge, when he corrected himself, 'To any of them!'

'And where will that be, and how will they know who will expect it?'

'They will know in time.' He replied unconcernedly.

She shook her head, Robbie thought her neat, black hair made her face beautiful as she did this involuntary movement, but good manners forbade him from commenting. 'Why did you do it then?' she asked with another smile clearing up part of the table and exposing a neat tablecloth, which Robbie had looked at with great interest while he ate and spoke.

'The horse will decoy the men to the hill-hut while I be about my business with you, Mrs Sellar!' he replied earnestly.

'With me! By the Lord! It would be better to wait until my husband is away on business, would it not?'

'Aye...it would! But that might have been in some time, and there's not so much of that around!'

They both laughed and the woman smoothed her apron. 'You're so like Grandmother, Robbie, full of life and a good-looking face to boot, God rest her soul! But to get back to what I was saying! I know that His Lordship has asked for only a partial clearance in some areas, at the request of the Marchioness, Countess of Sutherland.'

Robbie smiled. 'Is that so?'

'Yes!'

'I thought there must be some good in the Countess, her being of Highland blood!'

'Yes...there is! And they are both in London where they truly belong, and it will be some while until they return to the highlands...probably to the end of the year...if other precedents are followed.'

She thought for a moment. 'There's no reason for them to know that the township is not burned, but it would soften my husband's heart and make him forget what to do, if you could provide a few pounds for him and McBain.' Here the woman's face assumed a more fixed expression.

'McBain will abide by the agreement too?'

'Yes, he's somewhat afraid of my husband, but eager for money, he's the man behind the scheme!'

Robbie considered the situation. 'I will get word to my father, for twenty pounds and the same from Alasdair. But no more! For any more will surely render my parents paupers in time, for new fodder must be bought after the bad harvests of the last two years.'

'Twenty pounds for each factor, to be delivered here within the month, will be enough! I'll see to that, Robbie Sutherland!'

'Aye, I trust you, Mrs Sellar! My grandmother seems to speak to me now, and she tells me to have great faith in you! I know you'll keep your word!'

The young man stood up and placed the plate on a small table. 'I cannot thank you enough. There's no much more I can say...other than a man called Ian will bring the money as soon as it can be arranged. He will deliver it to this house, and the horse will be taken back early tomorrow. That I promise! So your husband can rest easy tonight!'

With a gentle bow Robbie turned to the door and prepared to leave his home, county and family - for many years, if not forever.

*****

Robbie set off the next morning at first light.

The black clouds of the day before had been shredded and then compressed into black smudges on the eastern horizon by a west wind that had sprung up overnight.

He gazed at the glens and lochs so familiar since his youth, then determined to travel by the coastal, flatter way. Thus he made his way along a narrow path, through broom and gorse, towards the sea taking as his guide the ancient Pictish tower of Kintradwell Broch, just visible in the distance.

Satisfied that he had accomplished his mission and realising it was more by good luck, in being helped by Catriona and the factor's wife, than by good judgement, he travelled with a jaunty step and a light heart. After all, his brother's home and the township had been saved from burning.

He was sanguine enough to realise that he had to stay out of Sutherlandshire, at least until the current situation settled down, or the Laird or his factors forgave him. He was saddened to leave his parents, but had sent a message to them with Ian. However, he was curiously ambivalent in his emotions towards Alasdair, not really caring about the parting, one way or another.

Yet there was one other person he would have liked to have seen...Catriona!

This curious longing puzzled him, for at times he felt detached from her, at others deeply involved. It was a curious amalgam of emotions. He also acknowledged that she had been party to his schemes, at no inconsiderable risk to herself.

He felt a curious kinship, a degree of love. But he reasoned that detouring southwards to see her was out of the question.

The mid-August day was intermittently warm and chill as the clouds passed rapidly overhead.

The noon stop was a half an hour's rest on the cliffs. Seeing the small fishing boats reminded him of sitting with Mairead a few days before and his closeness to her.

Once again he realised that not being with her seemed to diminish his love. It was an undeniable fact! As if her personality bolstered their closeness! But when apart, the spectre of his brother rose to reprimand him.

It was a curious feeling and, on balance, one that he did not like. Thus subconsciously he blamed the girl.

On he wandered keeping close to the shore.

There was the odd peel of thunder about four, but few sounds other than the gull's cries.

The path petered out at times and he had to turn inland past briars and nettles and gorse.

Still, he enjoyed the thrill of walking and feeling the fresh west wind on his arms and face.

Onward he walked towards Caithness, a double day's journey at his easy pace.

By six-thirty the sky had completely cleared and the wind dropped. The falling sun cast a long shadow eastwards towards the sea. Robbie watched the sun slowly descending. He felt hungry but not tired and settled down on the cliff top close to an old cottage. He surveyed the building for a while. Then he knocked on the door and waited.

Presently an old man shuffled to the window and inquired *'Hallo!'*

'It's a lovely day now,'(*Tha ibreagha, an-drasda*) Robbie rejoined

'It is indeed!' (*Tha gu dearbh*)

'Have you a drop of fresh water I could have?' Robbie sang out politely.

'There be no trouble with that! Would you be wanting anything else now?'

'Thank you, nothing! Only water! For it's a tiring walk despite the coolness of the day!'

Aye, it is that! Where are you heading man?'(*Cait' a bheil sibh a' dol?*)'

'To Wick!'(*Tha mi a' dol a Wick*)

The man called from the small kitchen. 'I ken it well! It's pretty (*Tha e snog!*) I hav' taken many a fishin' boat in the harbour mair times than I ca' tell!'

'Is that so!'

'Aye, that's so!'

'I could do with a boat now and a fair wind,' replied Robbie accepting the tin mug and draining its contents.

'Come you in man and rest y' legs fur a wee while!'

'That would be right welcome!' Robbie replied cheerfully.

'Are you married? Have you a family?'(*A bheil thu posda...a bheil ag teaghlach agaibh?*)

Robbie laughed. 'You're one for the questions, are you not? But it's no to being married and no to having children...I hope! (*tha mi 'n dochas!*). And that's as truthful an answer as there ever will be!'

Together they laughed and the old man shook his head and grimaced to acknowledge the joke.

'What are you called?' (*De 'n t-ainm a tha ort?*), the man asked after appreciating the joke with a further nodding of the head.

'Robbie Sutherland!'

'A fine Highland name, one to be proud of!'

They both settled on stools, one on each side of the window. The sun broke through with long beams and illuminated their faces, while giving a soft radiance to the cramped room.

'So you be going to Wick, eh! It's a fair journey but a pleasant one if the weather be right!'

'The signs are good for the morrow if the wind keeps from the south west as it seems to be blowing now,' replied Robbie sanguinely.

'That is true at this time of year! Have you family up there?'

'*Chan eil* (No)! My kinfolk are here but I have to travel to seek work, the factors in our area no being in favour with me, and they're none to my liking either,' replied Robbie.

'My eyes are dimmer now but I dinna like what I hav' seen. There is no place for all the grazing animals in the glens, although I'm o' fishing folk mysel'.'

They sat in silence for a while, the young man enjoying the rest and the warmth of the setting sun on his face; the old man contemplating with closed eyes, his lined face etched by the golden rays.

Suddenly he spoke. 'If ye ever need to sail from Wick, remember the name Angus MacLean.'

Robbie smiled. 'Angus MacLean, and where would I find him?'

'Anywhere and everywhere! For his brig sails the oceans far and wide, but he puts into Wick whenever he can!'

'Who should I say told me, then?'

'Say his brother. There's only one left now! And I'm near twenty years older, and still going strong.'

Robbie laughed.

Another half an hour went by before he left. They largely sat in silence, each contemplating their lives, Robbie's concentrated on the future, but the old man was content with the past, comforted by what had gone before, entertained in his own mind by the many embellishments he made with each recollections.

When it was time to go Robbie thanked him and shook hands.

The old man watched him depart and went back to reflecting on life and loves as the sun's rays sunk lower and lower.

By now Robbie had decided to sleep on the shore, using an area of soft, dry sand in the shelter of a cave, away from the possible incursions of the west wind.

Finding a way down the cliff side he finally slid and stumbled onto a beach of white sand with a soft, crystalline texture.

So fine was the sand that his footsteps disappeared almost as soon as he left them. Robbie laughed as he looked back on his invisible way.

Here the sea had become an emerald green with the shallow inlets a vivid blue.

And the water was almost devoid of waves.

Beside the paradise the young man walked for a mile or so before finding a small cave, which smelled fresh and was devoid of sea debris.

Assured of a comfortable, dry night Robbie quickly threw off his clothes and ran down to the sea.

No part of the northern sea is ever more than icy cold and this area was no exception. However, the still water soothed his aching body and as he lay looking at the sky he felt a tranquillity he had not experienced for many months.

Robbie had never been one to contemplate the future and his mind soon became blank in a period of sublime rest.

A snort of water, then another, made him turn.

He knew the sound well. Two grey seals wallowed in front of him for a moment, watching with bobbing rounded heads. Then in a cascade of spray and ripple, they dived and were gone.

Seeing that the sky was beginning to darken and a mist was drifting towards the shore, he hurried back to the cave and dried himself with his shirt. Then he hung it on a rock at the entrance of the cave. Putting on his thick jumper, which he had worn round his waist in the warmth of the day's journey, and then the rest of his clothes Robbie settled down for the night, content in the silence. He had just reflected on life, drowsed for half and hour or so and pulled his coat over his chest for added warmth, when he heard a muffled cry.

He sat up and strained his ears.

At first he thought it must be a gull's cry or the strange call from a seal.

Then it started once more, strangely subdued but echoing amongst the cliffs.

Anxious to find out what was happening, he threw the coat onto the sand and pulled on his shoes. He hurried outside and paused.

The mist had crept inland and the tide was flowing quickly over the shingle and sand. The lapping sound was all he could hear.

Then another faint cry!

It seemed to come from the small bay just around the promontory. Running as quickly as he could in the darkening conditions Robbie clambered over the low lying rocks, now filling with water.

He called out.

There was no reply.

Another call.

And this time a faint reply.

He made his way along the shoreline, through the thick kelp that strung inlands on the shallowing tide.

There sitting and sobbing on the sand just above the water's edge was a girl of about his own age.

Robbie raced up and knelt beside her. 'What's wrong!'

'It's my shoulder, it's all crooked and in pain!'

He touched the right shoulder and the girl winced. 'Here, let me lift you to your feet,' he said softly, 'and I'll get you home.'

As he raised the girl her foot caught on a long strand of kelp, tangling it around her ankle. In a moment she had fallen to the ground, letting out a scream as she did so.

'By the Lord, what is it?' cried Robbie in alarm.

'It's my shoulder!' there was a pause as the girl felt the injured part. 'The pain's gone! It's a miracle! And I can move it again! But it's a fair bit sore!'

'It's cured itself, whatever it was,' exclaimed the man. 'Here, take my arm...but this mist is dark and unholy. I cannot find a way up the cliffs tonight. Still,' he continued helping the girl towards the rocks, 'I've a fine, dry place for the night, if you don't mind sharing the same soft sand and coat.'

'Och! That's nothing,' she replied. 'After all you've done!'

*****

Once in the relative warmth of the cave, Robbie waited outside as the girl dried herself with his damp shirt.

'You can have my coat if you wish,' he called.

'That would be a fine thing!' she shouted back. 'Then I could hang my dress to dry overnight, that's if the mist doesn't sprawl into the cave with its dampness.'

'Well, that's settled then!'

The girl shouted back, 'You can come in now!'

Robbie wandered in quite unabashed.

The young girl was pulling on the coat, her body rounded, heavy breasted and largely exposed. Glancing his way, she quickly fastened the garment and sat down, her legs bare, his long coat was wrapped round her thigh just above the knees. For the first time he noticed her dark eyes and short black hair, framing a broad face with high-cheek bones more Spanish than Scottish.

'How came ye here?' she asked.

He settled down beside her. 'I'm returning north along the coast and had decided to rest for the night out of the breeze. How came you?'

'I was looking for crabs and the like to feed my parents and their kin. For there's no potatoes or oats where we come from and no peat to burn; 'tis the sea that gives up the shellfish and all!'

'Well, you should tak care of the tide for it has taken many an honest soul out to sea, in the past. Are you of fishing stock...I'm sorry...I haven't asked you your name?'

'Sine!'
'Sine!'
'Aye!'

"'S mise Robbie Sutherland! Co as a tha sibh fhein? (Where are you from?)'

'You have heard of Rogart?'

'Aye, I know it well! Don't tell me you were driven out o'there!'

'We were!'

'Then where did you go!'

'Eventually, after terrible hardships and events, to a small fishing village about a couple of miles from here! A place my parents were given. And what land! So poor! Narrow strips on the coast, so thin that the seed is blown into the sea, and if it springs up - the shoots are washed by a bog as the land takes up the winter rains and spray. We pay our dues with aught we hav'...brooches, rings and simple utensils that hav' been passed down from our ancestors. But we're no welcome. The Factor's right-hand man follows me...'she paused, 'even today!'

'What do you mean today?'

'He was here tonight! He was the man who threw me down as he has done before. But tonight it was mair violent! Each time it's mair violent...I think one day he means to kill me!'

'What manner of saying is that, Sine?'

'It's true...Robbie!'

'How came ye to know this man?'

'He was our neighbour near Rogart.'

'You know Alasdair Sutherland there?'

'You have kinship with Alasdair and Mairead, my friends.'

'I have truly, for he is my brother,' continued the troubled Robbie.

'Think no ill of thy kin for they were the best and truest of neighbours. But the same cannot be said o' Eanraig! How that man's gone bad!'

'I hardly know the man, for I have rarely visited my brother since he settled there after the wedding, and have not visited him at all in his new township since the first few days - when I gave him a bit of a helping hand. But the man you speak of is a tall body with long fairishbrown hair if I recollect rightly from the one time I saw him...and a confident manner.'

'That's him right enough,' said the girl leaning against him for warmth. 'Is not the night growing cold Robbie?'

'That's true enough! But you can keep resting yourself again me for warmth and I'll no be complaining. What else is there to tell!'

'You've heard aboot the shooting o' my husband and the rest?' Here the girl faltered.

'I heard about if from a friend,' Robbie replied. 'And I didn't ken it was you. It's a sorry tale!' he said in a solemn voice. 'You have suffered much Sine, what more can a man say to ease the pain, but I'm very sorry indeed.' He went silent for a moment.

She took hold of his hand. 'Well, nothing can bring back the past! And, do you know, I hav' put all behind me. I thought at first the pain and the grief would never end, but suddenly like the fever it vanished, I ken no how or why. I just feel I must find a new life and press on!'

Robbie nodded once more. 'You're young enough and pretty enough, Sine. The Lord will have someone for you, I have no doubt, if that's any consolation.'

'You think so? It seems just a short time ago that my life had ended before it began, as if everything was in reverse of the normal.'

Robbie put his arm round her shoulders. 'Tell me more about that man Eanraig, if you so wish...but I don't want to upset you in any way, and that's the truth!'

'It doesna upset me really. At first I thought he was only trying to help fur I was on my own. But his attentions became mair frequent and persistent until I could stand it no longer. I ken he was after our share of the township, Uisdean having no close kin. But I didn't want to upset his wife, Anna, who had been so caring in my grief.'

Robbie sighed. 'It's a difficult situation to be in. You were best to leave.'

'Aye, there was little choice. I couldn't have worked the land. I thought it best to leave. And yet he managed to follow me here. For he knew I wud be staying with my parents until I decided what to do. And if he is passing this way to his cousin's he teks a great delight in telling me to give up the land we were given, so he can hav' it for himself. He's a powerful man, for he's sided with the factors and informs on the poor folk whenever he can.'

'Is he about the shore now?'

'*Chan eil!* He's gone off to stay with his cousin and drive some sheep...aye sheep - that surprises you - to a market. He no so fickle as he should be!'

'Each man to his trough, Sine! But come with me...bring your family to Wick, fur the fishing's good there and out of the jurisdiction of the Great Laird.'

'I would if I could! And we have relations in Caithness. But my mother and father are crippled with the rheumatism, and we hav' no money to hire a cart.'

'Lord have Mercy! If that's all that troubles you, there will be a cart at your front door before the week is through.'

'There will?'

But he did not reply for a moment. Then he said, 'If the night gets any colder... there is no objection to you moving closer.'

'Is that so!' she laughed.

'Aye, that's so!'

'To my way o'thinking it is colder...now you mention it!'

She fell asleep, her shoulder still throbbing with the recent injury, and Robbie sat for some time, watching her and thinking on the vicissitudes of life in general.

Naoi air fhichead (twenty nine)

To Robbie it was more of the same but with a different motive and a different horse.

Furtively he enquired from a local store the whereabouts of the farm where Eanraig and his cousin were staying, and by the first light of dawn he had scaled the stable door.

The black gelding, heavy about the withers and legs, was not the finest horse he had seen, nor was the cart the best, indeed one wheel turned and groaned under the impediment of a noticeable buckle. Still it was a make-do-and-mend situation, a turn of circumstances that pleased him very much.

After the night in the cave he had spent a relaxing twenty-four hours with Sine in her parents' home.

He had never felt so warm and clean and comfortable for many a month, while the oatcakes were almost as good as his mother's.

He had slipped out of the house before the others were awake, although the old man who had tossed and snored prodigiously for most of the night had suddenly become subdued as Robbie was preparing to leave.

He sat quietly for a few minutes.

Perhaps he had disturbed her father after all. Then the bellowing and whistling had begun once more, and Robbie prepared to go.

Still his mission was for a good purpose this time, although taking the grey horse on the second occasion had also been for a good purpose too, he reasoned, with a smile.

How Catriona would laugh if she saw him now! Leading the gelding up a rutted lane with the wheels bumping and rattling as if to waken the dead.

It was a good thing that the two younger men were still asleep bound up in their dreams with sheep. For Eanraig and his cousin would have something severe to say when they awoke.

'After all no one likes to loose such fine possessions,' mused Robbie to himself with a smile, 'although I could do without the animal if there was an alternative.'

In such a light-hearted manner did he deliver the cart and horse to Sine and her parents.

And in an equally light-hearted way did he help the rheumaticky couple load up the cart with their meagre possessions.

'We canna thank you enough, Robbie,' said the old man hobbling forward to shake hands.

'*Tapadh leibh!* (Thanks!) Now you can be on your way to Caithness and out of reach of the Factor's whims.'

'Aye...we can that!' rejoined the wife. 'Will you be travelling with us and Sine?'

'I think not,' replied Robbie politely still gazing at the horse, 'I must press on by the coastal route but I will see you at your cousins in the cottage by Pulteney harbour, will I not?'

'Aye, y'will that!' said the father as Sine came out of doors with some fisherman's hemp to secure the belongings.

'Are ye departing now, Robbie Sutherland for Wick...(*A bheil sibhse a'dol a Wick*) she inquired, 'or waiting for us there?'

'I can't wait long in Wick, Sine,' he replied thinking of Mairead. But saying that, I can wait at Lybster for you to arrive.'

She walked up to the cart and stood close to him, motioning her parents aside. 'You will want to see me again, won't ye Robbie.' Her voice was a whisper but the slight pleading it conveyed was not lost.

'What makes you think otherwise?' he asked with a laugh.

'Oh! I have just a feeling that when I get there...someone else will be there!'

'Why do you think that?'

'Intuition!'

'Is that all! I thought there must be something more.'

'Is there anything mair?' she whispered. But in his hesitation she gained courage and continued. 'So there is!'

'Is what, Sine?'

'Is mair!'

He hesitated again. 'In Lybster and Wick there are friends and one relative. But a relation by marriage...my brother's wife.'

'Oh! It's Mairead...she's awful pretty, is she not...and speaks well of you!'

'Well, I'm the man who has to look after her now...for there's been a slight parting of the waves since they moved to that new township.'

Sine looked serious. 'I guessed there was something afoot, now I think about her face and manner. Yet Alasdair always was sae cheerful and loving...'

'Aye, he was! But Mairead was not of the same mind. Anyway, it's not mickle of our business, is it?'

She nodded 'It is my business if it concerns us, is it not?'

Robbie took hold of the horse bridle and turned the cart with the girl by his side. He did not speak until he had completed his task.

'I am still waiting Robbie,' she said.

He sighed. 'For what?'

'To know if it be of any consequence my coming to find you in Caithness? Perhaps I'm being foolish to think that you want to see me there...but I don't know...you have given me hope and to see it taken away so soon is hard to bear.'

'I am taking nothing away, Sine. In fact I'm leaving you with the cart and a horse as equally bad as each other!' He laughed. 'I'll be attending to some business for a day or two but will seek you out as soon as I can, and that's a promise. I didn't save you from being washed out to sea or strangled by kelp, for nothing! Did I?'

It was her turn to laugh. 'If you don't turn up within a week I'll be the first to strangle you with kelp when I find you, Robbie Sutherland, so mark my word.'

They both laughed.

'I must be bidding your parents good day, Sine and a safe journey. The cart's strong enough for them both to ride, but don't walk too fast or the old gelding may fall down in its traces. Cheerio for now.' (*Mar sin leat an-drasda.*)

With a final wave, Robbie Sutherland was on his way back to Caithness.

*****

The road stretched as a twisting dark ribbon of mud and stones, each boulder bumped and bent the rickety wheels; and the horse would stop in an aggravated stamping each time a deep rut was encountered.

Sine tugged at the bridle while her father beat lamely at the withers with a birch switch.

Progress was slow, painstakingly slow, and the girl's mother moaned on her uncomfortable perch, refusing to get down but cursing quietly in Gaelic each time the cart veered to one side.

The old man hobbled for a while by her side, rubbing his back, which was stooped and twisted with pain, muttering on the evils of the world and the Highland roads in particular.

Such an air of sustained aggravation made the girl bad-tempered, and her hauling on the bridle made the animal even more defiant at each obstacle.

The weather did not help.

Squalling rain seemed to beat on them at regular intervals, the girl's blue dress was imprinted against the legs - the hem dark, mud splattered and creased.

The man's hat was thrust firmly down, the rain dripping off the narrow brim onto his black jacket, the woman's plaid shawl wrapped comfortingly tight about her shoulders.

On this occasion the horse reared and stamped so that their meagre possessions swung one way, then the other, the thick rope straining with each lurching movement.

'What a hell of a place!' exclaimed the woman hanging grimly onto the cart side. 'The devil tek us fur fools!'

'Fools or no, we must move on,' yelled the girl beating the horse's flanks, 'and you sitting there like a brooding hen helps us not at all!'

'Aye, you wud speak so, what care you fur the likes of me!' came the reply.

' Haud y'tongue, the pair o' you! That's enough o'that!' The man swore in his annoyance. 'Y'r both cackling like old hens and my nerves are fair frayed with this road without a' that bickering.'

'Well, you can save y'breath then, the both of you! Haven't I done enough gettin' this horse and cart?' Sine shouted back as the journey slowly began again.

'Fifteen miles and no mair, and the sun on its way doon,' muttered the woman to herself. Her husband had climbed back onto the cart, groaning and muttering, and sat opposite her, his eyes closed. For the rain had suddenly stopped and a shaft of sunlight had broken unexpectedly through.

'I never thought I'd be leaving m'own land,' he said at length.

'Did you not!' Sine replied brusquely. 'Neither did I! But it's the will o'the Lord Almighty.'

''Tis a strange will then!' the woman added.

'Aye, it is!' was the man's only reply as he closed his eyes again.

'We must be near the bigger road,' thought the girl, 'and the night's shelter in that old barn father spoke about!'

She scanned the horizon but the patches of mist segmented the landscape, and a true bearing was hard to find.

'Is that Beinn na Meilich, father?' she inquired.

The old man opened his eyes and shaded his brow with gnarled fingers and surveyed the rugged peak. After a few moments he replied, 'Aye, it is!'

'Guid, we've only two miles to go!'

'Two miles,' muttered the woman, 'it will be the death of me in this shakin' contraption. Where o'earth did that man find it?'

'I didna ask and he didna tell me!' replied the girl.

'Huh! He seemed a decent lad...the brother of Alasdair, so you said!'

The girl nodded.

''Tis a pity you didna marry him!'

Sine turned angrily. 'What manner of mother are you? Uisdean was a guid man, that ye trow! And just over two months dead!'

'I'm not saying that he wasn't, but he had an unlucky omen about his birth, that I've heard!' said the mother in a factual way.

'Had he now! That's not what has ever been told to me!'

The mother shook her head, 'I ken how you have suffered, having lost twa bairns mysel, but y'r a young lass and there's a man fur you yet!'

Sine did not reply but walked on ahead, the horse three paces behind.

The wisps of mist were clearing under the challenge of a westerly wind. As a broad expanse of grey slowly dissolved the girl noticed two men on horseback on the horizon to the south of them. They appeared to be proceeding at a steady pace.

She turned towards the cart, and to her horror the buckled wheel suddenly jarred against a large rock and bent sideways making any further progress impossible

She swore and kicked the rim. 'Father, whatever do we do now!'

The old man stiffly descended and gazed at the wheel. 'A mallet wud knock it back!'

'Any fool kens that,' replied the daughter, 'and we have one on the cart. But who has the strength to swing it.'

'Well not me!' replied the man.

'That I ken,' said the girl hauling herself onto the cart. 'Can y'move aside mother so that I can rummage.'

But the woman suddenly produced the hammer.

It was heavy and the girl swung it with all her power. The sound echoed around the glen but the wheel only straightened a few degrees.

'Wait, Sine,' exclaimed the man. 'Twa men are approaching, they may be the salvation for us!'

The girl put down the instrument and rested her back against the cart.

As the figures approached Sine felt her heart sink. The distinctive form of Eanraig was clearly seen with his cousin, she presumed, a few yards behind.

Within minutes the couple had pulled up beside the cart.

'It is nice to see you, Sine and your kinfolk,' said Eanraig dismounting.

The cousin was a strong, red-haired man of about thirty-five, with a long face and warm, somewhat languid, eyes.

He walked over to the girl and shook hands. He then walked over and introduced himself to the parents.

'So you'll be having trouble then?' inquired Eanraig, smiling at the girl.

'Aye we are!' Her mother replied, 'and we'll be needing a strong hand to help us! I'll be thinking!'

'I can see that!' stated Eanraig laughing, 'but the next time ye borrow a horse and cart, make it a guid one!'

'It was fra Sine's friend, who meant well!' said the woman.

'Did he now!' responded the cousin.

'Aye he did that!'

'And who is this friend, I'll be asking,' continued Eanraig.

'Robbie Sutherland, the brother o'Alasdair!' Sine spoke quickly and handed the hammer to Eanraig.

'And where be he?' asked the man.

'I dinna ken!'

'Och! While we be fixing the wheel I expect you'll remember right enough!'

The girl looked at him angrily. 'Will I now!'

'Aye, I think ye will! For it may be a difficult thing to mend without help, is it not cousin.'

'Aye, especially since it's my horse and cart!' the cousin replied.

'What!' said the parents almost as one.

'Aye,' continued the cousin, 'we arrived back this morning to find the animal and the old cart gone, did we not Eanraig?'

'We did!'

'And lucky for me that the best horses were in a friend's fields. Or we may not have been able to catch you sae quickly!'

Sine pursed her mouth in annoyance. 'Well, we'll pay you what ever we can!'

The men laughed.

'I think it be about time to unload the cart and put the wheel in position, is it not, cousin?' stated Eanraig undoing the rope.

Within twenty minutes the hammering began in earnest, the wheel lying detached on a broad flat rock.

*****

The barn offered a dry refuge and a fire was quickly kindled to warm the inhabitants.

Sine and her mother cooked a simple meal and all five sat down on the pile of hay in the corner.

Eanraig lounged beside the girl, she tried to turn her back on him but he bent forward and whispered. ' It cud have been hard on you stealing, what with the bailie and the factors on the look out fur thieves, if I'm not mistaken pretty one!'

The girl gave a mock laugh, 'So you say, Eanraig! And well you may!'

The man went on eating, gnawing the meat off a chicken bone. 'Well, it's lucky I'll be thinking that me and my cousin are well disposed tow'rd you! About him, you couldna guess he thinks you fair pretty, could you?'

She suddenly stopped eating. 'It's your cousin now, is it?'

'Aye, he's a guid fellow and hard workin', there's no doubt on that!'

'And one for the lassies, like yersel'.'

Eanraig smiled and nodded. 'But not as agreeable and handsome as me, don't ye think?'

The confident way he said it made her smile. 'And what thinks your wife Anna, Eanraig?' she said sarcastically.

He laughed and whispered, 'And what manner o'business brings her into the conversation and spoils my meal?'

Sine turned to face him. 'Where lives this cousin then?' She spoke unaffectedly, without emotion.

'Yer no sae proud then! Did y'friend no tell you? I suppose not! Well, he has a holding, and a good one at that, by the coast and is well looked upon by the Great Laird's men having a fine way with sheep and he being not against the clearances!'

'You expect me to work for such a man?'

'*Chan eil*, not work! Marry the man...for he said to me just a day back that he was looking for a wife.'

For a moment Sine was taken by surprise. 'Indeed!'

'Aye, indeed!' He smiled. 'Think o'the future Sine! Your parents are getting auld and being infirm can offer little for the future. The past life is behind you, sad as it was...and I've always been one to help you when I can.'

The girl looked at the wall for a moment. 'How can I believe what you say, Eanraig, after all that pestering aboot me recently?'

'I do think o'you a fair bit, Sine and I'm much taken by you. But I canna provide for you and Anna, I realise that! And to see you fleeing from the land y've been raised on fair unsettles my soul, or what's left o'it!'

'You think him a fine man then.' For the first time in the conversation the girl had turned to face the cousin.

'Aye, I do!'

She considered for a while. ''Tis strange but he has a likeness of Uisdean, has he not!'

The man hesitated. 'Only a bit, in my way of thinking! But he has mair money and land than Uisdean wud ever have had. And if I've done you any wrong, Sine, this is one way to make up fur it!'

The girl smiled.

The cousin and her parents were warming themselves in front of the fire and engaged in conversation.

'If he asks me, then I may well take up the offer!' Her voice was emphatic and slightly excited. ' 'Tis true that there is not much in the future as things stand, and with the clearances, matters can only get worse.'

Eanraig nodded. 'And married to my cousin will keep us together, one way or another. Will it not? For we meet regularly.' He waited for a response then continued. 'They say the Laird has sent word from London that more hillside grazing is to begin and that boats are to be placed at the disposal of those who wish to emigrate.'

Sine looked in mute astonishment. 'Emigrate! Holy spirit! Whatever next!'

'Aye...'tis true enough! I have helped the factors and their men as best I can...but all they do is not o'my liking. But what can a person do when he has a wife and a holding...and risks losing all! I'm no so proud of what I have done – that I don't too have a conscience and some misgivings!'

'You have spoken honestly, Eanraig, and in some ways I can't blame you. For each must look to his own in these bad times...'

He interrupted. 'If you come to my cousin's, you'll be safe and y'r kinfolk will be with you! And all will have worked out well.'

Sine smiled and went on eating.

Deich air fhichead (thirty)

Three men were chosen from the village after much discussion. The women sighed and spoke firmly, the younger girls wailed and bemoaned their fate, while the children played, oblivious to their problems, outside the kirk.

The Minister was a Godly man in every way, a father of three and looked upon with respect for hadn't he studied in Glasgow some thirty years ago. His hair had receded, his nose was long but the eyes still held a compassion and understanding that had dispersed from the lineaments of many of his fellow ministers. The villagers looked to him for guidance from the Lord, and the Minister gave them as much common sense as mortal man is allowed.

He sat on the stool at the far end of the church. The evening light played through the colours of the stained glass window above the altar, a simple design that refracted the rays just enough to paint the plain embroidered cloth that adorned the altar, and to just touch the hewn oak pews to the right. The minister smiled and turned to Archie (*Eairdsidh*) a forty-six year old crofter with five children. His younger brother Fingal (*Fionn*), a stouter man by far - taciturn and more red in the face and hair-, sat beside him. The third man was called Simon (*Sim*). He was strong and broad shouldered, had fairish-sandy hair and was more placid, more pessimistic than his cousins – a man who had spent long days on the fells in recent months as a shepherd but not watching the lowland cattle as of old but tending the newly imported flock of sheep. Simon still felt ashamed of his new occupation that he considered to be, in some respects, traitorous to his companions. But with six children to support and an ailing wife, circumstance had given him no choice.

All three listened intently.

'You're not sure, are you?' (*Chan eil thu cinnteach, a bheil?*). The minister looked at Simon as he spoke.

'No, I'm not!' Simon replied.

Archie took a long breath and shook his head. 'There are problems Minister, that I know...but most of all...who will listen to poor folks like us?'

The Minister agreed but took hold of the man's hand. He looked him straight in the eyes and continued as if speaking to him alone. 'Aye, you may be right about that and all else too! But with my letter you can travel to Edinburgh (*Dun Eideann*) and seek help. I have contacts within the church elders and, most of all, in the Lord Provost's office. Simon, we will make a grand case to stop these wretched clearances. It was looked upon as beneficial at first...but matters have got out of hand. You can all do some good in Edinburgh, the three of you...but I wouldn't tell the rest (*chan fheum sibh guth a radh cach*).'

Simon smiled, but it was clearly seen that he wrung his hands in a nervous way.

'But what about the others, our wives and children... we cannot keep them in the dark?' Archie took over the conversation.

'When I say tell no one, I really mean keep the facts to yourselves as much as possible! No clan member will speak to the enemy, if that's what I can call them in this Holy House, but I do not believe in taking risks.' The Minister was emphatic.

'It's an awful long way to the Capital City,' replied Archie ruefully, 'and not one I'm so keen about.'

'Aye, that's true man,' replied the Minister sitting up straight and arching his back to relieve the ache, 'but there are rewards from going, and our cause is just!' Think of the widows and widowers and children who have lost their loved ones when the ferry between Sutherland and Tain went down with about a hundred drowned - bodies floating for days in Dornoch Firth. What destitution has been thrust upon them by this dreadful tragedy; who can blame them for taking any old plot of bog land that's given to them now, for they own nothing else and in their sorrow they're too mute to fight for more and better.'

The three stared at each other, and nodded in agreement. Simon spoke. 'Was is not another sign of the wrath of the Almighty on us poor folk, and have we not suffered enough in the last year and mair! Sometimes, I'll be thinkin' there's no end to troubles, one way or another. There's no luck about us Highland folks, and I dinna see much in going to the big city.'

'You can but try,' responded the Minister with a grave shaking of the head, 'you can but try gentlemen, and if it fails, you'll be none the worse off.'

This statement was met with silent contemplation for some time and then the mood lightened and the discussion went on for a further fifteen minutes, the arguments vacillating to and fro. But the worries and taut nerves were eventually calmed by the man of the cloth.

Still pondering their mission, the three men left the kirk .All felt heavy in heart chiefly through their lack of worldliness and they dreaded being pitted against the educated chicanery of those they had to confront.

'You're as good as any man, Simon,' his wife stacked the dishes in the low-ceilinged kitchen with a large bucket leading to a cold water tap, suspended halfway up the wall. She looked kindly on her husband. He had always relied on her for what he deemed 'common sense' and 'firmness in manner' and she rarely let him down. Thirty-eight, plump and cheerful she was the exact foil or antithesis of her husband. She walked over and kissed him. 'All will be well! I have no doubt! You're tired aren't you? (*Tha thu sgith, nach eil*?)'

'*Tha*!'

'You're a worry to me sometimes, my love,' she replied with a short laugh, 'but no kinder man drew breath, that we all know Simon MacCoinnich! And we all love you for it! There's no harm that can come out of the trip to Edinburgh town, and you will see I'm right.'

'You think so, Magaidh (*Maggie*)!'

'Aye, I do that!'

'What would a man do without a woman like you…only the Lord knows!'

'Does He now! But a woman's a mysterious creature, one minute as tame as the hind, another as wild as the cats that stalk the glens.' She laughed at the analogy that produced a smile of contentment in her husband.

'It'll be strange leaving you behind…but it's only for a day or two as Fingal said.'

'Aye!' she said pensively and left the kitchen to the man, who sat and contemplated their future.

*****

It was two days later.

Fingal put down his small glass, gazed reflectively at it for a moment, sighed and stood up. He was a genial, if taciturn man, but lacked the courage of his brother, Archie. His mind was full of indecision. Should he travel to the Capital or decline to go? He knew the consequences would be grave if the three stirred up too much trouble.

He made up his mind to see Ewen, a man who had a strong following. For he was in part a veterinarian whose spells and potions could ward off or neutralize the evil spirits, including the evil eye of animals.

Ewen also had little regard for the law. As a goat-herder, he firmly eschewed the fact that the Highlands were lands made for goats and goats were created as part of the land. No sheep would graze his pastures and fells, for he vowed to kill any he would find. In this respect his esteem had risen with the troubles.

Fingal quietly closed the pine door behind him, his wife dozed by the small peat fire, and he set off briskly in the fading light towards the far glen where Ewen lived, some three miles away.

He had barely traveled a mile when, on turning up a steep bluff as a short cut, he saw three soldiers sitting on the side of the path.

As was his nature Fingal instinctively wanted to turn back and in his hesitancy he was observed by one of the three, the other two facing in the opposite direction, and a voice called, 'Here man!'

His companions instinctively turned and they all quickly rose to their feet.

Fingal, still apprehensive, stood his ground.

'Here man! Come here!' called the taller soldier brushing a few brittle grass stems from his dark trousers, as casually as he could. 'You speak some English, don't you!'

Fingal proceeded towards them at a snail's pace.

'You're a goat man, yourself, aren't you?' the soldier inquired with a frown.

'Aye! That I am!'

'And you graze them on the far side of the Glen?'

Fingal nodded.

'Cameron's land, as it is!'

Fingal looked fixedly at the speaker. 'It has been our family's of a right for generations!'

The soldier paused.

'You see this! It's a spy glass!' he tapped on his bulging breast pocket. 'And through it we see the men who graze and where they graze!'

'Aye, I do! But I graze by every right of the law!'

'Indeed! Perhaps you did! But the laws are changing!'

'And why?' said Fingal slowly, puzzled by the rapid eloquence of the soldier but able to follow the gist of the conversation.

'Because that land is for sheep now, and you have been warned not to graze your goats there any more.'

'But that'll be the death of me and my family, I have no other way to feed them but by the goats and the trade in milk and hides they bring,' replied the perplexed herder. 'No other way!'

The soldier looked towards his companions who feigned nonchalant attitudes. He continued with a sarcastic smile at the corners of his mouth, which anyone but the trembling herdsman, lost in his confusion, would have noticed. 'There is a way,' he continued, 'to save your goats!'

Fingal looked up.

'Tell us the men who are planning an appeal in Edinburgh, we've heard about it you know, and the land will stay with you for generations.'

'I canna do that man!' he blurted in reply. 'Tell on ma own folks!'

The soldier waited. 'So you know then?'

There was a long pause. It was the turn of the other soldiers to smile. One said, 'Leave the old fool alone and let us away!' But the leader still waited.

'If I were to tell, it would be the death for me, I have no doubt! An' the disgrace!' Fingal shook his head, frowned and rocked his heavy frame back and forth for a few seconds as if contemplating his fate.

'No one would ever know, I give you my word on that!' The soldier took the pondering man by the forearm. He said slowly, 'No one would ever know! Think on that my man, and don't be a fool or a martyr or both!'

But Fingal was lost in his own thoughts as to the effects an eviction would have on his wife and two teenage children. He did not believe the soldiers or their laird for a minute, and he knew that in the harsh brutality of Highland life people might have little sympathy for his predicament. Each family faced starvation as a continued battle, little could be spared in the long run for others. He was suddenly faced with the threat of appalling suffering and destitution. Resettlement in a coastal village and employment at sea, were a distant and improbable prospect! He knew that the only life he could endure was the poor existence he had had for decades. Should he tell the truth and take that one hope to salvation, however small?

In those few moments of indecision were crammed a lifetime of emotions.

Fingal looked up. 'I canna tell! I do not know! *De a tha ann*? (What is it?) I've wracked my brains for a few minutes but I know of no such expedition.' His voice broke as he tumbled over the words in a mixture of Gaelic and English.

'Speak up man! We cannot understand you!'

'Chan eil! An urrainn dhut Gaidhlig a bhruidhinn?'
(Can't you speak Gaelic?)

But the three soldiers shook their heads in reply and wandered off down the valley, seemingly unconcerned as to the emotions that churned within the frightened man.

*****

The summer rain beat heavily on the corrugated roof of the two-bedroomed house, set back on a small indentation in the hills, sheltered by a few juniper bushes and gnarled pines. The thunder and rain could not dampen the man's spirit, they were dampened enough by the evening's events. The streaks of lightening went unnoticed.

Fingal looked at the smoldering embers of the peat blocks, inhaled the grey-blue slightly pungent smoke that seemed to drift leisurely around the small sitting room. There was just enough of a draught from beneath the pine door to hold it at bay from spreading out, mist-like on the hard baked-mud floors.

The man stared stonily and sighed imperceptibly. His wife and children were asleep, the room would have been surprisingly silent for the wind had dropped in the sweaty heat before the storm, but the rain kept up its staccato clamber and vied for his attention.

But it fought a loosing battle for his thoughts turned back and forth, from the confrontation with the soldiers, his fear as to what they might do, and the despair as to what he might do to rectify the situation.

It was in this troubled state of mind that the minutes passed, and so engrossed in thought was he that he did not notice the slow movement of the door as it swung open.

His gaze was fixed on the fire and he noticed a sudden rush of redness on the peat. Slowly he looked around.

In such a bleak state, this taciturn man would have rarely been surprised. But the sight of one of the soldiers standing behind him made his pulse race. Fingal made to get up, then in a strange apathetic despair, slumped back on his chair.

'What brings you here, soldier?' he inquired at length.

The soldier motioned to sit down. Fingal pointed to a chair opposite and closer to the glowing embers. A fine wreathe of smoke had suddenly curled upwards and the stranger coughed. 'Just another warning...about the warning you were given earlier tonight.' He spoke kindly however and the older man gained some comfort from the tone.

'Aye... a warning!' Fingal said no more and the soldier warmed his hands. For the first time the crofter noticed his wet clothes and pointed towards a black woven towel, that resembled a small rug, hanging on the side of the table.

The soldier smiled and got up. For a few minutes he rubbed his face, then hair and finally the top and front of his jacket so that the buttons resumed their former gleam and the red of the cloth looked less like crushed velvet and more like the robust material it was.

He resumed his seat and warmed his hands once more.

'*Tha* (Yes)...' said Fingal after another profound silence.

'Listen! There's more than a storm brewing in this Glen and many another!'

Fingal did not reply but nodded in agreement.

The soldier paused. 'You must move on!'

Fingal still stared in silence. Then he deigned to speak. 'I ken that full well! But where to?'

It was the soldier's turn to contemplate the fire. 'Take your family and be gone within the next forty-eight hours, that's all I can say!' He gave an apologetic sigh.

'But where soldier, where?'

'To the coast in Caithness, or towards the lowlands! I do not know any more than you!'

There was another silence.

The soldier took up the conversation once more. 'Have you a family in another area? Apart from your brother who lives close by.'

'Aye, there's one in Caithness, a cousin of sorts. But we're all poor enough, Heavens knows, and little to eek out as I ken full well.'

'Listen, my friend, they are hell-bent to burn you to destruction, possessions and all! If they find out I have been here I will be dismissed at the least and transported at the most. But I must warn you, Eilidh says it's only right and proper.'

Fingal smiled for the first time. 'She is a grand girl is Eilidh, that's for certain. You must be the soldier man I've heard about. Fancy that now! Fancy that!' He smiled again and then gave a low chuckle.

'Well, what you say could be right! I'll not deny it! But as far as you and your family are concerned, you do not know who I am and you never saw me again after the episode on the hill!'

'I understand English but poorly soldier but I get the gist of what you say,' he said with some words in Gaelic

The soldier smiled. Rising quickly he shook the man by the hand and almost silently left the room.

Fingal now had the knowledge and advice he had craved from Ewen but had been unable to get.

Then he went to bed, leaving the rain still fighting with the roof.

He would talk to Archie, Simon and their families. Had not the Earl of Selkirk slipped quietly into Sutherland? Had not he sung the praises of a new beginning, in a new land across the sea? Fingal could remember the name in English, "The Red River" in North America. Where North America was, he had only the haziest of notions; yet he knew it was much farther, a score or more times farther than Edinburgh...but they would be safe, healthy and prosperous there...the Earl had intimated as much.

For the first time in months, Fingal slept the sleep of the just, blissful in the companionship of his brother and his friend and their families, knowing they could escape the privations of the present by going to America. But he was unaware that being deceived by the Earl was only part of their future disaster, for in a journey which was to be plagued by inclement weather, disease and starvation, only a few would survive; and almost everyone would be decimated by a final savage massacre. A handful would escape into Canada. But no record of the survivors would ever reach home.

*****

Andrew Lockhart hurried away from the cottage barely noticing the downpour that soaked him more truly for the second time. Barely able to focus on events that had embroiled his life, and so many lives, in recent months!

He cared little about the highlands as a place to live, but had the highest regard for the people who lived there, families that now faced an added, almost insurmountable, difficulty to their existence.

And Eilidh?

He had loved her from the first. There was no doubting the fact. And now he was risking his future. The army would not forgive his betrayal if they found out.

He had heard the orders to burn and burn. To drive all dissenters or occupiers of prime grazing land out of the country! He knew of the hungry and helpless, the refugees searching for new lands across the sea.

Through the rain he wandered as quickly as he could towards the old hall where the 42nd were stationed.

It was well past midnight and not an animal stirred.

He stopped, conscious of his own heartbeat, and no other sound.

He listened.

It was a critical time, a time not to be caught.

What excuse could he give to be out on such a wild night?

He stealthily opened the oak door and peered within.

The sounds of men sleeping sonorously and at peace were welcome to his ears.

He smiled as he slipped out of his wet clothes, and shivering went to sleep, pleased that he had entered unseen.

*****

'Your name and rank?'

'Captain Lockhart, Sir!'

The Major paused and looked down at the papers on his desk. 'Your general attitude and behavior has been, to say the very least, suspicious, lacking in decorum and not befitting of a soldier and an officer. In effect it is common knowledge that during the last year you have been seen out on a regular basis with one of the local girls and, more to the point, supplying information to the Highlanders about military plans. Have you anything to say in this respect?'

Andrew bit his lip. 'The girl had naught to do with the matter, that I can affirm!'

'I see! Then you do not deny that two nights ago you stayed out late, in inclement weather, and were known to have been in the company of Fingal, one of the troublemakers who had intended to travel to Edinburgh and make a case, however, false against the Marquess and others. Now what do you say?'

'On my word the girl....'

'I am frankly not interested in "your word" knowing them to be half-truths at the best and lies at the most! You will face a serious charge that I can tell you now! The girl will be called as a witness, by the way. The dwellings of the troublemakers will be dealt with soon in the manner that you are well aware of!' The Major's voice had a quiet threat that was not lost on him. 'You are confined to this building!'

Andrew walked slowly down the corridor, took a rapid glance back at the Major who was busy writing at his desk, and within a minute was out of the front door and running for his life.

He expected a rifle shot at any second, but heard none.

Indeed there was an eerie silence broken only by the sound of his boots on the damp earth.

He did not pause.

Within seconds he was leaping through the heather.

At first it was in fear.

Then a strange exhilaration seemed to envelope him

A sudden rush of freedom; a feeling that his life belonged to himself, whatever the consequences!

He hurried for the croft where Eilidh lived.

'Would she be there?'

He briefly stopped.

'Perhaps down in the settlement…seeking the goats…visiting friends?' A whole rush of fearful thoughts raced through his mind in a near panic certainty that she would not be there.

He stopped for a moment to regain his breath.

Then on and on! He attempted to hurry across a shallow stream but the moss-covered steps made him stumble and jar his left ankle. He limped for a short while, hobbled as the pain grew worse and was forced to stop once more.

He rested on a mat of heather and pulled down his sock. The outer bone looked deformed and the blood was already accumulating as a pulsating weal.

He tried to stand up, couldn't, and sat down again in agony.

Once more he rose…once more the pain reduced him to the earth. He had to do something drastic, there was no other course!

Taking out his knife he prodded the pulsating mass, the pain tore through his body with the initial cut, but a curious numbness took over and in an instant fresh blood burst forth. Hurriedly he pressed his palm across the bleeding half-inch slit. Then miraculously there was a 'snap' and the pain suddenly lessened as the outer bone of the ankle flew back into place.

He waited for fifteen minutes until the bleeding had stopped; tore a flap from the front corner of his white shirt and bound the ankle as firmly as he could.

Andrew hobbled on in pain but determined.

After a half a mile he reached the dwelling where Eilidh lived. At first it was eerily silent, with only the rushing of water from the mountain stream nearby.

He waited. Then, to his relief, he heard her laughter through the byre door. Slowly approaching partly due to apprehension and partly due to pain, he paused at the doorway and listened.

The girl was humming softly as she went about her tasks.

'Eilidh!' he whispered.

There was no immediate response.

'Eilidh, are you alone?'

'Is that you Andrew, what brings ye here so soon?'

He still could not see the girl.

'Come quickly, Eilidh!'

She hurried to the door. 'Gracious, why the rush? And why are ye hobbling so?'

'Never mind that for a moment! Will you come away with me...forever!' The words barely passed his lips such was the tremble in his voice. 'I'm in sore trouble, Eilidh, that you may be sure of!'

Eilidh flung her arms around his neck, and the soldier winced in pain. She backed off.

'What's the matter then, Andrew?'

'The Commanding Officer knows that I've been a traitor, that I've told people where the intended burnings will take place and when. The Military have it in for me, the Major has said as much. So I'm away, to catch a vessel to another port, I know not where!' It was not just the crestfallen look nor the words, but his whole manner that affected the girl.

The soldier waited for what seemed an eternity. At last she spoke, 'I have no money Andrew, nothing to help you with, ye must ken that before I say "yes".'

'Bring just yourself Eilidh...that is enough for me. So the answer is "yes"?'

She laughed. "Aye, it is, for better or worse...and probably the latter in my case.'

He kissed her for a moment, 'But hurry, Eilidh, we have little time to loose before we head for the coast. Tell your parents that we'll be back again soon!'

'They'll not care that much, with one less mouth to feed...and me a lady in the making. A soldier's wife sounds awful grand for a lassie like me...does it not? Still, I'd better say my farewells, should I not?'

Within the half hour the couple were hurrying through the heather, the stems still drenched from the storm of the night before, the girl's dark dress snagging on the tough spindly shoots, the soldier's steps more cautious and controlled to spare him from the jabbing pain in his left ankle.

They climbed as quickly as they could, through a misty land of heath and ravens; saw the shores of Dornoch in the distance but headed away from the Marquess's stronghold and the Factors and the military stationed near the cathedral.

As they walked on the sounds of swirling streams came from every direction, converging into a boggy terrain, which although the cold water gave comfort to the broken ankle, caused the girl to stumble and sink at times so that her shoes squelched mud and churned moss.

As if to add to their problems an icy rain whipped down from the sharp peaks and blew full into their faces.

Then in an erratic manner, the black clouds would suddenly part and a few bright yellow rays would encourage them into more mud and ooze

They crossed the mountains and after a further four miles, Andrew collapsed onto the wet earth. 'I cannot go any further, Eilidh, what fate have I brought you to?'

She put her arms around his shoulders to support him. 'You must realise how much I love you, Andrew. All else pales into insignificance before that!'

He smiled, 'One day I'll tell you how much I owe everything that's good in my life to you!'

'Will ye now! And what about how much of my life and love I owe to ye? Answer me that my bonny soldier!' It was her turn to laugh and kiss him.

'This is a dreadful way, Eilidh, to begin a married life. But things can only get better, and I'll make sure they do!'

'Let this food staunch the chattering, Andrew. I brought along some cold meat, and a bit of bread, a couple of eggs and some drammach.' It was his turn to kiss her, and despite the rain beating in their faces it was a long, lingering show of love born of respect and adoration.

Andrew looked into the distance. 'We'll make for the crags over there and shelter by them for the night,' he said after some consideration, 'I can only guess at the time, but the brightness to the west would indicate about eight o'clock although the clouds are fair shutting out the light.'

'Aye, it's awful gloomy and a drenching night for newly weds, for that's what we be now. And the only sounds are the gushing torrents not the cry of the sea birds by a golden shore. I always wondered how my married life would start, and never expected such an icy trickle down my back!'

They both laughed and headed for the crags and the sparse shelter they afforded from the storm.

Aon deug air fhichead (thirty one)

McBain drank his whisky by the tumbler-full and in a state of bemused anger, and an air filled with oaths, stumbled out to his horse.

Thirty constables and a dozen soldiers waited in the courtyard. They had been given liberal spirit, exhalted not to be cowards or to flinch from duty; then given more drink! And they gathered in little clusters and began to talk amongst themselves.

They set off on their mission, boisterous and brash in confidence. At the first sight of Archie's dwelling they got a surprise that made many draw a deep breath of alarm. For approaching was a group of twenty women from the settlement – their husbands being at market. The soldiers stared in amazement for there was not a man in sight.

In years to come, this was the infamous battle; folklore told of the women's determined fight, and how the dogs of the district licked up the blood for days to come and how the grass grew spattered with red for weeks and how it was left uncut as a token of brutality.

It was a crofter's wife who approached as a spokeswoman.

But the Factor plunged forward to meet her, pushing the small army to one side, his eyes blazing with rage and intoxication.

There was hardly a time to speak, a time to reason, before a broad stick had clubbed the woman to the ground. As she lay unconscious blood spurted from her head. With a scream of rage another woman, heavy with child, rushed forwards. The baton descended again, fracturing her collar bone and ribs with a sickening crunch.

All the women joined in the melee. They attacked the men as best they could, shouting for their rights, outraged at the behavior. They were determined. 'Keep your summonses!' they cried, 'and we'll keep our land, our forefathers' land and our children's' land'.

But driven wild by their taunts and defiance the Factor, the soldiers and constables rushed forward.

It was an outrage that was never to be forgotten - the scars, the deformed and bruised limbs, the many broken bones were an eternal reminder of what happened to the women of the township on that defenceless day.

So the clubbing continued until all were prostrate, and lay in heaps of humanity, many severely injured, most in a pitiful condition. Then they were handcuffed together or tied with ropes, thrown into carts, and in that huddled, pathetic state driven off to prison.

Amongst the tall grass were strands of hair, waving in the wind, strands of black and brown and red, many still attached to patches of scalp, incongruous against the backcloth of the colours of the flowers.

Once again there was no justice, for the Lord Advocate of Scotland dismissed the injuries, 'had not the women resisted and defied the Law, and had not the majesty of the Law to be observed and attended to?'

He was certain that it had.

The women nursed their wounds and injured limbs, and the returning husbands cursed and declared vengeance, and it was not long in coming.

*****

A day went by.

Murdo McBain watched the smoke sweep down to the sea.

The buildings blazed.

First Archie's, the thatch dry and tinder sharp; then Fingal's - deserted but substantial and homely. Last, but not least, Simon's shone red in the sky, silhouetted against the grey of the cliff-side, a roasting inferno that had been homes. Two dozen houses followed, until the valley was hung with acrid smoke.

'Aye, they'll never come back, right enough!' Murdo said quietly. 'And good riddance to them and their scrawny bairns!'

He turned his horse, the whites of its eyes glowing red like a demons in an inferno.

'Come men!' was his only cry.

The constables and military men had been warming themselves before the fires with a curious mixture of pride and satisfaction - for the operation had gone well.

On hearing his voice, they turned almost as one and marched in dissolute groups down the narrow path, stopping occasionally to watch and listen as some beam or roof burst into flames with an explosive force that scattered red embers into the palls of black smoke.

McBain rode steadily ahead. Almost without thought and certainly without conscience!

Another loud explosion and a scattering of sparks!

Yet within the tumult of noise and movement three score of men and women poured down a short, steep incline and into the mass of constables and soldiers.

A shot rang out, a soldier had fired, and a girl of seventeen fell dead. But such was the turmoil and mayhem that her lifeless body was trampled by the struggling hordes.

McBain crashed from his horse, a broad pointed stick thrust firmly into his face just below the eye. Tears welled in the agony and he writhed on the ground.

Other constables lashed out with their batons – but for once they were overwhelmed – a dozen were felled unconscious within a minute. More groaned in agony as they were remorselessly beaten as they lay on the ground, even more of the soldiers were pulped in a frenzy of attack. The rest fled.

The sixty or so Highlanders hurried off, it was their turn not to look back.

Dha dheug air fhichead (thirty two)

On the second day the wind blew even more keenly and until the sharp bursts of air cleft the low, sombre clouds apart. The couple meandered within the mountains, first striking north by north-east and then after an hour's wandering finally, and ultimately, returning to the pinnacles of rocks they had recently left.

There was little said and their spirits became broken by the unusually harsh summer weather.

Eilidh watched every hobble, every agonizing step with fear and trepidation that Andrew might suddenly stop. But grimly and bravely he plodded on, refusing her arm as a support.

'What have I brought you to?' he asked several times.

But tired of repeating the same encouraging response, she let him wander along in silence finally ignoring the recurring question. Yet she loved him still, more than ever as she recognized his sacrifice, the risks he ran from the military and the pain he endured.

Only once did he stop to take off the sodden stocking and examine his ankle. But the cold water of the peat bogs has so numbed the area and turned it a reddish-blue that he just shrugged and set off again in a slow, purposeful step.

No apology was needed, none given by the soldier. She looked at him as he walked just ahead on the winding, stone path; noting his kindness and courage; and these thought made her redouble her effort in the battle against the storms.

'If I cannot make it, Eilidh, let me lie here and the ravens' can have my bones!'

She looked at him keenly, for a moment lost for words.

He sat down and sighed.

'Even in the worst of times, Andrew, I would never leave ye to your fate!'

'The pain in my leg is like a thousand sword thrusts, Eilidh, and I fear that soon I cannot go on!'

'If ye can't, nor can I!'

'It's a sorry…'

But she interrupted him, somewhat sharply, 'We can't grumble and cry for help here Andrew, there's no one to help. Are ye sae daft or befuddled with pain to think that I wud leave ye here. There's no fate that can keep us apart now! So draw yersel' up and lets walk on, take my arm, and dinna be so proud.'

Conscious of the sharpness and admonition in her voice she kissed him on the cheek and held him close to her wet body for a moment.

He smiled and stood up. 'You are right! There's no point in moaning or looking for pity, even if we are lost.' He gave a brief laugh for the first time in hours. 'If only we could get our bearings….that must be the north-east!'

'I have a little of the mutton-ham left Alexander,' she said smiling, producing some meat from a small bag that had been fastened to the inside of her coat.

'You must eat it Eilidh!'

'No! I'm fine, thank you!'

He looked into her face and saw the resolution, so started to eat slowly but beset with worries.

'You look sae weary, Andrew, that I thought y'needed some refreshment…but that's all I have!'

'I am weary,' he replied with a sigh. He sat looking into the gloom. 'I did feel sickly and in a mind to give up, a few minutes back. But not now! Yet I feel guilty in taking the food but it has settled my stomach. It must be the nagging pain that affects me so, body and soul' His voice quivered for a second like the wind in the reeds. Then he resumed in a more cheerful voice. 'I know we can make it to Wick, and there'll be a boat waiting to take us to lands where the sun always shines on a serene sea, and the waves are never more than ankle-high.' He laughed as he said "ankle" and she laughed too, not quite understanding all the words but comprehending the underlying deep emotion.

****

They rested for almost an hour as the wind threw the elements around and the rain became fitful but spiteful in bursts.

'I think it may take another day or so Eilidh, or even longer with the bad leg,' he sighed and then gave an apologetic smile.

She responded by another kiss and then slowly got to her feet. Her hair was flattened and her clothes dripping wet, the water trickling towards her feet as pattering, incessant droplets.

She took hold of his left hand and helped him up.

Slowly they moved up the hills towards a mountain pass and on reaching the summit they paused and looked behind towards her home in the far distance.

But the cloud was low and obstructive.

So they trudged down the swampy path, avoiding the puddles at first and then splashing on oblivious to the water that swirled around their feet.

Once again they proceeded in silence apart from the elements. Suddenly Eilidh stopped. She peered into the gloom, only able to see a few yards ahead.

'What is it, Eilidh?'

'Och! I thought I heard a voice, that was all!' She strained and focused her sense hoping to hear the sound once more. 'There it is again, Andrew! I'm sure I heard it this time!'

Motioning him to stop Eilidh hurried forward until she was lost in the mist.

To her surprise there was a small building ahead and a faint curl of smoke issued from the roof. Eilidh turned and ran back. 'It's a house, Andrew,' she said excitedly, 'and there's someone home.'

The soldier smiled and hobbled forwards as quickly as he could.

There was the small building and the whole setting looked comfortable and inviting.

Andrew walked up to the door and knocked.

He knocked again and in exasperation gave a staccato burst.

There was a man's voice and a command, 'Who's there by the Lord!'

'Only two weary travellers on the road to Wick,' shouted the soldier trying to be as apologetic as he could.

'Are you of the Laird's or Sheriff's men or constables?' the voice demanded.

'No!' replied Andrew, 'I'm a soldier with a girl from near Dornoch.'

There was a long silence and a woman's voice was heard and then her voice descended into a whisper. Eventually, the man spoke. 'Be awa' with ye then, for I'll no have a soldier in this house!'

'But we are wet and exhausted. Have some pity please,' pleaded Eilidh. 'There's no way we can go on in this horrible weather.'

'I ken that!' said the woman slowly but emphatically, 'I've known this weather for many a long year, as ye no doubt appreciate!'

The soldier shouted, 'You cannot keep us out man, anyway take in the girl before she catches her death of cold.'

'But what soldier are ye,' asked to woman cautiously.

'A deserter, and proud of it!'

The woman paused. 'We'll ye can stay aboot the house for the rest of the day or until the weather breaks, if that suits your plans.'

The door slowly opened and a couple in their mid-fifties, the woman plump and grey, the man stooping and bald, confronted the couple.

Eilidh and Andrew ate some warm gruel and had a drop of whisky to warm their bones. They sat on the floor in front of a peat fire which was supported by three stout pine logs that occasionally threw sparks into the room like miniature shooting stars.

The warmth made the young couple drowsy, their eyelids grew heavier and their eyes unfocused, and their necks gave small, convulsive nods.

So they succumbed to a deep sleep for the next three hours!

Andrew awoke with a start. He could see the sky through the narrow window. The clouds had blown away, and the late afternoon's sunshine had roused the rock pipits by its heat into twirling song. For a moment he was lost in his surroundings, confused within that period when the mind ascends from the unconscious to normality. Shaking his head to clear his thoughts, he stood up and glanced around. The small room was empty. Andrew looked outside, quickly opened the door and walked painfully around the house. He hobbled to a small promontory to survey the valley. The view was clear and uninterrupted for about two miles.

He could see no one.

He felt uneasy and a slight shiver crossed his frame.

As quickly as he could he was back in the house, his ankle agonizingly painful from the sudden exertions.

'Come, Eilidh,' he said putting his arm around the sleeping girl's head and feeling the wet hair, curling and dark as it dried.

'What is it?' asked the girl looking round bemused.

'They've gone and I don't like it. There'll be a bounty on my head, and threats against those that help...I have little doubt! Something tells me we must be away, gone in a moment if we can.'

Placing a few pence on the table as a gesture of thanks for the shelter and food, they hurried out of the door. Andrew paused and glanced towards the sun. 'They know we're heading due east for Wick and have seen me rubbing my ankle. They'll be pleased that I'm lame and none more so than the military.' He stopped to think. 'They'll expect us to continue on this path so we'll turn west for some while and then cut back towards the sea.'

Eilidh nodded in agreement and linked his arm. Thus they proceeded forward in a sombre mood, anxious but not afraid.

****

Andrew and Eilidh were faced with a dilemma, they had no food, only peat water from the mountain steams and little hope of dry shelter for the night. Their overall ninety-mile journey was also to be extended by a further fifteen to twenty miles.

Sill, they set off in good heart, compatible in their one aim, united in the fresh flush of love and excitement.

They had tuned west for about four miles, when on the descending slope of the valley the soldier found he could not go on. His ankle was too painful and his left foot had begun to swell alarmingly in his boot.

He sat down and looked despairingly around. It was Eilidh who spotted two fallen pine trees with a good crown of leaves in the distance.

They hurried on as quickly as the pain would allow.

True enough, the ground was as dry as anything they had encountered since their wild journey began. With relief they slumped to the ground, unable to believe their luck.

The soldier was anxious at first to take his boot off, then remembering that the foot had started to swell alarmingly the last time he tried, he suddenly became afraid that he might not be able to put it back on. So he sat with the leg resting above his reclining body, the limb being supported by a generous flush of leaves on a stumpy bough.

'We will rest here, Andrew, as long as we can.' The girl spoke cheerfully and stroked the soldier's cheek. 'It's a strange wee hame for us, there's no doubting that! Still, it's better than none!'

The soldier stretched his hand towards her and she took hold of it. 'We'll make haste tomorrow when the larks spring up, but the food's a problem, right enough.'

She laughed. 'Guess what! Do you mind when you first saw me?'

'Aye, I do!'

'Well then, there's some berries about, and they'll be as easy to gather now for the rain's drenched them and in this bright sun they'll be nicely full of juice.'

She walked thirty yards or so from the soldier and began picking in earnest.

Soon she returned, still laughing, with several handfuls scooped in her dark coat. 'They make a mess right enough, but there's little mair that this poor coat can endure.'

They ate in silence. The soldier put out his purple tongue and she laughed and she did the same, and his laughter was a gratifying break in the worries he had suffered over the last few days. Then she licked both cheeks and spread the blue-purple dye horizontally beneath his eyes. 'Ye're mair a wild-looking chief now than ever, Andrew.'

So the sun slowly sunk into the west in a curious blood red glow, but the couple had long since fallen asleep in a state of exhaustion.

The dawn came brightly, a star heralded the first rays, that roused the sleeping birds, and their first songs awoke Andrew. The girl stirred uneasily beside him in her sleep.

He sat up and cautiously pulled back the covering branches of the gnarled trees.

The valley was bathed in steamy summer warmth as the vapour rose from the rushing becks and drying bracken. The purple of the heather was fresh, sweet smelling and alive with innumerable insects. He rubbed his eyes and yawned. Then he looked again.

Five specks of red were seen close to the small loch about a mile away; five specks slowly moving from side to side and then forward; examining each clump of bracken, beating at the foliage with their rifles.

'Wake up, Eilidh, wake up!'

The young girl took a few moments to answer his request.

'There's soldiers coming, we must slip away as best we can.'

Without any further discussion they crept out of their cover and headed, crouching as low as they could amongst the bracken fronds.

Slowly and cautiously they made their way along the side of the valley towards a small promontory of rocks, the granite glowing pink in the rising sun.

But Andrew's ankle still pained and, in a briefest of moments, it gave way so that he stumbled and then slipped a few feet down the hillside.

Eilidh grabbed hold of his jacket to try and hold him, but she was weakened by the recent hardship and exertions, and they slid and tumbled a further dozen feet together.

Andrew lay still against the damp earth with Eilidh a few yards away, crouched and watching the approaching soldiers. Her knees were scraped and impregnated with grit, his ankle had become more swollen and his toes gone numb.

They hardly dared breathe. They watched the advancing soldiers but there was no response. The couple lay still and waited for what seemed like an eternity. Then suddenly two shots rang out.

Andrew and Eilidh leapt to their feet. He knew that he had to put the pain out of his mind. Gritting his teeth he managed to keep up with the running girl as she hurried back up the hill towards the rocks.

Another shot whistled and fell close by.

They threw caution to the wind and swept around the first rocky defile as quickly as they could.

But Andrew could not go on.

There was another ominous crack and he fell to the ground in agony holding his ankle. The joint had dislocated and was rapidly filling up with blood.

'Hurry away, Eilidh! Save yourself, they only want me anyway. So be off. They'll not follow, that I trow'

'What have I said a hundred times, my love?' and she sat down beside him stoking his brow and talking in a quiet comforting voice as a mother would to a child.

They heard a rustle of stones and fearfully looked up.

'I think I'll always be finding you in some strange mountain place, Eilidh, this is the second time, or my name's not Robbie Sutherland.'

'Perhaps its not, ye look different without that beard!'

'In what way…?'

'Och, for goodness sake, why are ye blathering on like this with our lives in danger?' she said curtly although smiling at the man none-the-less, and then laughed. 'Y're a terrible tease Robbie Sutherland.'

He sat down beside the soldier. 'I've been watching the happenings for some while from that rock face and here's what's to be done. There's a small cave the foxes use by the side of that rock, and it fair reeks too!'

'Does it now!' interjected the girl.

'Aye, it does!'

'Well, go on!' said Andrew impatiently.

'It's only big enough for one, that I ken, but you can hide in there Andrew, and in a wee while I'll be back for you!'

'But they'll search hereabouts until they find me, why would they go on after you?'

'Easy!'

Eilidh looked at him curiously, 'Have ye been in trouble with the law as well?'

He smiled, 'Aye! Here and there! But not enough to be shot at! Anyway, in that fine red coat I'll be fair game running down the hill side, so off with it!'

'Robbie, I cannot let you risk your life for me, not for a second.' Andrew shook his head.

'I'm not really risking it...and if I was it would be in part for Eilidh,' he said laughing. 'Hurry man, they're getting that bit closer by the minute...although I will lead them a merry dance,' he said emphatically.

They changed coats and Robbie pointed out the lair about thirty yards away.

'Come on, young lady, you've still got a soldier man as a companion...although the jacket's a bit tight and short in the arms for my liking. But what can those men see,' he pointed to the valley, 'only one as brazen as themselves. I wouldn't like to wear it at a cheilidh, though!' he continued with a smile.

With a kiss from Eilidh, Andrew crept slowly towards the small entrance and safety.

Robbie motioned the girl on. 'Head towards the left o'that track yonder, and wait by that rich clump of heather. The land's fair smooth and green there and it's just for my liking.'

Eilidh hurried off and Robbie waited.

The soldiers, realizing that they were near to their quarry and trying to flush them out, began shouting; their voices echoing through the sculptured rocks. Satisfied that Andrew was invisible, Robbie walked along the hillside towards the girl who had reached the desired spot. Now he was clearly in view.

A couple of shots rang out. By this time Robbie was by the girl's side. 'We make a fine couple do we not?' he asked good-naturedly.

She just nodded and glanced apprehensively behind her.

'Don't worry! We'll pick our way through this heather bog, and I know the route grand and true. They'll be up to the knees in mud and slime within five minutes, and trapped like a mountain goat...that you can be sure!' He laughed uproariously. 'Of that you can be sure!'

Tri deug air fhichead (thirty three)

Alasdair Sutherland forked the dry straw and hay into the corner of a small barn adjacent to his new cottage. The lean dog hung around the outbuildings, looking for rats and mice. The odd hen and rooster scratched in the manure heap, but there was an ordered tranquillity about him.

The dog pricked up his ears and turned, watching a rider slowly cross the pastures, driving the kyloes to one side.

The man pushed open the wooden gate with his foot and turned the horse towards the barn where the swish and scrape of the hayfork continued unabated.

Alasdair's mind was on other things, life had been sourer in recent months. After the initial shock and anger his thoughts had returned more and more to his wife, accompanied by a deep longing to see her.

Mairead had suddenly become the young girl from the next township again whom he met on the way to the kirk or school, the young girl who made his life a little less serious and a lot more positive than he could ever imagine.

With this concentration on past events, he was not aware of the approaching man until he turned to see a figure standing in the doorway.

Alasdair rested on his hayfork, 'What brings you here, Factor Sellar?'

'A whim, Alasdair!'

'Aye, and what whim is that?'

'To see what dues you will pay for the right to remain here!'

'For dues, y'say!' Alasdair said blandly.

'I do say that!' replied the Factor impatiently.

'It is a wasted journey to my way of thinking, Factor, a wasted journey!'

'Don't be so confident man, for if you'll no pay the dues then this cottage will burn.

Alasdair still rested on his fork. He did not reply.

'D' you hear me, man?' Sellar demanded. He raised his hands in an appealing gesture.

'Aye, and I'd prefer not too!' was the blunt reply

At that moment there was a further sound of horse's hooves clattering through the yard.

Alasdair ran to the door, pushing the Factor to one side.

There was a sheriff's officer, astride his black pony. 'Hallo!' he called.

'What is the manner o'things, Officer?' asked Alasdair.

'I have been sent by Mr McBain to get his due. I see Mr Sellar's mare, where is the man?'

'In the barn!'

The officer dismounted. He hurried over. 'Between you and me...McBain means no good, man!' he whispered.

'Is that so?' Alasdair asked in flat voice, 'that's nothing new!'

'This time it is! McBain's hell bent on razing this land after what has happened and he wants his money.'

'I thought McBain would have told Sellar what was spoken between us and what was agreed to be the due!'

Sellar approached them in the yard. He heard what had just been said. 'I know what was agreed! But there's no stopping McBain now, he's too much drinking the whisky, for my liking' The Factor adopted a tone half sympathetic, half admonishing. 'His brother was an educated man, but McBain is no intellectual, he has no profession other than taking money when and where he can.' Sellar gave an apologetic smile that had a serpentine quality in its finality.

Alasdair turned away suddenly and walked into the barn. He pushed through the doorway in an impulsive gesture, his face fixed. Factor Sellar kept close behind.

'Good day to you, Factor!' said Alisdair

'Wait! You know what brings me here, what is your answer man?'

'Aye, money flushes ye out as always, Factor! And it's my business that has to pay for it, one way or another, I'll be thinkin'.'

'That's true!' muttered Sellar.

'Well, Alasdair Sutherland, what have ye to say about it?' inquired the officer.

'What I have to say is this - get yourself out of here before there is more trouble than you both can cope with!'

The officer did not answer. He looked as if anger had solidified his features into marble. Without a word he slowly pulled a pistol from inside his dark coat, it was a controlled threatening gesture that made Alasdair step back.

'Put that away, man!' warned Sellar stepping forward.

'You're a canny man, Factor Sellar,' replied the officer slowly, 'and willing to take as much as you can for yourself and those that employ you! But there are others wanting money for this land, McBain has his mind set on it.'

'I have shot one man in the past, Officer, for less impudence. And the thud of a bullet whining into flesh is not of my liking, but I'm willing to do it again, if the need be!'

'Aye! You may swing one day if it comes to that!' replied the officer,' You must have no fear of death to linger about this land. For there's plenty about that would kill you a hundred times over, perhaps a thousand, by my reckoning.'

'Maybe so!' replied Sellar calmly, 'but the dues from this township belong to me and no other, of that you may be certain!'

Alasdair looked hard at the speaker but did not say a word. He slowly gripped the handle of a pitchfork that was propped on the wall next to him.

This action was not seen by the two others, for Sellar had taken out his pistol and cocked it. The noise made the officer look in the factor's direction. Sellar spoke, 'The charge is ready to fire, man! Put down your weapon! Or we shall both perish as one, that I have no doubt!'

'Put it down Officer!' said Alasdair firmly. 'Now there's two of us, and two may die, but one of them will be you! A pitchfork is as deadly as a gun, and the chest is a fine target at this range.'

The officer laughed. 'Aye, but one of us will die and each wonders which it'll be, and that's a handicap, is it not? Not knowing who will be first...while you man (he looked at Alasdair) have not the spirit to kill...McBain has told me that...so I would be of a manner of thinking that the Factor could die, and me...if I'm not in luck!'

Alasdair slowly turned the handle of the hayfork and thought of the penalty he would have to pay if he killed. He thought of eternal damnation, and what would his parents think, what would Mairead think? These thoughts flew in an instant through his consciousness. He threw down the pitchfork. 'I'll have none of this nonsense. Tell me my due, and I'll get it!'

'Thirty guineas!' the officer looked pleased.

Alasdair nodded. 'You'll have to wait while I go to fetch it!'

'That's no trouble!'

Sellar watched Alasdair walk to the doorway and into the yard. The dog ran to greet him.

He shouted, 'Factor Sellar, could you spare a moment, please?'

The factor shrugged his shoulders and walked outside.

The air was fresh and cold after the sudden excitement. Alasdair adjusted his coat, pulling it up around his neck. 'I will not say you have done right by us Highlanders...but you've perhaps seen a more Godly way in recent weeks…so I've heard but…I do not know. That will be for the Lord to judge, on the day of reckoning! But I ask you one more kindness, in the spirit of your wife's goodness! I'm away now, with what little money I have left. Make sure that the other houses in this township are not burnt, that I beg of you! And give me thirty minutes or so...one for each guinea (Sellar laughed!) To get away!'

The Factor took his hand. 'My wife has spoken well of your grandmother. I'll deal with McBain and the officer! Do not forget my ways are the ways of the Laird, but I'll respect what you have just said and the place will be saved. McBain is a strange man, and always has been, there's no doubting that! Keep your money and be gone, Alasdair... and God be with thee!'

Ceithir deug air fhichead (thirty four)

From Robert MacKid,
My Dear Brother,
The troubles that have befallen me since the trial, and the hardships placed on our family, have been greatly alleviated, in part, by your unending support and generosity. That you should direct us to your friends in Caithness, whose kindness matched your own, is a blessing for which we shall be eternally grateful. Life had not been without its vicissitudes, and the constant problems of raising monies to support our growing family, has been at times almost overwhelming.

However, I have often thought of being a writer of sorts, and with this in mind will bring to the public's notice the harsh reality of life, as we know it to be in the Highlands.

Yet, I fear there will be little response in the rest of Scotia, for in the North we appear to be a race forgotten or if not forgotten, deemed to be of so little worth in the eyes of our fellow country man.

There have been a few honest souls who have written to the newspaper proprietors, and a few reporters have ventured north, but what overall effect there has been to ease the hardship and deprivation, I cannot ascertain as yet.

It has occurred to me, marooned in an isolated cottage for the present and, I hope, away from the constant harassment of the perpetrators of our misfortune, that it is an ideal time for contemplation and learning.

As I often walk the shore and gaze out across the wide oceans, all thoughts of my position, indeed all man's position, in God's bountiful firmament fills my mind.

This morning I contemplated on Homer and his precept of the artificiality of humans within the City life, and the freedom of expression within the countryside and nature. Much of the Lucretian theory of the aggravation of particles at birth and their dissolution at death seems to be a random phenomenon at variance with the concept of an Almighty. And yet the events within our natural world would speak of randomness within a world where the wickedness of man flourishes. Perhaps within the Garden of Eden, the solitude and communion with nature had to be broken.

Still, there is always a balance within life between good and evil, tempest and sun, love and hate, and much more. Thus it was with a cheerful heart that we heard of the dismissal of that incarnation of the devil, Sellar, by his Lordship recently - for some lack of trust and weakness in resolution, I believe, rather than the man's cruel deeds of the past.

I am well aware that he still has land and enough prosperity for the future. But we cannot believe, and will not believe, that he will not suffer eternally when he meets his Maker. These thoughts, although in most respects against the scripture's teachings, have sustained us, I regret to say, during the recent weeks since we heard the good news of his downfall; although strangely due to some good he had done for a change. His failure to carry out orders and also contradict his Lordship's bidding for the first time, was as surprising as it was unusual.

Thus I write to inform you of this matter, our continuing good health, and our felicitations and regards to you and your family.

I remain your loving brother,
Robert.

*****

From Robert MacKid
My Dear Brother,
Having received your communication, following my epistle of three weeks ago, I write to tell you of a change in plan occasioned by more judicial chicanery. Once again the staff of the law, heavily disguised as incompetence, has been wielded in the customary legal manner, which I have experienced myself.

Having read the following details, and having given the matter some consideration, especially a detailed and frank discussion with my wife, I have decided to embark on a career as a lawyer, armed with the practical knowledge of the past events and my time as a sheriff.

The matter concerned a stonemason who married a lady from the parish of Farr. His father-in law died and a whole family of children was left entirely on the resources of the stonemason, Donald MacLeod.

The helpless family was in such need that Donald gave up his job in Edinburgh and hurried back to his native Highlands, where, stung by the oppression and injustice around him, his frank words and decisive actions soon brought him foul of the sycophants who exist in certain areas in the North.

The enemies hatched a plan, according to his testimony and indeed supported by the genuine populace at large, and he was brought before the courts by a factor for the sum of five pounds and eight shillings, not an inconsiderable sum when one considers the family circumstances.

As events turned out the factor was the judge, a worse scenario one could not imagine.

The judge wasted no time until he challenged the hapless stonemason. 'Well, Donald, do you owe this money?'

'I would like to see the pursuer before I would enter into any defence,' he replied.

The judge's retort was instant, 'You see him in front of you…and I will pursue you, man!'

'I thought you were my judge, sir.'

Another angry retort marred the proceedings, 'I'll both pursue and judge you – did you not promise me on a former occasion that you would pay this debt?'

'No, sir!'

At that point the judge ordered a constable to seize the defender.

Then followed an incarceration for several hours as a common criminal until the judge demanded his return to the bar. 'Well, Donald, what have you got to say now, will you pay the money?'

But the stonemason continued to deny the debt most vociferously.

The judge unleashed his anger with the words, 'You're one of the damn'dest rascals in existence, but I'll pursue you between heaven and hell, I'll make you pay it, and I'll get you removed from the estate.'

Donald was defiant and replied, 'Mind, sir, you are in a magisterial capacity.'

I am told that there followed a volley of the most foul execrations to which Donald MacLeod calmly replied, 'Sir, your conduct disqualifies you for your office and under the protection of the law of the land, and in the presence of this court, I put you to defiance!'

That was not the end of the sorry matter, for after writing to the Marquess and Marchioness of Stafford, he received a reply much more cordial than my own. It was their wish that the stonemason could remain and continue as before until the case was reviewed by a Mr Loch on his arrival in Sutherlandshire.

But the case was judged and decided before Mr Loch left London.

It was with confidence that Donald MacLeod produced the receipted documents that proved his innocence before Loch, and the courteous, soothing words of the arbitrator indicated that the outcome would be good. He bade the man go home to his wife and family, and make himself easy.

His wife was of a more pessimistic disposition, and she proved correct. For when the stonemason was at work, forty miles away, eight men entered the house just as they had finished dinner, they threw out the occupants in a violent manner, with some bedding and articles of furniture; then in a few minutes nailed up the doors and windows in the face of the helpless woman, with a suckling infant, and three other young children - the eldest child being of eight years and comforting her as much as he could.

Wind, rain and sleet ushered in a night of extraordinary darkness and violence, even for that inclement weather.

The woman was too terrified to comprehend the situation for some while and stood mute in the storm, soaked to the skin and freezing cold; the children shivering by her side, afraid and tearful.

But the calamitous events did not end there. For on coming to her senses she sought help from neighbour after neighbour. To her astonishment the doors were barred against her. Messengers had been dispatched warning the surrounding inhabitants, at the peril of similar treatment, against giving shelter, or affording assistance to wife, child or animal of Donald MacLeod.

The once kindly people did not dare offer any help, help they would have once offered to an enemy's dog on a night such as this one.

Seeing that all attempts were fruitless, the poor woman erected a makeshift shelter from what furniture she had. But the howling winds scattered them down so that she stood pitiless with no covering but the frowning heavens, and no sounds in her ears but the raging storm and the cries of her famished children.

Want and necessity are hard taskmasters and drive people on in desperate times. Such was the sheer fear and desperation of the woman that she placed all the children together, gave them strict orders to remain where they were, and to listen to the wishes of the eight-year-old who was put in command.

The only choice left was to set out on the fifteen-mile journey to Caithness. As she set off she had the cries of the children ringing in her ears, but knowing that they all faced death, and even with such a slender hope of keeping them alive, she hurried as fast as the wind and rain would allow. She feared that the youngest could not survive more than a few hours without her. In this agitated state she barely paused, finding some strange force almost beyond human comprehension.

Within a few miles, and still a long way from her destination, she was met by a good Samaritan under the name of Donald MacDonald, who disregarding the danger he incurred, opened his door to her, refreshed and consoled her, and then took her to the dwelling of William Innes, esq. of Sandside, Caithness.

He made available a house and while taking her there met her husband, Donald, who under one of those strange and supernatural occurrences known only to God, had decided to return home from Wick; having laboured the day before in great uneasiness of mind and spirit.

He almost ran the remainder of the way. To his intense surprise and delight he eventually found them safe and sound. But it was a dramatic story! For under the care of the eldest boy, who had decided to take the infant on his back, and with the other two holding him by the kilt, they travelled in darkness, through rough and smooth, bog and mire, until they arrived at a grand-aunt's house, where finding the door open, they bolted in, and the boy advancing to his astonished aunt, laid his infant burden in her lap, without saying a word, and proceeding to unbuckle the other two, he placed them before the fire without waiting for an invitation.

The man of the house rose and said he must leave the house and seek a lodging for himself, as he could not think of turning the children out, and yet dreaded the ruin threatened to any that would harbour or shelter them, and he had no doubts his house would be watched to see if he should transgress against the order.

His wife, a pious woman, upbraided him with cowardice, and declared that if a legion of devils were watching her, she would not put out the children or leave the house either.

But the man impelled by his fears did obtain a lodging two miles away. The father collected them the next day and took them to Armidale, the dwelling they had been promised.

This is indeed a salutary tale and one that does little credit to the fairness, hospitality and kindness of the people in this area. We seem to be in the hands of cruel and despotic factors and judges and graceless ministers who support them.

Your loving brother,
Robert.

Coig deug air fhichead (thirty five)

Mairead sat on the cliff top, scanning the path ahead at intervals and then watching the gulls in their lazy flight above the waves. The rocky promontory bearing the 14th century castle was precariously perched before her, the steep escarpment lapped by an untamed sea, while close by were Neolithic ruins still undisturbed and at peace.

She had spent as much time as she could, away from the fish cleaning and boning, which had been intense from the moments the fresh shoals of herring had arrived in Wick.

Her job had been to smoke and salt. She could still smell the smoke in her hair and rubbed her fingers through the auburn locks in annoyance. Twice she had washed her hair that morning, yet still the aroma remained.

But she was troubled. Waiting patiently for Robbie to return was not one of her strong points. But even more disturbing were the numbers of Highlanders who had crowded into the town for the two ships.

Ships that were bound for Canada.

The narrow streets jostled and were alive with families, single men, widowers, and the aged. Begging for hospitality that none could refuse, but none could afford.

The visions of the multitude floated before her - here a painfully thin child, limping on swollen feet wrapped in rags; old men and women bent and hobbling with sticks or broken branches fashioned as stoutly as it was possible. While the gutters ran foul; and the cheap lodging houses were brimful and stagnant.

The noise never ceased.

It still rang in her ears on the cliff top.

Mairead pondered on the future of her kinfolk and watched the busy swoop of the puffins, trailing seaweed to the nesting hole.

She had just stretched back in the sun, her cream dress a beacon in the brightness, when she heard a distinctive sound that made her leap to her feet.

The jaunty step of Robbie, the cheerful wave, the long call, were happiness personified.

'Hurry!' (*'Greas ort!'*)' She called back and suddenly she was running towards him.

It seemed like an eternity.

And then she was in his arms. 'Oh! *Robbie*! *Robbie*! *'S thu!* (It's you!) How I have missed you!'

The man laughed. 'That's the sweetest sound I have ever heard, Mairead!'

'Is it?'

He laughed again putting her down after swinging her round.

'It is!'

'And what have you been doing?'

'Oh! All manner o'things!'

'Such as?' She linked his arm as she walked along, still smiling.

'Helping some friends to leave their township where all is not well!'

'Not well!'

'No! The clearances continue as ill as before, to my way of thinking. There seems no end to it all, Mairead!' he shrugged his shoulders. 'And I have seen that Eilidh gets to Lybster.'

'Eilidh!'

'Yes, It's a long tale, Mairead.'

She went silent for a moment and felt some of her confidence ebbing away. She brightened up as Robbie continued. 'Andrew her soldier friend has deserted the military and in his journey north, he damaged his ankle, broken to my way of thinking. Anyway, his Majesty's loyal band of brigands were in some danger of having to do some more taking of innocent lives. So I swapped to the soldier's clothes and they set off after me, with Eilidh close behind, across the braes. They're as slow as a cow with a full udder, and not so useful. Well, we gave them the slip and I set the girl on her way to Lybster. There she has a friend who's a Captain on a boat that oft sets for Holland and such like.'

'What about her friend?'

'He had a comfortable journey to Lybster as any man had; for I sent old Sinclair, Chisholm the tinker's friend, to pick him up. Neither have truck with the lairds and factors after what happened to auld Morag. So, I have no doubt that the soldier had a comfortable ride on that piebald pony of Sinclair's, all the way to that wee port.'

He laughed and Mairead kissed him in pleasure and admiration. 'I dinna ken how you do all these things, such kindnesses Robbie Sutherland.'

'For that matter...neither do I! It just comes oddly and....naturally.' he said with mock emphasis on the last word.

'Have ye seen...?'

'Alasdair? No!'

She went silent.

'What is it, Mairead...did you want me to?' (*De a tha ann, Mairead?*)

'No! I just wondered, that was all!' She brightened up. 'Have you heard the news about the brigs?'

'*Tha!* (Yes!) I have!

'What do ye think then? Of going away together and leaving it all behind!'

Robbie stopped for a moment and held her close. 'Would you like that?'

'I wud, really I wud!'

He paused and looked out across the harbour. 'Do you know any of the name of the Masters?'

She laughed. 'So we can go then?'

'I didn't say that, Mairead!'

'No, that's true! I did hear that the big ship belonged to Captain Angus MacLean!'

Robbie picked up the girl, swung her round and kissed her once more. 'Then it's fine by me, Mairead, if it's fine by you?'

She laughed and clung onto his neck for a few moments. 'Do you think we could live as man and wife in Canada?'

'*Tha!* (Yes!) I do! Who's to know?'

'The Lord!'

Robbie sighed. 'That's true, but He will forgive us...all that's gone on!'

'Y' think so, Robbie!'

He laughed again. 'Let's find the brig and be done with it!'

They hurried down the path. The noise grew louder and louder before five minutes had passed. Robbie looked in amazement at the crowded streets, the urchins and barking dogs. Fisher women yelled their wares and handed out split-herring to the eager crowds. But Mairead recoiled at the smell that haunted her and hurried on towards the quayside.

There stood the ship, its sails stored, its hull newly tarred, and scrubbed to perfection.

Robbie called to a sailor swabbing the deck. '*Hello!*'

For a few minutes the man did not look up. 'What do you want today?'(*De tha sibh ag iarraidh an diugh?*)

'Is there a Captain MacLean on board?'

The man went on swilling the water to and fro.

Robbie repeated the question, but in a shriller voice.

'Aye!'

'Could you fetch him please...say it's a good friend of his brother.'

'Aye!' was the curt reply. Then the man vanished.

It was barely two minutes until the Captain appeared, stout, grey and whiskery, but resembling his brother. 'What ails you, friend!' he bellowed.

'Have you passage for two?'

'*Chan eil!* (No!)'

'Did ye say "No!"'

'I did that!' the round figure attempted to disappear but Robbie's loud call brought him back.

'Your brother said that you would give me passage because I helped him when he was ailing!'

'Did you now?'

'Aye, I did!'

'Ailing -from what then? He never ailed a day in his life!'

'Well, this time you're wrong!'

'Am I now?'

Robbie nodded.

'What was it man?'

'The ague, but it passed in a week!'

'In a week you say!' The Captain reflected for a moment. 'We're full to the topsail!'

'There's only two newly weds who have been treated right sorely by the Laird of Sutherland.'

'Och! That Sassenach! But what is different about you! A' the others hav' been treated the same shameful way...and paid their fares to boot!'

'There's no much more I can say then?'

Then Mairead called. '*Ma 's ur toil e* (Please) help us Captain MacLean, you seem a fair man!'

The Captain gazed at the girl for a moment. 'I cud never resist a pretty face and my wife, the Lord bless her in repose, had hair like yours. But I'm telling you one thing! There's no much comfort on board and we sail on the first tide tomorrow! Good day then!' (*Latha math an-drasda!*)

With this closing remark the Master left the sailor swabbing the deck, oblivious to Robbie's further questions.

Sia deug air fhichead (thirty six)

From Mr Robert MacKid,
To the editor,
Dear Sir,

I feel it is my manifold duty as one who has seen and has suffered under the Clearances, to point out to those citizens involved in seeking a new and better life in the Colonies of the dangers inherent therein. I know that many of the people driven to despair and departure will be unable to read the following epistle, but those kind citizens who do, and who have the linguistic skills to impart such knowledge on these unfortunates, will take heed of what has gone before.

I will not list all the many voyages and tribulations but will concentrate on the early settlers travels to Nova Scotia. Their journey was on the ship *Hector* for Pictou, Nova Scotia. The *Hector* was owned by two men who had shares in land there and engaged an agent John Ross, to bring out as many colonists as they could induce, by misrepresentation and falsehoods, to leave their homes. They offered a free passage, a farm and a year's free provisions to their dupes. On his arrival in Scotland, John Ross drew a glowing picture of the land and other manifold advantages of the country. The Highlanders knew nothing of the difficulties awaiting them in a land covered with dense unbroken forest; and tempered by the prospect of owning splendid farms of their own, they imposed upon his promise. Calling first at Greenock, three families and five single young men joined at that port. She then sailed for Lochbroom in Ross-shire. Where she received thirty-three families and twenty-five single men, the whole numbering about two hundred souls.

Thus in July 1773 they bade a final farewell to their native land, not a soul before having ever crossed the Atlantic save a single sailor and John Ross, the agent. As they were leaving, a piper came on board and the captain ordered him off, but the strains of the music affected those on board so much that they pleaded to have him allowed to accompany them, and offered to share their own rations with him in exchange for his music during the passage. Their request was granted.

The pilgrims kept up their spirits as best they could by song, pipe music, dancing and wrestling through the long and painful voyage in the miserable hulk of a ship.

The ship was so rotten that the passengers could pick the wood out of her sides with their fingers. They met with a severe gale off Newfoundland coast, and were driven back by it so far that it took them about fourteen days to get back to the point at which the storm met them.

The accommodation was wretched, smallpox and dysentery broke out among the passengers.

Eighteen of the children died, and were committed to the deep amidst such anguish and heart-rending agony, as only a Highlander can understand. Their stock of provisions became almost exhausted, the water became scarce and bad; the remnants of provisions left consisted mainly of salt meat, which, from scarcity of water, added greatly to their sufferings. The oatcake carried by them became mouldy, so that much had been thrown away before they dreamt of having such a long passage; but, one of the passengers more prudent than the others, gathered up the despised scraps into a bag, and during the last few days of the voyage his fellows were too glad to join him in devouring this refuse to keep souls and bodies together.

At last the *Hector* dropped anchor in the harbour, opposite where the town of Pictou now stands. In celebration of their arrival, many of the younger men donned their national dress – to which a few of them were able to add the *Sgian Dubh* and the claymore; while the piper blew his pipes with might and main, its thrilling tones, for the first time startling the denizens of the endless forest, and its echoes resounding through the wild solitude.

But how different was reality.

The whole scene, as far as the eye could see, was dense forest. Their hearts sank within them. They landed without the provisions promised, without shelter of any kind. Their feelings of disappointment were most bitter, when they compared the actual facts with the free farms and the comfort promised them by the lying emigration agent. Many of them sat down in the forest and wept bitterly; the few provisions were soon devoured. It was now too late to raise any crops that year. To make matters worse they were three miles into the forest, so they could not partake with ease of fish that might be caught in the harbour. The whole thing appeared an utter mockery. To unskilled men the work of clearing seemed hopeless; they were afraid of the red Indians and the wild beasts; without roads or paths they were frightened to move for fear of getting lost in the unbroken forest. They refused to settle on the company's lands, so in consequence when provisions arrived they were not given any. So John Ross and the company decided to leave them to their fate. The few of them that had a little money bought provisions; while others exchanged clothes for food; but the greater number had neither money nor food and they soon were left destitute. Thus driven to extremity, they asked to have provisions; once again they were refused. In fury they seized the agents, tied them, took their guns and hid them at a safe distance, told them they must have food for their families but were willing to pay in time. One powerful man was left to guard the agents until the others had escaped. Then they were released and informed where they could find their guns.

It would be tedious to describe the sufferings that they afterwards endured. Many of them, men, women and children, bound themselves as virtual slaves in other settlements for mere subsistence. Those who remained lived in small huts, covered only in bark or branches of trees to shelter them from the bitter winter cold, of a severity that they had no previous conception- not even coming from the Highlands where the winters are as severe as anywhere in Britain. They often had to walk eighty miles through the forest and in deep snow to the nearest town for a few bushels of potatoes or a little flour in exchange for their labour.

In the following spring they set to work. They cleared forest and planted crops; hunted moose, cut timber and sent a cargo to Pictou, which proved profitable. The population had diminished, but they laid up supplies of oysters and clams for the winter, piling them as large heaps on the seashore, covering them with sand, although in the winter they were often obliged to cut through ice a foot deep to reach them. Plagues of locusts and field mice often destroyed their crops but they fought on and eventually formed a thriving colony.

Thus I chronicle this account, not to totally deter the travellers but to warn of the hardship of foreign lands.

Yours sincerely,
Robert MacKid.

Seachd deug air fhichead (thirty seven)

The dawn rose fitfully and Robbie slept badly, tossing and turning on the hard mattress in Mairead's friend's house.

It took no effort to get up and wash as best he could. With almost forty pounds in his pocket and as many clothes as he could pack into a small bag, he embarked on the journey of his life.

The cobbled street was deserted as he made his way to the cottage where the girl stayed. Her cousins were already awake and Mairead stood flushed with anticipation and excitement.

She linked his arm and they walked towards the harbour.

As quiet as the streets seemed on the edge of the town, the harbour was packed with subdued figures, many having already been allowed on board.

Mairead trembled as she stood in line.

She looked around at the roof -tops and the gulls lazily grooming themselves in the early morning sun.

Then she thought of her home, her remaining family and friends, the places she loved and began to cry. Already she had a deep-seated feeling of loneliness, a strangely anticipated feeling of being home-sick.

Robbie put his arm around her, 'Hush, sweet one! All will be fine, getting on board will put us in a rare mood to travel and start a new life.

She put her head on his shoulder but did not reply.

Indeed they would have stood in silence, like so many around them, had it not been for a familiar voice.

''*S toil!* (Yes!) 'tis me, for my sins!' Alasdair slapped his brother on the back and reached over to softly kiss Mairead on the cheek.

She gave an involuntary jump, which made her husband step back with surprise. 'I'm truly sorry if I startled you!'

She held out her hand. 'It wasn't you, as such, but the shock o'it!' She felt the inner tension, a moment before her hands had been relaxed and cheerful.

Robbie laughed, but did not know whether to feel glad or sorry. "What's doing? (*De tha dol?*)' He quickly recovered from his surprise and added, 'What brings you here, Alasdair?'

'The same as you, no doubt! The brig! The troubles didna leave with you Mairead but got worse. Factor Sellar helped me escape the clutches of McBain, that evil man. I have told Mother and Father, and they were saddened fur me to leave. I fear they will be sorely set out for they had no heard of you doing the same, Robbie!' he looked at Mairead, scrutinizing her response.

Robbie shrugged his shoulders. 'I'm feeling guilty at the thought of it. But never considered leaving until yesterday, and my kinfolk never came into my head what with the rush of getting ready and all that! But I'm truly sorry not to have told them, now I think of it!'

Alasdair did not reply. But he glanced furtively and suspiciously at his wife once more. He marvelled at finding them so soon, but he found it was impossible not to be angry with them. He tried to disguise his feelings, assess how the situation would proceed. He knew it was an absolute certainty that Mairead was in love with his brother, it told in her glances and the tremor in her voice. As for Robbie? He was in part the same bland, jocular brother who was a master of hidden feelings and surprise moves.

The crowd shuffled forward until Robbie and Mairead reached the gangway. Alasdair was a few steps behind. A sailor strode towards them and checked their names on a broad scroll of paper. 'You be the new travellers that Captain Angus MacLean listed yesterday?'

'That much is true!' responded Robbie.

'Welcome on board then!'

They stepped up onto the long wooden gangway that led to the crowded deck. Robbie hesitated. He turned to his brother, 'Come with us, Alasdair!'(*Thugainn comhla ruinn!*) Then he looked at Mairead's pale face.

To their surprise Alasdair needed no second bidding, 'All right!' (*'Ceart gu leor!'*) He began to follow them up the gangway, Mairead hurrying ahead in confused silence.

One of the sailors reached out and caught Alasdair by the sleeve. 'There is no room for you!'

For a moment the astonished man did not speak. 'What do you mean?' he faltered. 'I have booked a passage for today.'

'You cannot fool me, man, I recognise you from last night, I was there when you booked a passage on another brig that docks today, the weather being fair and the tide just! You're not listed for the brig *Neptune*.'

Robbie had turned at this point and retraced his steps. 'There is no room for him on this ship?'

'None! And never will be! This man is booked on the *Sulivan*!'

Mairead also hurried back in alarm. 'Did ye say the *Sulivan*?'

'I did!'

'She's an auld schooner that couldna make the outer islands never mind Canada!' Mairead said emphatically.

'Rubbish woman! She's already made one trip to our liking and mair t' come!'

The girl stared at the old sailor for a moment and then hurried up the gangway. Both men paused waiting for the other to proceed. In that moment's hesitation Robbie called, 'Mairead.' And turning to Alasdair said firmly, 'It should be you going with Mairead, I've been thinking!'

The girl, hearing these words, turned back - her face full of anxiety.

She started to speak, but the words "what are you saying?" stuck in her throat. She saw the sadness etched in her husband's features.

She hesitated. 'If that be your wish, Robbie?'

He paused and took hold of her hand, wrapping his fingers gently around it, leading her slowly up the gangway. Robbie could not look at her as he said. 'It is meant to be!'

Alasdair did not speak.

Robbie pushed him up the gangway, the girl did not look round.

He waved and shouted, 'Goodbye!' (*'Mar sin leibh!'*) But only for now! For I'll be following you, all the way! In the good ship *Sulivan*!'

But she stared fixedly ahead, with her husband three steps behind. He stopped, 'You have my blessing Robbie, God be with you!'

The two men exchanged glances. 'And God be with you both, I love you both!'

Mairead heard the words and turned her tearstained face towards him. 'We'll see you soon, I hav' no doubts about that!' She tried to laugh, bent her head so that her hair fell naturally around her shoulders to hide her feelings, then hurried onto the deck, leaving Alasdair to give a final wave to his brother.

Ochd deug air fhichead (thirty eight)

The wind was unseasonable and came in from the northeast, with a biting chill and chopping waves. The brig *Sulivan* reared and bent in the gale, the sails taut and lashed with spray.

Captain MacLean's vessel the *Neptune* had left twenty-four hours before, while *Sulivan* had been checked and the mainsail repaired. Still it was an unwholesome vessel having been used to bring livestock to the highlands and take barrels of herring away.

The rank dampness was not helped by the constant retching and vomiting of the despairing passengers, some one hundred or more, who packed the two lower decks.

Quarters were cramped and fouled. Children sat in bemused boredom and despair, while wretched women nursed babies on their laps and cuddled them with lullabies, a strange Gaelic lament which unsettled Robbie as they left the land behind.

Even in their greyness the mountains seemed to beckon him home and for the first time he felt his spirits sinking.

The ship shuddered and groaned, and at times appeared to almost swivel ninety degrees in its tack as a large wave struck it broadside.

The crew raced to and fro adjusting the sails, scrambling up and aloft until they seemed to perch like gulls above the waves, dark specks of men in imminent danger with each rearing of the bow.

Robbie wandered onto the top deck and watched the men fighting the gale. The mainmasts groaned ominously and the vessel took another lunge to starboard.

After four hours the wind seemed to fall and the vessel made some progress towards the north. Then long, thin storm clouds, heavy with rain and hail, were driven in on the wind and hung low as black masses above, insinuating themselves into the very whiteness of the waves. How the sea suddenly darkened, almost ink-hued, in its confusion. Then the air burst into life, shaking the sails and rolling the sea back and forth.

Now the gale was from the north and the vessel zigzagged without making any inroads into the fury.

Silently the highlanders huddled in the lower decks despite the smell, starting at each resounding crash and roar as a giant wave flung itself against the wooden hull.

There was much shouting on deck as the men grimly clung to the ropes and rails, lashed with rain and cascading water. Hair and beards were one streaming lank mass, their clothes flattened to their bodies.

'Hold fast there!'

The cries came and went. They were lost in the roar of the gale to those huddled below, but not to Robbie Sutherland who sat on deck his leg entwined by a rope attached to the gunwale. The water ran down his face. His body shivered in the constant cold. Yet he thought it better to be almost alone than be crowded in the squalor below.

More and more waves, all Arctic cold, pounded the ship.

Ever more frantic were the groans from the timber frame, while the main mast set up a discordant vibration on its own, as if one vast fiddle had been plucked and tuned at random.

Robbie watched the sail tighten and twist to one side then another.

How long they had been sailing was difficult to determine, for the clouds concealed the sun, but he reckoned about five hours.

Then the noise began to reach a crescendo.

Wave after wave burst heavenwards, heaving the ship one way and another.

His stomach churned as waves of nausea flowed over him.

Robbie grasped the rope and the wood to which it was attached.

He pressed his semi-recumbent body against the heaving timbers. He heard a voice cry, 'For God's sake hang on!' Robbie froze with the fear and then followed a violent retching as if from the very bowels of the earth and a huge sea roared towards them at a frightening pace.

The ship seemed to fly into the air for a moment and then fell back with a crack.

So sudden was the sound and so short the motion that it almost seemed to be a dream. Then came a second almighty wave; so immense that it appeared to take the vessel into the cup of its hands and fling it first one way then another, finally lifting the brig so high that it was flung head over on to the beam.

There was cry and screams and more screaming. But with the sudden tilting Robbie was cast off the ship and clean over the bulwarks. The sea plucked at him like a feather, carrying him higher and higher into the raging, curling torrent.

And yet higher!

Suddenly the swirling mass of water was above him and he was cocooned in a rolling wave.

Then down into a stark, chill darkness, ever deeper and blacker. Bubbles and foam rose about him in his descent.

As he felt he could go no deeper, another giant force sucked him down.

He felt the rope about his legs and tried to kick free. Down he went choking for air, then up again into bubbles and foam.

Then down once more, airless and afraid.

The huge piece of wood passed him, fleeing upwards though the water, striking him on the chest, spinning and turning in its bid for freedom.

Around his body coiled the rope like a giant snake, now twisting him upwards with a sudden jolt, hurling him along so that his body was wracked with pain, beaten and choked into submission.

Then just as he felt he could take no more, and his eyes seemed to dim, cold air shocked his face, as the giant wave cleft asunder, leaving him bobbing like a cork on a calmer surface.

Robbie coughed and spluttered, shaking his head and retching to relieve the pressure in his throat and lungs.

For a moment froth poured from his lips!

Then the air, sucked in - cool in his mouth and chest.

He gulped deep breaths, as another wave hurled towards him. He looked round and was amazed to see wreckage on the ink-black water, wrapped in foaming turmoil, bristling with a steady stream of bubbles that poured out of the deep as a final tribute to the ship. But no one else was visible although he had difficulty seeing for his eyes were misted over and stung with salt. He was amazed at how far he had travelled from the debris. He called out once or twice and then let the elements howl to themselves and tried to consider his next course of action.

But the binding rope and wood were his salvation. They rode the waves serenely, up and down, dragging him behind. After a minute or two he became used to this strange trailing motion, and felt more secure in the water. He did not feel terrified, not even afraid. The feeling was uncanny as if he had departed his body for a different life.

Then his legs began to feel numb and he kicked them as wildly as he could, but the rope tangled him more. So he relaxed and awaited his fate.

As quickly as the elements had vent their irrational fury, the wind seemed to die and the waves began to flatten and calm.

At first Robbie thought it was some sort of heavenly happening, as if he was floating to the promised- land.

He felt curiously elated, watching every ripple and cascade around him.

Suddenly he heard the roar and turning saw rocks not fifty yards away. Now his fate was to be dashed upon the jagged, white foam-wet barrier to the shore. Once again he kicked furiously but to no avail. Still the rocks flew closer and closer, until there was a crash as the very object that tied him down struck a pinnacle and flew back into a narrow gully and then into calmer reaches. Another roaring wave sped in. Backwards he was tugged with intense force. But the guardian wood pulled him clear and, with a resounding crash, it was hurled against a huge mound of a rock.

He felt the rasp of sand and shingle. Then he was dragged back again by the tide. He cried out in fear, felt the blows that bruised his body and saw the breaking waves that struck his face with bitter saltiness.

For a moment, a brief moment, a huge wave seemed to resemble the grey horse of the past, and fleetingly he thought of the girl.

But the memory was gone in a second, as the struggle for survival continued.

Endlessly, so it appeared, the waves tugged at his body, while wood that held him prisoner snagged between two rocks.

Each breaker battered his face and chest, so that his body became a mass of bruises and scraped skin; while the salt burned the wounds in one crescendo of pain.

But the endless toying ceased abruptly.

With a sudden snap the encircling rope swept free, unleashing one coil at a time, so that with each convulsive movement his body spun until it was propelled into the shallow water of the raging sea.

Robbie knelt, the sand was smooth and firm, with the kelp ebbing around his feet -like the girl he had seen once before- and prayed fervently in gratitude for his salvation.

With that indomitable highland spirit he rose to his feet after a few moments of intense pain and difficulty breathing -for his ribs ached with each movement. He managed a short laugh and staggered to the soft, dry sand of the Sutherland shore. In a shambling run, with his body starting to shiver, he made for a small cave in the cliffs. He found a narrow stream just leaving an inlet. Parched, with a sore throat and aching head, he drank his fill and lay down.

The sky was becoming blue in small patches and the black trailing mist was beginning to clear.

Suddenly he sat up, looked and listened with a beating heart.

There was no sight, nor sound, of the vessel - and of those who travelled with her.

Their journey had been brief, with no reward.

He hung his head in despair.

*****

Robbie waited after his long journey into the heartland of Sutherland, not sure as to what rewards of capture were still in force, wondering if he was still a marked man. He made his way towards the coast cutting across to the Castle. He had a longing after his near brush with death to see Catriona. Instinctively he felt that she was the one to reassure him. He had not experienced such a need for a woman's comfort since his early childhood days. His parents knew that Alasdair had set forth on a new life. But what they knew about Mairead and himself, he could only guess. Still he would see them soon and explain their new life, omit the details that needed omitting, and accentuate the positive features of their happiness. How he hoped they would be safe. But the *Neptune* had looked a different vessel from the rotten ship that had cast him into the deep, along with countless others. He pondered on how many could have survived, how many would have had his luck, and whether there was any reason for his good fortune. Perhaps there was! That thought consoled him from his past demeanors. His father, pragmatic to the Highland core, often repeated the simple creed "God's will be done!"

Now Robbie agreed.

His journey home was in many respects an image of many journeys, as reflections are spread in perpetuity from parallel glass mirrors. The same steep mountain passes, the fertile glens - green and harvested - inlaid like a jewel within granite crowns. The rough tracks, whose steady twists and turns gave a rhythm to his stroll. The rushes and moss covered bogs - dark and green but now surprising fresh looking and inviting - were all around him; the long smooth meadows in their twining, twisting, serpiginous course danced to the tune of the meandering rivers.

These were scenes he knew by heart and loved by heart.

Yet the sylvan beauty had scars, charred broken walls, rubble with crushed and rotting doors, window frames twisted as if some gigantic upheaval had consumed the earth. Gables roofless, broken fences and walls, fields of corn black as any volcano's larval spread. There was no smoke from the stunted chimneys, no laughter, no voices of man or beast. The odd crow, magpie or jackdaw picked through the rubbish in areas of desolate landscape.

He wandered into the odd township, eerily silent, looked for familiar faces, listened for familiar voices, but the ancient heritage had all turned to ruin. Clansman, crofter, tenant and tacks man, mothers, wives and children had been erased from the land before him.

He startled a black cat that hissed and after racing up a demolished wall, thought better of its rashness and returned meowing pitilessly for food. Robbie looked round for a few scraps but there were none and he gave up the search after some minutes. The animal followed him for a quarter of a mile before relenting and sloped back to the ruins, with a gaze fixed on a jackdaw as it ran stealthily forward belly-down.

The nearby coppice was a charred, mangle of tree stumps - part apple trees, part oak and ash.

Robbie looked at a squirrel as it sat grooming on a spared branch, but noting the white streak of fur underneath and the weasel-like face, he stopped to study one of the feared hunters of the hills. 'Aye, the pine martens as beautiful as any of the Lord's creature,' he surmised as he watched the animal for five minutes.

Meagre crofts were now empty shells. Tiny pastures which once supported a black cow or two or a few kyloes were amalgamated into broad undulating swaths, many overrun with sheep. 'The four footed Highlander,' he had once called them.

It was with relief that he arrived at his parent's house. They were subdued by the news of Alasdair and Mairead, his mother fearful of their new life, her silence underlining the despair that she might never see them again or any grandchildren. His father was taciturn and composed, hoping that they would have a good, Godly and fruitful life; but dejected behind all the platitudes. It was with some relief that Robbie set off on his journey to Dunrobin the next day.

Now as he approached the great castle he could only hope and wait.

*****

It was with some trepidation he heard the sound of a horse's hooves coming up the cobbled path.

It was with dismay he saw the figure was Murdo McBain. Not the man of old, that he quickly ascertained, but a man with one eye and a face crumpled inwards on the right so that his mouth was distorted in a horrendous leer.

Robbie sitting on a small grassy knoll could have easily hidden, being on the blind-side of the approaching horseman as he turned round a sharp bend, but curiosity forced him to remain.

The factor, preoccupied and still in pain (for the scars showed a livid hue on approach and part was still weeping from the proud flesh under his right orbit), would have probably rode by but for the Highlander's call. 'McBain!'

The voice was recognized in a moment and the rider turned. 'It's you, you damned rascal, have you not been hung yet?'

'It seems not, or if I have, my spirits are in good voice.' Robbie studied the wounds with intense curiosity. He had not seen anything like them before. He refrained from commenting.

'So you ken me then,' asked the Factor.

'Aye!'

There was an uneasy silence. 'It's no so difficult to recognize me?' McBain pointed to his face.

'No! There's enough left about you to recognize.'

The factor gave a grunt of satisfaction. 'Enough, in what way?'

Robbie ignored the question. 'Have you seen Catriona?'

The Factor took a deep breath. 'I've got little to lose from telling you her whereabouts. For I have been dismissed by the great hypocrite, the Marquess of

Stafford.' He took a deep breath. 'Man, you do all his dirty work and with clean hands he washes you away.'

'Well...', inquired the young man standing up, '...where is she?'

'Gone inland to see some friends. Towards the west coast near Croick! She took off in a rare huff!'

'Did she now! Were the friends male...or female?'

'I suppose it's some importance to you, Robbie, so I can tell you...female...although there'll be men about, never fear.'

'Aye, well, I do fear, and that's the truth of the matter!' Robbie replied earnestly and with some agitation. 'But I'm of little worth in her eyes, I don't doubt it, me, a humble highlander of little money and in some ways less worth,' he said, his voice tinged with dejection.

'More worth than me, Robbie, I can tell you! I lost my wife several years back, Robbie and my brother and finally my soul. My brother wasn't as good a man as he would have many believe; at least I took the path to destruction willingly. He was a weak man, Robbie, and would waver to and fro in whatever winds circumstance made. Choosing like a lot of those men of the kirk, the easiest route to a fine living. So it was for many a year! And my wife, God rest her soul, could not put up with his vacillations, never having any plan in his life, never wanting to work. We were as like in appearance as mortals were ever made, yet different in spirit. I had a good job once Robbie, I can tell you, and we were happy until she took ill with the cholera and died, a short painful death. Where's the Almighty in that, I ask you? I had never touched a drop of alcohol until then, had never said an unjust word until that time, yet from her death the world became sour and I slowly began to hate those around me, those who had survived, Robbie, when she hadn't. Sounds incredible, but that's where the wickedness took root, from the day I lost her. And my brother,' for the first time he paused and considered, 'he didn't send one word of commiseration, not one word! But as God is my witness, I didn't kill him, I didn't touch a hair of his head. He ran towards me full of hate, stopped and fell down and was dead in an instant. It was a peaceful way to an eternal life. Maybe we'll meet again, who knows, I have my doubts on that...after all I've done. But it would have been nice to see my loved one once more, and if there's a redemption, I will!' McBain gave a curious half smile that caused an accentuation of the twisted mouth. 'The loss of my eye is but a small matter! If you can recognize me so will my Maker.' He turned his horse to go.

'Mr McBain....'Robbie paused.

'Well...'

'It seems that not one of us comes out of this mess without some hurt and sacrifice unless it's a few lairds, a minister or two and the odd factor. It's a pity it ever began.'

McBain paused. 'What you say is true, what has been done is done...and there'll be more to come, I fear. But for me I'm on my way to Perthshire and in the eyes of the Good Shepherd "pastures new"

Robbie watched him ride away, whether he felt pity for the broken man he could not decide.

Suddenly the Factor stopped and turned. 'She was in a rare mood when she left, Robbie, full of passion and anger about the clearances. Took herself off to a fine house near Croick in the county of Ross-shire, to see some friends, as I said, but I often heard her asking if they had caught you. Aye, she seemed mighty pleased each time I said they hadn't. And I'm mighty pleased too, Robbie, mighty pleased!'

Naoi deug air fhichead (thirty nine)

Robbie decided that the journey west to the county of Ross was his last remaining hope to meet Catriona. It was, he believed a futile expedition. But after weighing up all the pros and cons, his mind was set on this course of action.

He turned his back on the eastern seaboard, confident and curiously elated since his near tragedy that his life had been guided by divine hands. As he cut across the land towards the west he knew that he must pass close to his parent's home, and for a brief moment pondered about seeing them again, so soon.

He wandered along for ten miles in the taciturn company of a shepherd of one of the lairds. Robbie quizzed him about his livelihood, the reasons for this existence and other matters appertaining to his situation, but the man, in his late fifties, kept up a stoical silence, punctuated by sundry grunts and the occasional monosyllabic remark. Still, it was company and Robbie felt jaunty enough in the man's presence to occasionally break out into a raucous whistling, but not to the discomfort or approbation of the strange companion. Robbie noticed that his kilt had been replaced by coarse trousers and an English-style shirt adorned his back.

As they approached the pass close to the strath by Loch Shin, the young highlander suddenly had a yearning to see his parents once more, in part to see how they were taking Alasdair's abrupt departure. Despite the pragmatism he had worried about them for the last two days, especially his mother whom he loved dearly.

There was no farewell between him and his silent companion, for they both peeled away from each other like birds in flight and Robbie hurried down the fell side to the cottage he knew so well.

Both parents were pleased to see him so soon. Robbie noticed the strain in their faces and wondered what embittered arguments, what recriminations had passed between them since his last visit. Their mood lightened as he sat down.

He stayed three days - days sometimes full of happiness at other times quiet and reflective, but as he wandered up the hillside to begin his journey west and to regain his former route he somehow wished he had stayed away. Not that there was any ill feeling towards himself, Alasdair or Mairead.

No! The sudden realisation, the significance of his brother's departure, had been brought into sharp perspective by his parents.

They hadn't meant to upset him.

Indeed, just the contrary.

His father had smiled. 'The farm's yours now son,' he said placing his hand on Robbie's shoulder.

'Aye! It's yours!' his mother had confirmed cheerfully.

He remembered the inward dismay, and how he had tried to hide it by being cheerful, and wondered if his parents had seen through the contrived joviality.

He stopped as he climbed up the pass to gaze at a mountain goat walking sedately along the path ahead. Then it looked round and hurried off. He watched its nimble ascent to a rocky pinnacle and then it disappeared.

The curious disappearance, the change of circumstance in this small creature's life, made Robbie collect his thoughts. His initial impulse had been to accept the farm, yet he knew that a crofter's existence was not for him. Indeed, as far as he could reason, his ambitions would vanish like the goat before him, lost in an abyss of mediocrity.

There was little hope of a friendship with Catriona, he could not bring himself to consider more than being friends, if he remained on the family's small holding. How ludicrous it would compare with her fine homes.

As he turned the corner, Robbie laughed. The goat had appeared in full glory, head down and refusing to budge from the narrow path. As Robbie walked up the hill, so did the animal. As he walked down, more of the same. Waving his arms did little more than make the creature step back a few feet, but at the same time it took up a more rigid and defiant stance.

Since the September sun was warm, and the journey in his mind had an indefinite conclusion, he had no other option but to sit down and admire the animal's stubbornness.

The goat seeing the man relax, began to rasp the short grass with a curious shaking of the jaw and a swishing motion of its spiky beard, content in its victory. Robbie soon lost interest and began to study the rolling clouds, that seemed to drift as tenuous columns of white infantry men, mostly in step until some gale close to heaven spurred on a lagging column so that it collided with the others into a rolling, puffing swell.

He must have dozed for a few moments, for when he blinked a few times, yawned and fully opened his eyes the goat had gone. 'So far this journey has brought little in the way of companionship,' mused Robbie as he brushed himself down and slowly ambled on his way.

It seemed a long and tedious journey now, punctuated by periods of apprehension, which grew with each step. Perhaps he had made a false start that was impossible to rectify. Stealing the horse, the brashness and impromptu meetings were hardly likely to endear any man to any girl, at least not one as sophisticated as Catriona.

As he descended down a rugged hill-path Robbie stopped and listened. There was the wail of the bagpipes - a sound he had not heard for almost a year. He had not noticed their silence during the troubles, but the mournful notes made him pause and lament the past. Within the echoing sounds was pictured the suffering of those unfortunate beings whose only involvement in this tragedy was by location of birth, lack of money and political power.

The crags trembled in the noise, its ethereal purity exhilarated the young Highlander. He threw up his arms towards the blue and shouted in a strange mixture of joy and relief, as if a weight had arisen and been born away on the music. It was with a curious feeling of relief that Robbie turned for home. His mission ended! He recrossed the paths of a few hours before, thought he saw the goat in the distance, whistled shrilly to attract its attention, but getting no response, he continued on his way in a buoyant state of mind that would last all winter.

Da fhichead (forty)

Robbie worked hard all winter. It was a particularly mild winter and the animals fared well. Most were retained for the following summer. The feed had lasted, the greenery had come early and the burns were fresh and overflowing. Not withstanding, his mother had been delighted to have her youngest son as a daily companion, while his father had recovered from the joint pains that had so nearly ended his farming life in the September before.

'You know, father, I've been a drifter far too long, don't you think?'

'That may be the case Robbie, but all young people need some time to wander and learn, 'tis part of growing up in man and beast. Look how the creatures of the moors – stag, wildcat and others – roam at will and fight at will until the day they establish their own domain. Ye're nae different from their kith and kin, Robbie Sutherland! Ye'll settle down one day!'

Robbie thought of his brother for a moment, reflecting on the vagaries of marriage and continued, 'Aye, that might be the case, but not for a wee while. The troubles will go on, what do you think, father,' he said earnestly.

'They will, I have nae doubt on that!'

'A year ago I was full of glory and ready to shed blood, but so much has stained the Highlands that I feel like going away. Yet I cannot leave you and mother.'

The father looked long and hard at his son, 'Y'can if you wish, there'll be no stopping you…although I hope it's no abroad like Alasdair and Mairead, or it'll be the death of your mother.'

Robbie shook his head. 'I was thinking of going to Caithness, father. It's been in my mind for some time to go to sea, I've no fear of the sea in any way, fair weather or foul. But to see the fish they're landing there, it's a bonny haul and with bigger boats there'll be more to haul in, cod and the like as well as herring.'

His father reflected for a moment. 'What you say has a ring of truth and commonsense about it, Robbie. But bigger boats will cost bigger money, and we havena got it!'

'Aye! That I ken. But a few of us could put our heads and hearts together and raise enough from those that lend money, and working in Caithness will take those that will join me out of the Marquess's evil ways.'

His father smiled, 'So you've been thinkin' it out then, Robbie?'

'I have that!'

'We'll, I've little fear of ye no doing well, for ye have determination, and that's as good a part of a man's power as bravery and strength.'

Robbie went about the day's tasks in a light heart. He stopped and looked at the first spring flowers showing through the dead grass, and listened to the first bees and midges as they orchestrated the air around him.

'Somehow,' he said confidently, 'I don't think I can fail.'

The next day he decided to embark on his new venture. However, he realised that he had not seen Domhnall and Ealasaid since the first frosts. He was determined to take his leave of the kind old couple. At daybreak, he set off on the eighteen-mile journey to their home.

When he arrived, Domhnall was packing his belongings on a cart. The horse stood obediently, head down.

But it was a sad and bent old man who seemed to have aged since the last time Robbie saw him, aged beyond recognition.

'She's dead!' was his greeting to the younger man and the old man broke down and wept.

Robbie asked no more. There now had to be a change of plan.

For Domhnall had decided to visit his daughter in the county of Ross and Robbie had to help.

He insisted the old man sat in the back of the cart, his bent shoulders against the side with a few belongings stacked around him.

The journey would be painfully slow. As they set off up the steep incline the old man took one last lingering look at his cottage and waved to Robbie who had tarried behind.

With that signal he hurried indoors and soon dark smoke appeared from the windows, and fumes reddened on the thatch.

Robbie came running up the hill. 'That's it, Domhnall!'

'*Tapadh leat!* (Thank you!) Aye, it's a blessing that nae one can live there after a' the happy times we've had. None o'the factors' men and any other evil body! That gives me some consolation!'

There was another uneasy silence. Domhnall muttered a prayer and then firmly said, 'Goodbye to the place I'll always love, Ealasaid, but never as much as ye!'

Robbie remained silent and left the man to his contemplations, reliving his life and the good times that seemed to have vanished like the cottage where he had given and done all that was possible in his confined world.

Aon air da fhichead (forty one)

The girl, her hair bright and fair in the May noonday sun, read the *Times* with an expression of dismay.

It said: "When Gustavus Aird took me to the glen," she glanced to see the name of the correspondent, "all the cottages were empty with the exception of one, and in this one Hugh, a pensioner, was dying. The rest of the people were seated on a green brae, the women all neatly dressed in net caps and wearing scarlet or plaid shawls; the men wearing their blue bonnets and having their plaids wrapped about them. There was a simplicity extremely touching in this group on the bare hillside, listening to the Psalms of David in Gaelic and assembled to worship God. They sang the Psalm "The eyes of all things wait on Thee, the Giver of all good."

"Behind the church in Croick, a long kind of booth was erected, the roof formed of tarpaulin stretched over poles, the sides closed with horsecloth, rugs, blankets and plaids. Their furniture, excepting their bedding, they got distributed amongst the cottages of their neighbours; and with bedding and their children they all removed on Saturday afternoon to this place. In my last letter I informed you that they had been round to every heritor and factor in the neighbourhood, and twelve of the eighteen families had been unable to find places of shelter. Cottages were everywhere refused to them."

"I am told it was a most wretched spectacle to see these poor people march out of the glen in a body, with two or three carts filled with children, many of them mere infants; and other carts containing their bedding and their requisites. The whole countryside was up on the hills watching them as they silently took possession of their tent."

"A fire was kindled in the churchyard, round which the poor children clustered. Two cradles with infants in them, were placed close to the fire, and sheltered round by the dejected-looking mothers. Others busied themselves into dividing the tent into compartments by means of blankets, for the different families. Contrasted with the gloomy dejection of the grown-ups and the aged was the not less melancholy picture of the poor children thoughtlessly playing round the fire, pleased with the novelty of all around them."

"There were twenty-three children, all under the age of ten, and seven of them were ill. The most were over forty, but some unmarried men and women were present. They crowded about me, shaking hands. Their Gaelic I could not understand, but their eyes beamed with gratitude. This unsought, spontaneous and grateful expression of feeling for being their friend is what their natural protector – their chieftain – never saw, and what his factor need never hope for."

"They have dignity and pride yet there is a puzzling docility. Were such clearances attempted in England, I leave you to conceive the excitement, which it would be certain to create, the mob procession, the effigy burning, the window smashing."

"It is a cold calculating heartlessness on them that is almost as incredible as it is disgusting."

Dha air da fhichead (forty two)

Robbie and Domhnall journeyed on for two days stopping to sleep under the cart for the weather had become suddenly mild. At Ardgay they entered a strangely silent country, turning left off the main track and then following a narrow level path that ran south of the River Carron towards a tangle of hills and glens to the west. It was a lonely land with the odd isolated farm and lodge sheltering behind clumps of woodlands and rhododendron bushes now out of bloom. The road then crossed to the north bank of the river and after a mile or two of rough grass and thistles petered out near Croick.

It was the morning of the third day and the couple slowly wound their way up a short incline, the horse pulling-on ahead.

Domhnall's step was brisker now.

As they reached the top of the grassy knoll, the old man stopped and stared.

The small township was deserted.

Robbie ran down and looked into the first cottage. It was empty.

Then the second, then the third and fourth!

There was no sign of life.

Despondent, he turned to the old man.

'Where to now?'

Domhnall considered the situation. Then said slowly. 'I didna think o'the clearances here!' And went silent.

Robbie put his arm on the old man's shoulder. 'We'll inquire at the Manse in Croick. They'll know the whereabouts of your cousin John!'

Domhnall gave a brief smile but his face was careworn and sad.

So they walked on, halting for the old man who suddenly felt weary as if the enthusiasm for life was draining away. He spoke briefly. 'I ha'e walked the fells and mountains for many a year and never felt sae tired.'

'Och! Away with you, Domhnall!' He laughed. 'There's not a stouter pair of limbs in the whole of

Scotland, you fair outpaced me over the years, even now!'

The old man smiled and resumed a firmer step.

The Manse was reached in just under the hour, the men having stopped to drink water from a trough and eat a handful of oatcakes.

As they approached the Manse, they could see the Minister's wife in the garden.

Robbie approached and asked politely, 'Good morning! (*Madainn mhath*!) Is the Minister in the house, please?'

The woman shook her head and pointed father down the road. There he could see the small church with its strong stone walls and fringe of trees.

'Is there a funeral then?'

She smiled. 'No! A gathering for prayer!'

They walked back to the cart and led the horse to the verge where it could crop in peace and not disturb the gathering.

Robbie walked ahead and the scene in the graveyard amazed him.

The old man gasped with surprise.

For ninety people - eighteen families- were crowded around the graves with makeshift shelters. Amongst the throng was Domhnall's cousin John, who, on glancing up, gave a cheerful wave.

The two men waited until the prayers were over.

Then the old men hugged each other with the words of Gaelic streaming forth.

At length John turned to Robbie and said, 'We're here to seek shelter with our families and pray for guidance and help!'

'How long have you been here? asked Robbie.

'About two weeks or so! But the Minister is a kind and guid man and will get help and relief from the great men who provide it in the South. Only a few days back a newspaper man came to see us and did he make notes, and a fair time he was aboot it, to tell of our plight in England.'

'And what plight was that?' Robbie enquired.

'Well, Glen Calvie where we lived was poor and rocky enuf, but we were asked for fifty-five pounds ten shillings as a rent, tae much fur us! Yet we paid it, only to be asked for mair, and when we wished to speak aboot it, we were told they would make "friendly discussions". Aye, that's the very words! Instead the "friendly words" were formal notices to leave our hames with decrees for removal. Everyone was hunting here an' there for shelter and only six found any. So we sit near the graves of our brave ancestors and face the elements with a stout heart. Death may take us to join our forefathers beneath the sward...who can tell! But I never thought my home would be a kirkyard!' John sighed and looked at the two companions.

An old man, sick with palsy, had been listening. 'I've recorded it here...forever...that I'm fair certain aboot!"

'What?' Domhnall asked.

'Glen Calvie people, the wicked generation.' He went silent and ambled off to join a group in the far corner.

'Aye, he's written it in the kirk,' said John in a matter-of-fact way, but did not say any more.

Robbie looked at the temporary, flimsy dwellings set amongst the juniper trees. 'Do you never go inside the Kirk for shelter?'

'No, that is not right and holy, dressed and uncouth as we are! It would be a desecration of the Holy House,' was the firm answer. Things may change...next week...next month...sometime. (*an ath sheachdain...an ath mhios...uair-eigin!*)

As they spoke the sun broke through the clouds and an eagle called high on the hillside behind them.

Robbie thought of the wedding day less than two years ago as it trailed its talons in the sky. So much had changed.

Then his thoughts returned to reality. 'So we're to make ourselves as comfortable as we can here,' he asked at length, 'if we have a mind.' He glanced at Domhnall.

'You're right welcome to do so!' replied John.

Robbie thought for a moment. 'I would be more of a mind to wander to the coast, Domhnall, and seek my fortune there,' he said at length. 'Have not the waves delivered me for such a purpose?'

'Aye, they hav'!' replied the old man cheerfully. 'They have!'

'Will you come with me?'

'Now I'm of a mind to think I will, Robbie Sutherland!'

So the two men departed with a sad and final farewell to the families sitting in the graveyard. But John ran after them, 'Here, as poor as we are, there's something to help you on your way.' He pressed a few provisions in Domhnall's hands.

The old man gazed at his cousin, grasped him warmly and held him close for a few seconds. 'We will never forget ye all. Never! Even in the long journey ahead. God be with ye and take care of ye all.'

As he waved a final goodbye Robbie turned to his old friend and put his arm around his shoulder.

'There's not much here (*Chan eil moran an-seo.*). We'll make out just fine elsewhere! Me as a fisherman and you the laird.'

The old man laughed. 'Me a laird! Time will tell, Robbie Sutherland, time will tell!'

They gave a long, lingering look at the kirk as they climbed slowly up the hill, the horse wandering behind them.

It suddenly began to whinny.

Robbie turned. In the field on the horizon, about half a mile away, and framed against the blue of the sky, stood a grey stallion; its whiteness gleaming in the sunlight. 'By my life, it cannot be...but it is!' He smiled. '*An t-Sultain!* (September!).

His companion caught the mood of pre-occupation.

'You'll never believe this, Domhnall! But my life is about to change! Perhaps for the better, I'll be thinking!'

The old man paused and laughed. 'I ha'e nae doubts, Robbie, for if a man waits long enough the wind always blows fair and dry in time, does it not?'

For the last time, they stopped and surveyed the valley. The villagers were just visible in the distance, still sitting quietly in the churchyard.

Robbie called, '*Beannachd leat!* (Goodbye!)'

Then turning to his friend he remarked, 'They're a fine people, Domhnall! And will long be remembered in the Highlands. Did you see the window of the kirk?'

'No!' (*Chan eil!)*

'They've all written their names on it, including that old man's prophesy. It's a rare and wonderful sight! And it's a story in just a few words that will be remembered as long as a Highlander draws breath'

'On the kirk window...in the name o' the Lord God...whatever next!' was his friend's only reply.

Tri air da fhichead (forty three)

Robbie was in a serious mood, unusual for him and keenly noted by the old man, who said not one word, despite being inquisitive as to what course of action would be taken next.

Robbie contemplated as he walked ahead, putting four paces between himself, Domhnall and the horse.

The white stallion, if it recognised his former temporary companion, deemed not to look up and Robbie felt the portents to be poor, noting how it had adopted the aloof mannerism of its mistress.

He crossed to the edge of the field and, reaching over the wall to stroke its nose, said, 'Well, how are you and your mistress?' His sudden laugh made the stallion start backwards. Then spying the old mare that ambled beside the two men the white horse directed its equine attention towards it with a finely tuned whinny.

'It's a fine stallion Robbie, I didn't see aught o' it the last time ye took it. But if the animal's here, the girl must be here or here abouts. There's but one way to find out and I'll take myself along this lane and rap on the door, like a factor.' They both laughed uproariously and the old man assumed a strange, stern countenance and a more determined upright stance.

Robbie watched him disappear around a sharp bend towards a stone manse, its aspect welcoming despite the small dark windows and grey stone roof. 'It's better you dinna come,' Domhnall had said, 'there's no knowing if one o' those damned factors or sheriff's men are about and still in league with the aud Laird, even if we're in another part of the country.'

The door was answered by a slim woman of forty-five, with dark hair pulled neatly back with precise manner and an engaging smile. A golden retriever stood behind her wagging its tail. Domhnall felt at ease and patted the dog on its broad head. 'I dinna want to trouble ye, ma'am, but my friend and I are seeking the whereabouts of a young gentle lady of the name of Catriona.'

'Catriona? Well, between you and me, she's in London at present, or is it Shropshire, I do not know!'

Domhnall paused, not wishing to sound too inquisitive or rude. 'Will it be a long time then, until she comes back?'

'It could that! For she's a headstrong girl and the trouble in the Highlands is not of her liking.'

'Nor mine,' said the old man frankly and without thinking. 'Could ye tell her something?'

The lady nodded.

'Tell her, that a man named Robbie called about the horse, him seeing it in the field and a' that,' he replied hastily. 'And,' he paused until a bright idea struck him, 'if she ever needs the animal tending to while she's away in England, she can always find us, I mainly mean Robbie, in Lybster harbour, or by Latheron.'

'But Latheron's a fair sized place and nearly as big as Thurso, so will you be easily found?' she inquired, stooping to pat the dog.

'Och aye! Every one knows Robbie Sutherland far and wide,' Domhnall replied with a laugh.

The young highlander watched him walking up the path with a pleasant smile. 'Is everything settled then?' he asked.

Domhnall laughed, 'Aye, in a manner of means.'

Robbie waited but there was nothing forthcoming. 'Well....'

'Well what?'

'Well, where is Catriona?' His voice was an amalgamation of exasperation and suspense.

'I dinna ken!'

'Give me your horse!' Robbie grasped the bridle and proceeded to lead it along the road eastward. 'I'd rather be leading that white stallion than this old mare any day,' he muttered. 'What on earth did you come back grinning like a goat and then tell me such bad news.'

'Grinning like a goat eh! That's all I get for my pains, and foresight,' was the bland reply.

'And...come on Domhnall...there must be more!'

'No, there's no mair, I'm afraid.'

Robbie sighed again with exasperation. 'I'm fair disappointed Domhnall, for when I saw the horse I was sure it was a lucky omen.'

The old man stopped walking and surveyed his companion. 'Good luck comes in bits and pieces, Robbie. That's the first bit…for ye ken where she'll come back to, do ye not? The second bit o'luck is… that I've managed to give her our address.'

Robbie laughed, 'We've no got one!'

'We have…Lybster harbour, and they'll all ken ye there, with a whole fleet of fishing vessels named after you.'

'Aye, and we'll all be in Latheron churchyard by then.'

Domhnall took over the bridle. 'Ye mark my words, Robbie Sutherland, there a lot mair to come…from all quarters, don't y'think?'

Ceithir air da fhichead (forty four)

The small harbour had a river that rushed down the steep hillside, yellow with primroses in spring and now a profusion of purple thistles, red willow-herb, and the tints of numerous ground weeds - colours so attractive splashed about that Robbie paused to survey them before hastening down the path to where the sea washed into the narrow rocks and threw spray high upon the cliffs. A dozen fishermen were mending their nets. With a rhythmical movement of the hands and a relaxed concentrated look, they lounged with their backs propped against the harbour wall, some with pipes dangling from their mouths in an abstract way. Two women carried the small morning's catch in white buckets, counterbalanced one in each hand against their broad black skirts –which hung full and almost to the ground, so that the wooden clogs, peeping shyly out, clattered on the stone steps in a curiously hypnotic sound.

Robbie said, 'Good day,' smiled and stood aside as the women passed him on the steps. But his gaze was fixed on the small working group.

'*Hallo, Ciamar a tha sibh*?' (Hallo, how are you?)

The men looked up, one took his pipe out of his mouth, surveyed the young Highlander. '*Tha gu math, tapadh leibh.*' (Fine thanks).

'I'm Robbie Sutherland, I've come to see Captain MacInnes about his boat.'

There was nothing distinctive about the elderly man, his face traced with fine lines like the ocean charts he knew so well, drawn by the winds of countless years at sea. He held his pipe and pointed towards himself. 'The very man! Captain and principal proprietor! And I'm a wonderin' what manner of inquiry it is?'

Robbie smiled, 'Indeed! You have a boat for sale?'

'I'm of a mind to think you're right,' he said dryly. The man surveyed the highlander, puzzled by the request from one so young, and not knowing whether it was in jest or in earnest.

Robbie smiled again. The other fishermen stopped work and listened attentively. 'How much for the fishing boat that I've been told is up for the selling?'

The captain considered the situation for a moment and sucked on his pipe, which gave a shrill sound like miniature bagpipes. 'How much have ye got?'

'About fifty pounds to put down!'

'Hardly enough!'

'There's little more to be said then,' Robbie said emphatically.

The captain removed the pipe from his mouth and thought. 'I don't know what y're thinking of, but we could go halves in the venture. I'm a man who's not afraid of a gamble and I like your honesty and ways. Is that of your likin'?'

'Aye, it could be when I think more of it.'

'What crew have ye?' the Captain added after some reflection.

'I can raise a dozen men, perhaps more. Most have been cleared off their land and out of their homes, so they're ready for any work that comes their way.'

The captain studied the situation and turned to a young man of muscular build and tanned, weather-beaten face. 'We could make up the rest.'

The sailor nodded. 'Aye, there's enough and some mair…to crew a boat, and the fishing's good to the north as the autumn sets in.'

The captain took up the conversation, 'There's good fish to be had far north and towards the west, big spouters, slow and easily killed by the harpoon. A few o' them can make a man rich for years, and a few mair for years after that! But it's a hard life and one no without risks.'

'That I ken full well, but I've never shirked a hard life and it will be the making of our fortunes if all goes well.' Robbie fell silent for a moment, 'if all goes well, so be it; if not …I'll take the consequences.

'That's fair enuf,' said one of the fishermen mending the nets, 'as long as y'ken the risks.'

The captain, who had been sitting all the while, stood up and shook hands. 'My son will take you down to the brig. It's worth a lot mair than fifty pounds to share. But I'll take your mair out of the next season's catch until we own half o'it apiece. Take a step back and look east by south east...at those ships.' He pointed, 'What's agreed is agreed and that settles the matter! You are now part owner and full fisherman, whatever your experience...and I suspect it be very little. But we've a captain for it who has sailed the seas and never shirked a wave, big or small. That you can take for a fact! For you're speaking to the very man himself.'

Robbie smiled and for a minute considered the curiously round about way the agreement had been made. But his general impression was favourable.

'What have you seen of the world,' the captain continued at length.

'What world?' Robbie replied laughing.

The captain laughed. 'It's a bit bigger than y'think, but for a start go and look at the ship and give me y'final thought o'the matter. I've risen from cabin boy, when I knew as little as ye, to mate and captain. There's plenty to learn at sea and a lot o'time to do it in.'

As the sailor led him down to the harbour wall, Robbie heard the captain say, 'Aye, he'll do!' in a satisfied voice. He walked a pace behind, thoughtful and slightly uncertain, until the sailor stopped and pointed out to sea. Just anchored in a quiet reach was the brig. Robbie had observed the topsail, amongst others, but had been unsure as to which vessel he was buying. Now he looked in earnest and with some degree of apprehension, his body tingling with excitement.

It was a ship that had seen better days, of the old school in design, but still clean and neat in trim. It was smaller than he had expected but weather-moulded and seasoned by the equatorial sun and Atlantic squalls. The hull was nut brown from these encounters like a veteran of the sea, the decks scrubbed but undulating from past encounters with the waves, but the gold, red and black fittings, the pure white of the sails, the crisp taut oakum coloured ropes, and the polished ivory bedecked her like an empress. A handful of men were clearly visible, hurrying to and fro for not only were new sails being hoisted, old sails were heaped on the decks prior to being mended, and mounds of rigging squirmed in neat triangles beside them. Unpanelled open bulwarks, a turnstile wheel at her helm, the quarterdecks scrubbed and shining in the sun, filled Robbie with pleasure. It was the moment he knew his luck had turned.

*****

'Y're as braw as any seafaring man, Robbie, and after less than two months at sea.' Domhnall's voice was full of admiration as they walked up from the harbour in Lybster.

'And, we've earned more money in that time than I've done in a lifetime, so far,' his companion replied. 'The way things are, Domhnall, the grand old ship will be bought in no time, or my name's not Robbie Sutherland!'

'Well…it is and in that way of thinkin', I've got to believe ye,' responded the old man with a laugh.

'Any news of my father and mother?'

'Aye and they're bonnie and well, for the clearances seemed to have escaped them and Sellar and McBain are nae mair about, which is a blessing although some of the others can be just as wicked, for there's no end o'them, that's a fact!'

They climbed the short, steep hill from the quayside, Robbie noticed his companions subdued manner and just palpable lack of warmth. The gulls cried incessantly overhead as they witnessed in their delight another boat heading for the shore, the aroma of heaped fish drawing the birds forward.

They walked side by side but rarely speaking for almost an hour.

Robbie stopped and turned to his friend. 'I have more than enough to buy a property in Latheron, Domhnall, and a good one at that. I have only got a week before I'm away again, but we'll settle something in that time, I'll be hoping.'

The old man did not reply.

'Is aught wrong, Domhnall?'

'In a manner of speaking, "yes".'

'In what manner is that?'

'I ha' a feeling that we will part in the near future Robbie, and it's no of my likin'.'

'Nor mine!'

There was another pause as they reached the broad summit of the hill with the small cluster of houses that constituted the village of Latheron in the distance.

Domhnall proceeded slowly. 'I have had two visits since you left, Robbie, visits that may or may not please ye, although I suspect the former.'

'Aye!' Robbie waited.

'From the girl with the horse.'

'Catriona?'

'The same!'

'Why should I not be pleased then, Domhnall, such news is always welcome.'

'That I ken, but she came about some business.' They had stopped while the discussion took place and Robbie scrutinized his friend's face.

'Did she come with a factor or such?'

'No! None but a young man...'

'What manner of man?' interjected Robbie hastily, the disappointment was obvious in his voice and manner.

'Oh! Some young fella and his girl, I dinna really know much aboot that! But it's no the point! She was asking about ye an awful lot.'

Robbie laughed, 'Was she now!' Then he said in a serious voice, 'It was no bad news, was it?'

Domhnall shook his head. 'She was inquiring about one thing and another and said she had come into some money from her old aunt in England...and to get to the truth of the matter...had a mind to put a farm in your way and help a few others.' He paused and watched the sea polishing the damp rocks that glistened in the autumn sunshine. 'I said you were a seagoing man now and might not be settling down for some while.'

Robbie considered the last sentence. 'Well, that's the truth as the matter now stands. But I'll just have time to see her if she's about in the Highlands, before I sail again...although I was hoping to visit my mother and father.'

Domhnall laughed. 'Anyway, I told her ye'd be back within the week so I have a mind to think that she'll be waiting for us when we get hame. Least she was when I left!' He laughed again. 'I was none too sure that it would meet with y'r approval, Robbie, knowing that ye wanted to cut yourself off from your former ways.'

Robbie slapped the man on the back and laughed too. 'Ah well, we can only wait and see what she has to say, but with a mile or two to walk, we must be on our way.'

*****

'How's the horse?' It was a tentative beginning. He smiled.

'Not stolen recently!'

'That's just as well, or you wouldn't be here.'

Catriona laughed. 'You're right, Robbie Sutherland, the horse comes first...mostly.'

'That's a blessing, it gives me some hope.'

'Does it now! You're in business as a proprietor of a fishing boat, I hear.'

'I am that!' He still felt unsure of his welcome and in what manner to continue towards his final objective, which was to find out her future, and by inference and hope, his own.

'Did Domhnall tell you that I came the other week?'

'He did!'

'I just had to see you Robbie, and don't interrupt with one of your remarks, like "Did you now" or such like, in the manner of querying or affirming every word or sentence I say, as you have in the past!'

He was just about to say, 'He wouldn't!' but decided to keep quiet, listening with great interest and secretly pleased that she had admitted to coming all this way to see him. He found himself pondering on that pleasant thought and suddenly had to collect himself in case he was missing what she was saying.

'This is why I came back, Robbie! At first I found it hard to believe that my relatives could be so harsh...cruel is a better word, on the people in the Highlands they were supposed to be looking after. When I read about the poor, starving men, women and children in the churchyard at Croick, it disgusted me so much that I resolved to do everything I could to relieve some of the suffering up here. No one knows what happened to those poor unfortunates huddled in that churchyard, they seemed to have melted like the first frosts of winter into oblivion. I have enquired, but I can't find out how many have left the county, how many have emigrated, how many have suffered and died. Those matters have brought me great distress in recent weeks. You know, the Lord and Lady Stafford try to think well for the Highlands, but they haven't the inclination to spend any time here and resolve all the difficulties that the sheep grazing brings. They still leave the day to day running to bailies, factors and the like who have their own interests at heart. However, I haven't come here to dwell on these matters, but to make you an offer.' Catriona looked earnestly into his face. 'That is the reason I have made a long journey, and it's not to take no for an answer.'

'If you want to help those that have truly suffered I can give you a few names, but it is a few of many.'

She hesitated. 'That's not what I am meaning to say, Robbie Sutherland. I have a business venture to propose. Simply, I would like to be a partner in your fishing enterprise.'

'If you ken as little as I did when I began a few months back, you'd soon realize that I needed a partner from the start. And I have a good one to boot! Captain MacInnes! What he would think of having another partner who speaks English and lives hundred of miles away...I really don't know!'

'He can think what he likes!' responded Catriona with indignation, 'it's what you think that matters.'

Robbie thought for a moment. 'For my part I would welcome you as a partner...'he stopped in mid sentence.

'It would be business only. I can assure you of that!' Yet Catriona smiled and took hold of his hand. They were sitting overlooking the cliffs, sheer and white, and the drift and roar of the waves on the shingle lulled their senses in the October evening sun. Catriona was resting on the grass, with Robbie by her side. 'I must admit Robbie Sutherland that I haven't met anyone before or since quite like you. But, I repeat, for the present...it is business only. My aunt has made me rich beyond what I would have ever expected. My plan, and I've discussed it with my friends, is for you to buy one, two or even three more ships. We will have a small fleet, Robbie, and give employment to those that have been displaced by the clearances. Only good will come of it...you believe me!'

*****

'You know Ealasaid, this is a grand house and as big as a manse, how that Robbie Sutherland has made so much money in the last seven years, I dinna ken. But he's a fine man - all the fishermen know that! And his wife, Catriona, and the three bairns are awful' good to an auld man. I would have liked you to have seen them, my dear, but the Lord decreed otherwise. Anyway, it's a providence living with them and Latheron's a bonny place, but it was better in our auld home in Sutherland before the troubles began. It drove most of the Highlanders away. Do you remember the lovely wedding of Alasdair and Mairead? They went across the sea, to Canada, and they're doing well! But there was nae vengeance on Factor Sellar and some of the other factors, their men, the ministers, the chiefs and all who betrayed the people. They have only profited by the Clearances.

And the Great Laird and his wife live much as they did before, not really troubled by what they have done. I often think of you at dusk, Ealasaid, when the birds are calling and come home for the roost, we often talked in the gloaming, did we not?

'Aye, I can still recall the wedding and the start of it all. And how we laughed, my luv, when I said, 'Sometimes you're a vain body Robbie Sutherland.'

*****

(The grazing, the burnings, the lootings, the emigration and the premature deaths of young and old led to the steady depopulation of the Highlands of Scotland that continued for almost a century. This was a regal land that has never recovered and today remains one of the least populated parts of Europe. And in the words of the young men of Sutherland asked to fight in the war against Russia, they issued a declaration in the newspapers of 1854 rather than besmirch the honourable name of the fighting men who had distinguished themselves at Waterloo and other major battles. "We are not allowed to marry without the consent of the factor, the ground officer being always ready to report every case of marriage, and the result would be banishment from the county. Our lands have been taken from us and given to sheep farmers, and we are denied any portion of them and told we should leave. For these wrongs and oppressions we are resolved that there will be no volunteers or recruits from Sutherlandshire. Yet we assert that we are willing as our forefathers were to peril life and limb in defence of our Queen and country were our wrongs and long endured oppression redressed, wrongs which will be remembered in Sutherlandshire by every true Highlander as long as grass grows and water runs."

Finally, if you are ever in the Highlands visit one kirk before all others.

For the window of Croick church is an abiding testimony to humility and suffering - name after name, after name, after name...all written on glass.)